CINEMA/POLITICS/PHILOSOPHY

FILM AND CULTURE SERIES

FILM AND CULTURE

A SERIES OF COLUMBIA UNIVERSITY PRESS

Edited by John Belton

For a full list of titles in this series, see pages 233–237

CINEMA/POLITICS/ PHILOSOPHY

NICO BAUMBACH

Columbia University Press

New York

Columbia University Press
Publishers Since 1893
New York   Chichester, West Sussex
cup.columbia.edu

Library of Congress Cataloging-in-Publication Data
Names: Baumbach, Nico, author.
Title: Cinema-politics-philosophy / Nico Baumbach.
Description: New York : Columbia University Press, [2019] | Series: Film and
culture | Includes bibliographical references and index.
Identifiers: LCCN 2018017877 | ISBN 9780231184229 (hardback ; alk. paper) |
ISBN 9780231184236 (trade pbk. ; alk. paper) | ISBN 9780231545372 (E-book)
Subjects: LCSH: Motion pictures—Philosophy. | Motion pictures—Political
aspects. | Film criticism. | Art and motion pictures.
Classification: LCC PN1995 .B3186 2019 | DDC 791.4301—dc23
LC record available at https://lccn.loc.gov/2018017877

Columbia University Press books are printed on permanent
and durable acid-free paper.
Printed in the United States of America

Cover design: Chang Jae Lee

CONTENTS

4 RETHINKING THE POLITICS OF THE PHILOSOPHY OF CINEMA
170

CINEMA/POLITICS/PHILOSOPHY

INTRODUCTION

The Politics of Film Theory and Its Discontents

Walter Benjamin's 1936 essay "The Work of Art in the Age of Its Technological Reproducibility" advances the following claim: for the first time in history the "function" of the work of art is political. The evidence: cinema.[1] According to Giorgio Agamben, perhaps the most Benjaminian philosopher writing today, "Cinema essentially ranks with ethics and politics (and not merely with aesthetics)" and is "proximate" to philosophy itself.[2]

These provocative claims get to the heart of the subject of this book. But what allows us to make the connection between cinema, politics, and philosophy? Is cinema just an art or entertainment, or can it be an ethics, a politics, or a form of thought?

Benjamin's essay is all too familiar today, but the assumption that cinema cannot be separated from politics, while frequently taken for granted, is not always closely scrutinized. What came to be known as "film theory" in the American academy, as it took shape in the 1970s, is often seen to share Benjamin's emphasis on the intimate connection between cinema and politics. But a subtle reversal had taken place. Film theory was understood to be a political project, but cinema's politics, it was implicitly assumed, tended to be obscured by ideology. The political dimension of cinema could be wrested away from ideology by theory. Theory was entrusted with the power to isolate and demonstrate the politics of films.

We can see this clearly in "Cinéma/Idéologie/Critique" (Cinema/ Ideology/Criticism), Jean-Louis Comolli and Jean Narboni's highly influential 1969 editorial statement for the newly politicized *Cahiers du Cinéma*.[3] "Every film is political," Comolli and Narboni claimed, in what might be taken as an axiom of 1970s film theory. In the wake of the upheavals of May '68, the great French cinephile magazine, cofounded by André Bazin in 1951 and once known for its passionate, impressionistic celebrations of filmmakers working within the Hollywood system, now framed film criticism's mission as guided by the rigorous and systematic analysis of any film's location within capitalist ideology. This position would help set the agenda for the emerging discipline of Anglo-American film studies over the following decade.

But when Benjamin claims that cinema is political, he means that it has a revolutionary social function. Comolli and Narboni used "political" to mean "ideological." "Every film is political," they argued, "inasmuch as it is determined by the given ideology which produces it."[4] Cinema's essence in this understanding is not political so much as antipolitical. Only certain films, the authors went on to explain, the ones that managed to disrupt the dominant ideology by thwarting the dominant codes and conventions of cinema, could be revealed to be political in a positive or affirmative sense. Theoretical criticism was needed to distinguish these films from the ones that were only holding up a mirror to ideology. Theory, as Laura Mulvey would later put it, was needed as a "political weapon" against the pleasures of mainstream narrative cinema.[5]

Christian Metz provided a succinct description of the basic operation of film theory at this time: "to disengage the cinema-object from the imaginary and win it for the symbolic."[6] Here semiotics and structuralism, Marxism as rewritten by Louis Althusser, and psychoanalysis as rewritten by Jacques Lacan all seemed to find a point of convergence in the fruitful moment that began in the 1960s in continental Europe, especially France, and spread throughout the Anglo-American academic world in the 1970s. Cinema was a machine of the imaginary, and theory,

by imposing questions of representation and the subject onto a phenomenological experience that effaced those questions, was a political intervention.[7] The "symbolic" in Lacan's sense (not to be confused with how
the word is normally used in English) was political because, as the domain of the circuit of signifiers, it was another name for the material
conditions of our seemingly transparent, and hence "imaginary," lived
experience of reality.[8] As Pier Paolo Pasolini claimed, the work of theory was to add something to our knowledge of its object and hence to
separate itself from "the obscure ontological background" that arises
from "explaining cinema with cinema."[9] By thinking in terms of the
symbolic or structure, theory produced what Althusser called a "knowledge effect" to save cinema from the ideological immediacy of the
cinematic experience.[10] As the example of Pasolini should remind us, this
period was not anticinema but was firmly committed to a cinema of the
symbolic, whether in the "camera-stylo" of Nicholas Ray or John Ford
in which the mise-en-scène functions as écriture to reveal the contradictions of the film's official narrative, or in the more overtly oppositional
cinema of a Godard or Pasolini in which the cinematic-imaginary is per-
petually under erasure.[11] The concern, according to Godard, was not
with the reflection of reality but the reality of reflection;[12] that is, not with
the imaginary but the symbolic.

The assumption that the goal of cinema studies is to wrest the political
(understood as the symbolic) from individual films continued in modified form in the cultural studies that became pervasive in film studies in
the 1980s. While less suspicious of the pleasures afforded by mainstream
films and frequently more ambivalent toward Marxist, psychoanalytic,
or structuralist theories, cultural studies approaches still invariably proceeded from a commitment to a critical or resistant position in relation to
dominant ideology. Despite its significant differences, in this specific
sense, at least, it continued the legacy of seventies film theory.[13]

But today this position has come to be viewed with suspicion, and
from the nineties into the first decade of the twenty-first century, numerous books and articles have reevaluated this tradition of film theory
as problematic and dated, if not faddish, obscurantist, and incoherent.[14]

Despite the agreement that recent decades have seen a "historical turn" in film studies, there is little consensus about what theoretical approaches are currently central to the field.[15] David Bordwell and Noël Carroll's 1996 edited collection *Post-Theory* sought to usher in a new era by dethroning "Grand Theory" in favor of a more modest "piecemeal" approach, offering cognitivism as the most promising new avenue of investigation.[16] While cognitivism has not yet had the traction within film studies departments the authors may have hoped for, the polemical dimension of their book seems less and less like the contrarian position it was announced as at the time. A stated polemical distance from "Theory" (with a capital T) should be familiar to anyone who has read the introductions to books on film published by academic presses in the last twenty years or so. As recently as 2011, Bordwell expressed concern about academics who "smother living work under a blanket of Grand Theory."[17] All too often, the Anti–Grand Theory position might better be understood as Grand Anti-Theory, because it reenacts the very move it criticizes by lumping a wide range of material into a single monolithic category that, once rendered in caricatural terms, can be easily demonstrated to be worthless. But it would be unfair to conflate this totalizing dismissal of Theory with more nuanced critiques that sought to shake off the most sterile tendencies of academic theoretical doxa in favor of new avenues of thinking about film form and history.

The era of anti-theory has subsided because consensus seems to accept that the anti-theorists have won. While the *Post-Theory* volume may not have inaugurated a new dominant paradigm in American film studies, and indeed this would have gone against its stated intentions, it can, at the very least, be seen as marking a turn that was already in place toward more modest and circumscribed scholarly ambitions within the academic study of film. And the "piecemeal" approach could be used to characterize the work of many scholars who may not share the same antipathy to psychoanalysis and Marxism as the book's contributors. Bordwell's own pursuit of formal and stylistic histories provides one example of a not-always-explicitly cognitivist "piecemeal" approach, as do the growing body of writings on cinema from the perspective of analytic philosophy or ordinary language philosophy, as well as more empirically based histories focusing on regional and/or national cinemas, "early cinema," and so on. Since interpretive work and historical scholarship cannot so easily do without theory (as Bordwell and Carroll would agree), we have also witnessed various "returns" to interesting, and not so interesting, avenues of the history of film theory that may have been forgotten about or dismissed in its Althusserian-Lacanian phase—whether phenomenology; questions of bodies and embodiment, aesthetics and beauty, or ethics and morality; or the theories of Henri Bergson, Jean Epstein, or André Bazin.[18] Malcolm Turvey explicitly defends his interest in returning to an earlier generation of film theory by arguing that "classical film theory tends to be much more piecemeal. . . . Early film theorists are focused on contemporary issues, and they're not, for the most part, trying to route claims about cinema in some larger metaphysical or sociological doctrine."[19]

Yet the renewed interest in classical film theory in recent decades points not only toward a more historical, piecemeal approach to theory, but also in an opposite direction—toward an ontological or metaphysical turn that has been taken up by new forms of film and media philosophy. In the seventies there was an attempt to develop a rigorous theory of cinematic signification that displaced many of the central concerns of classical film theory, especially the question of what makes film an art. At the same time, the emphasis on the relation between form and politics meant a renewed interest in early twentieth-century political aesthetics, in Benjamin and Bertolt Brecht and the theories of Soviet filmmakers, especially Sergei Eisenstein and Dziga Vertov. Today, the interest in classical film theory is less likely to focus on the relation between aesthetics and politics. Yet we should not see the new interest in classical film theory as a victory only for piecemeal theories and sober, empiricist scholarship. Classical film theory has also been summoned to buttress a renewed fascination with cinema as a form of thought and an experience of being.

Under the banners of film-philosophy and media theory, a new strain has invaded film studies in which Agamben's claim about cinema's ethico-political essence is seen as realized by digital technologies in the information age. If the post-theory turn was often justified by a clearer delineation of the film object against ostensibly extrinsic concerns such as politics and culture, the increasing lack of clarity about what the object of moving image studies is today becomes an opening for a new more expansive theory of mediation in relation to transforming notions of body and mind in a post-human world.[20] Here we find a subsumption of film theory into media and technology theory that do Benjamin one better by announcing the convergence of philosophy, politics, science, and aesthetics in a techno-metaphysical paradigm no longer weighed down by troubling questions about "the base," or mode of production, that for Benjamin made the analysis of art's relation to technology possible. One advantage of the media-technology-centered philosophical perspective, to the extent that it still is interested in the moving image, is that it can incorporate a large range of new objects, from video games to artist videos, YouTube, and smartphones—the spectatorship of the feature film reduced to only one possible form of interface between user and screen and perhaps an increasingly outmoded one at that.[21]

Despite their explicit opposition in many respects, what the piecemeal approaches share with the media and technology ontologists is a shift away from analyzing the logic of the film text or film work and toward a focus on the realm of sensory experience.[22] The proliferation of English-language books on Gilles Deleuze and cinema as well as the recent returns to phenomenology in both film theory and new media studies privilege what is no longer called the imaginary but is now referred to as affect or sensation. An emphasis on signification has been replaced by an emphasis on asignifying intensities, on the haptic and tactile, on bodies and pleasures. Most of these writings would wish to separate themselves from Bordwell and Carroll's "post-theory," but if the cognitivists' studies of perception and comprehension grounded in "biological propensities" and "cognitive universals" would strike the Deleuzian as too normative and not properly nomadic, let's identify what they have in common: a refusal to see media in terms of either the subject or representation and an unqualified dismissal of the utility of concepts such as identification, ideology, or any terminology derived from psychoanalysis or Saussurean linguistics.[23] Across a wide range of approaches, the tendency is to reverse the Metzian dogma. Today, the dominant assumption of theoretical or philosophical writing on the moving image is that the goal is to wrest it from the symbolic and restore it to the imaginary. A film, we are often told today, should not be interpreted but rather should be understood immanently as a heterogeneous bodily and/or cognitive and neurological experience.

Lacan's use of "symbolic" is just as out of favor as his concept of "imaginary," so it might be better to say that what is rejected is the logic of interpretation contained in Metz's call for winning cinema for the symbolic. Broadly, what is rejected is a certain Marxian tradition of critical thought in which the analysis of film proceeded deductively from the political premise that the hierarchies of a class-divided patriarchal Western culture are embedded in the viewing practices we take to be normal. Noël Carroll claimed that film theory "mystified movies,"[24] but it might be more accurate to claim that what he was rejecting was the *demystification* of movies or the modes of discourse that took as their premise that movies *could be demystified* and that they were not merely the sum of their parts. After all, as Jacques Rancière argues, demystifying requires an element of mystifying since it is a literary as much as a philosophical or theoretical gesture.[25] As Marx claimed about the commodity form, it does not *appear* mysterious; its metaphysical dimension, not its use value, is revealed by analysis.[26]

While film studies has tended to move away from psychoanalysis, Jacques Lacan is kept alive in a new eclectic Lacanian cultural criticism associated primarily with Slavoj Žižek.[27] Here too there is a shift away from the symbolic, but it is toward the failure of symbolization—not a materialism of the body, but the way that films and generally filmic narratives reach an impasse in the traumatic void of the third prong of the Lacanian triad—the Real. The Real for Lacan is not the "reality effect" focused on by seventies film theory, which for Lacan is imaginary, but rather the void or "object-cause" that both is absent from being counted within yet sustains the functioning of any machine, language game, logic of coherence, reality- or subject-effect. Žižek explicitly attacks the post-theory turn for renouncing the promise of film theory. He seizes upon Bordwell and Carroll's claim that psychoanalysis is *the* fundamental problem with film theory as a discipline,[28] but those of us still faithful to psychoanalysis might notice here a displacement on the part of the post-theorists.

Psychoanalysis is a convenient scapegoat for a rejection of seventies film theory because the assumption is that it is a scientifically dubious hermeneutic without any necessarily political valence. Post-theory's attack on the vacuity of theory is, true to its logic, conceived on epistemological and not political grounds. The politics of theory, they claim, are a smokescreen; hence, their emphasis on psychoanalysis. What is dismissed is that its use in seventies film theory was explicitly part of a feminist project as well as firmly within the tradition of Marxist ideology critique. In the following decades, psychoanalysis also would play an important, if sometimes more contentious, role, in certain strains of postcolonial theory, theories of the representation of race, and queer theory. The post-theory or anti-theory position thus needs to be seen, at least in part, as one attempt to erase from academic film theory the influence of the political convictions that emerged out of the sixties—a project that linked both theory and political cinema. Post-theory ignores that theory itself, as one of the ways of talking about and experiencing film, has a history that is not extricable from its object.[29]

This entwining of theory and praxis is a central component of what D. N. Rodowick, following Sylvia Harvey, had in mind when he diagnosed seventies film theory as "a discourse of political modernism." It is one of the many virtues of Rodowick's work—from *The Crisis of Political Modernism* (1988) up to and including the trilogy *The Virtual Life of Film* (2007), *Elegy for Theory* (2014), and *Philosophy's Artful Conversation* (2015)—to treat film theory historically. In his reading of film theory from the late 1960s through the early 1980s as a "discourse of political modernism," Rodowick grasped the extent to which "theory" stood for a position that advocated for a new form of filmmaking practice. Ideology critique was tied to an idea of a counter-cinema that performed within film practice the very function of theory. Rodowick argued that this position led to a deadlock:

The ascription of "theoretical practice" as a function of "materialist" film practice, the differentiation of film form according to criteria of epistemology, identity, and the body, in short the identification of critical practice and knowledge as a property of these forms, all contributed to marking theory as a relation *external* to the "the text." Implicitly, the theoretical discourse that articulated these concepts became a supplemental relation: an adjunct to "political/aesthetic" practice but not a part of it.[30]

Or as Rodowick put it in 1994, political modernism's tendency to suggest that the subjectivity of the spectator was a product of the film text or apparatus foreclosed the possibility of thinking "the potential of film criticism and theory for actively constructing meaning in relation to film and creating new positions of reading."[31]

Rodowick's argument is, in effect, the opposite of Bordwell's critique of seventies film theory as Grand Theory. Whereas Bordwell claims that Grand Theory places all power in the hands of theory, Rodowick suggests that "political modernist" discourse denies any power to theory whatsoever because it suggests that it is only a film that can achieve the goal to which theory aspires—a properly materialist text. This is because theory, in this logic, is "external to the text." Film theory recognized a critical and political dimension to aesthetics, but it tended to fail to think its own aesthetic dimension. For Bordwell, on the other hand, not only is the aesthetic dimension of theory extrinsic to the substance of its arguments, but the critical or political dimension of a film is similarly a distraction from any understanding of its function as an aesthetic object (except in very specific instances). According to Bordwell, when theory "reads" a film's politics or ideology, it actually imposes a political interpretation onto a film. The "politics" attributed to films by theorists derives only from the Grand Theory itself, which sees it everywhere.

Bordwell is one of a number of contemporary film theorists or philosophers of film who argue that "theories generally underdetermine political viewpoints."[32] By releasing film theory from the burden of having to be guided by political and ideological agendas, they have helped usher in a host of new research programs and methodologies derived from analytic philosophy, cognitivist psychology, or philosophies of mind that do not assign any a priori political stakes to their theoretical inquiries.

Rodowick, for his part, has resisted the idea that theories of culture can ever achieve the kind of apolitical neutrality that the sciences aspire to. Instead he claims that such theories can only ever be matters of soliciting agreement about sense and meaning. Therefore he aligns himself with a philosophical turn in film studies—his stated models are Deleuze and Stanley Cavell, but it is Cavell who helps define his approach to philosophy as marked by an "ethical" commitment to "epistemological self-examination."[33] Politics in this approach is viewed no longer as intrinsic to cinema and a necessary guiding force for film theory, but rather as a commitment that one is ethically obliged to acknowledge if and only if it informs one's methods and conclusions. Despite Rodowick's insistence that he has not abandoned the project of film theory, we are a long way from the claim—from Benjamin to Agamben, and including the seminal essays of sixties and seventies film theory—that, as Comolli and Narboni put it, "every film is political."

It is the argument of this book that both Bordwell and Rodowick are right to suggest that film theory in the 1970s tended to undertheorize its own position in constructing the link between cinema and politics. The diametrical opposition between their claims about the role theory played is due to a fundamental ambiguity in seventies film theory, a failure to think through the relation between aesthetics, theory, and politics. Bordwell and Rodowick, in very different ways, seem to take this failure as evidence that one needs to abandon the axiomatically political approach to film theory. Do we follow the lead of these thinkers and cut the knot that that entwines film theory with political and ideological questions? In a moment when literary theorists are proposing we embrace a quasi-neutral descriptive practice of "surface reading,"[34] when the latest forms of continental philosophy to be embraced by the art world, such as "object-oriented philosophy" or "speculative realism," prioritize metaphysics over politics,[35] when academic consensus seems more and more to accept Bruno Latour's once provocative claim that "critique has run out of stream,"[36] should film studies fall in line?

Is this the inevitable conclusion when, as Rancière has frankly acknowledged, the investment in theory as a discourse that could provide a way of definitively comprehending whether a given film, an auteur,

an arrangement of shots, or a camera movement is "idealist or materialist, progressive or reactionary" was ultimately a lost cause? As he
puts it, "How can we close the gap, how can we conceive the equation
between the pleasure we take in the shadows that are projected onto the
screen, the intelligence of an art, and that of a vision of the world—this
is what we thought we could expect from a theory of cinema."[37] Theory,
in other words, promised to unify the pleasures of cinephilia with an
argument about what cinema is and with an ethics or politics. This unity,
Rancière argues, is impossible. Where one searches for it, one finds only
gaps (écarts) or else the willed unity that leads only to dogma and
contradiction.

But if one cannot definitively tie a tracking shot to a moral claim, as
Godard (following his colleague Luc Moullet) once asserted,[38] and if the
films that have most haunted us or given us the most pleasure cannot
necessarily be connected by a straight line to the idea of art or cinema
we find most compelling and to the political ideals we wish to see es-
poused, it is not because cinema is nothing other than the sum total of
individual films reduced to their empirically specifiable properties and
must be definitively separated from discourses about art and politics. The
mixture of discussions about artistic practices with ideas about the world
we live in is not, as an analytic philosopher might tell us, "a category
mistake."[39] Rather, as Rancière argues, these gaps make possible "a common space of thought," and "thinking about cinema circulates within
this space, exists at the heart of these gaps and tries to determine some
sort of interconnection."[40] This is a thinking that is as present in films
themselves as in film theory.

———— ∞ ————

This book proposes that we cannot separate pleasures and affects, ideas
about what cinema is and the politics of cinema any more than we can
effectively unify them. The chapters of this book offer different ways of
conceptualizing politics in relation to film and philosophy that will show
us how we can cut through the false choice between theories that assume
that politics either overdetermine or underdetermine theory.

To rethink the politics of film theory and philosophy today, I have focused on three contemporary European thinkers and their ideas about cinema: Jacques Rancière, Alain Badiou, and Giorgio Agamben. And I have situated each figure in terms of another important figure in the history of film theory and philosophy: namely, Althusser, Deleuze, and Benjamin. This is a way to engage not only cinema and media studies today, but also their history and, more specifically, the role that continental philosophy has played in defining the terms in Anglo-American film studies of how we understand what makes theory and cinema political. Critics of "Theory" tend to be right in at least one respect: the latest theories, often associated with new master thinkers and reductively summed up by a limited set of ready-to-hand concepts or slogans, all too often are posed in stark opposition to the theories that are no longer considered fashionable and earlier arguments get dismissed and forgotten, awaiting resurrection at some later date. (Academic knowledge production thrives as much off of *returns* to earlier paradigms as it does off of claims of radical newness.) By situating these figures in the context of earlier generations of influential thinkers, I hope to rethink the history of theory and philosophy in film studies, acknowledging both continuities and ruptures. One goal is to show that seventies film theory remains a useful starting point for considering the politics of cinema even as we must rethink and reject certain of its dominant assumptions.

Rancière, Badiou, and Agamben are part of the latest generation of radical continental thinkers to become fashionable in American humanities departments and the art world, but they nonetheless remain relatively ignored within film and media studies. The purpose of this book is to provide a critical introduction to their specific contributions to thinking about cinema in relation to the history of film studies. More specifically, I show how each of these thinkers conceptualizes the relationship between theory, cinema, and politics in the context of the history of film theory and the influence of continental thought on Anglo-American film studies. What I demonstrate are the generative ways that each of these thinkers preserves the legacy of film theory as part of a political project in contrast to many other new trends in film studies.

Despite significant differences among them, these thinkers share the following significant traits: First, unlike the analytic, cognitive, or ontological approaches in film studies today, all three maintain the centrality of thinking the link between cinema, politics, and art. Second, at the same time, they all pose this link as a problem that needs to be rethought, and they reject significant aspects of both the "political modernism" and cultural studies approaches that dominated film studies in the seventies and eighties. They offer an approach to film theory that assumes neither that all films or theories are political (as was often claimed in the seventies and eighties) nor that politics underdetermines theory (as is often claimed today), but rather suggests that we analyze both theories and films in terms of how they might be seen to construct connections between cinema and politics. To think of cinema *as politics* becomes an axiom of film-philosophy rather than a normative claim. Third, they are all interested in asking once again, "What is cinema?" and they provide ways of thinking about cinema not only in terms of the projected feature film, but in a more expansive sense that can help us account for transformations in how moving images are produced, distributed, and exhibited in the twenty-first century. Fourth, all three thinkers conceptualize cinema in terms of a relationship between being and appearance, but attempt to do so outside the tradition of phenomenology. Fifth, none of these thinkers privilege the symbolic over the imaginary as was done in seventies film theory or political modernist discourse. Nor, on the other hand, do they privilege affect over textual signification, as is often done today. They all point to cinema as an arena for rethinking the relationship between sensory experience and signification in a nonhierarchical relationship. Sixth, all are interested in following Deleuze in reversing the relationship between film and theory. Theory is no longer applied to film, but rather conditioned by it. Finally, the politics of cinema, though never definable outside of specific instances, always concerns the affirmation of equality against a logic of control.

Cinema/Politics/Philosophy argues for the value of the approaches offered by these thinkers at a moment when the retreat from seventies film theory all too often means a retreat from politics. At the same time, it shows how in their search for solutions to the deadlock of earlier forms of politicized theories of the arts, these thinkers run up against their own limitations: Rancière is not able to entirely escape the ambiguities and confusions that he brilliantly exposes in so many other attempts to think the relation between aesthetics and politics; Badiou's strict division of modes of truth is undermined by his understanding of cinema as an impure mass art; Agamben's refusal of dialectical thought tends to return to a quasi-theological conception of art in which salvation is always just beyond our grasp. Nor, as we will see, do these thinkers all agree. On the contrary, there are numerous tensions and outright disagreements in their conceptions of cinema and philosophy. Nonetheless, the critiques of each of these thinkers and the tensions between them are meant not to dispose of any of these thinkers, but rather to open up new ways of thinking about the relationship between film theory and politics. In the final chapter, I offer notes toward an egalitarian and emancipatory cinema philosophy for the twenty-first century.

A NOTE ON THE THEORY/PHILOSOPHY DISTINCTION

By framing this book as one on continental *philosophy*, it may seem as if I am locating it within a recent "philosophical turn" in film studies. There is some truth to this, and I will address why the thinkers I examine (especially Deleuze, Badiou, and Agamben) might be better understood as philosophers rather than theorists, and why this is not merely a semantic distinction. On the other hand, this reading is open to misunderstanding because each of these thinkers is chosen because of the ways he continues the legacy of what Badiou calls the "anti-philosophers" Marx, Nietzsche, and Freud, and therefore also the legacy of critical theory, critique, structuralism, and poststructuralism—in other words, the significant modes of critical thought that have tended to be grouped under the category "theory" in the American academic context and that all at various times in various ways have been defined in opposition to philosophy proper. In other words, each of these thinkers might be understood in terms of the history of film theory and to be outside, or even against, the dominant currents of what might be called the new philosophies of film.

ON WHAT NOT TO EXPECT FROM THIS BOOK

A note about film examples: It is common in introductions to philosophers on film to supplement the analysis with an example that applies the work of the philosopher to a particular film. I have made a conscious choice to avoid this tactic. The approach of this book is largely philosophical or theoretical, and by investigating the relationship between aesthetic and political philosophy, it may appear on occasion to take us far afield from cinema itself. The subject of this book is not merely film theory, but cinema within the larger context of contemporary continental theory and philosophy and its influence in Anglo-American film and media studies. Numerous films and filmmakers will be mentioned over the course of this book, and certain ones will be given closer scrutiny, but my decision to avoid the model common to a book such as this in which each philosopher's ideas are coupled with a particular film example meant to illustrate the ideas is intrinsic to the argument of the book as a whole. A philosopher's thought, as Deleuze rightly argued, should not be grasped as a grid that can then be applied to its object. The chapters in this book are not meant to provide a series of options for ready-to-hand application. This is not intended as a handbook for Rancièrian or Badiouian or Agambenian readings of individual films in such a way as to update and reproduce a certain academic relation to theory that has been all too common. Rather, *Cinema/Politics/ Philosophy* is an investigation into different ways of thinking about cinema and asking the question: in what sense is cinema political? The hope is that this book will inspire philosophical approaches to new forms of cinema today that draw from these thinkers. But such approaches will be not merely examples to demonstrate the value of the philosophy, but rather new philosophical ideas that emerge out of new forms of cinema.

Additionally, the reader of this book should not expect much in the way of biography or even intellectual history, insofar as the latter focuses on the specific histories of institutions that shaped the ideas being discussed and the chronological trajectory of each thinker's thought. This book emphasizes the importance of looking at film theory historically, but it does so with attention to the history of debates within Anglo-American film studies, on the one hand, and the historicity of the philosophical arguments in relation to larger historical forces shaped by the development of global capitalism, on the other.

Finally, the charge will no doubt be made that as a book with politics in its title there is little here about the actual politics of specific films. I decided to limit this book, as best I could, to what may be called metapolitical questions related to the history of the theory of cinema. These are questions that I believe are preliminary to any analysis of specific films. Political readings of individual films are in great abundance, but what is often lacking in these readings is an explicit and self-conscious conceptualization and understanding of how theory or philosophy understands art or cinema as political. That is the subject of this book.

There is no single right way, no invariable formula, to determine the politics of a given film or of cinema in general. On the other hand, to isolate cinema from politics in the name of art is always reactionary and foreign to our experience of a medium so central to how we live in this world. This book offers an approach to the politics of cinema for the twenty-first century to free us from the dogmatism of so many past attempts to define the politics of cinema or deny its possibility. We need a new philosophical approach to thinking through how cinema can alter our ability to conceive of what is possible and imagine new forms of life.

1

CINEMATIC EQUALITY

Rancière and Film Theory After Althusser

T hough he wrote absolutely nothing about film, perhaps no thinker was more influential to the cutting-edge currents of seventies film theory than the French philosopher Louis Althusser. By reading Marx to the letter through the lens of structuralism and Lacanian psychoanalysis, Althusser's seminars and writings in the 1960s offered the tools for analyzing the internal structure of texts in relation to both subjectivity and history.[1] In the wake of the political consciousness that emerged in the 1960s, new forms of agitational independent cinema, and an upheaval in university curricula informed by revolutionary student demands, there was an increasing desire to take mass culture and film seriously as a subject for academic study understood as a priori political. Althusser's thought supplied a method for reading cinema politically that seemed to answer the call for a new, more rigorous film theory in fidelity to the political events of late sixties.

Introductions to Jacques Rancière frequently begin with the story of his parting of ways with his Althusserian past over his realization that the mode of reading Althusser attributed to Marxist science required assuming a position of mastery. One of the four students who collaborated with Althusser on *Reading Capital*,[2] the seminal 1965 volume that helped codify the conception of textual reading that grounded the practice of much seventies film theory in France, the United States, Britain, and elsewhere, Rancière in 1974 published *La Leçon D'Althusser*, announcing a definitive break with his former professor in dramatic fashion. He revealed the "lesson" of Marxist reading as defined by Althusser to be complicit with what it sought to subvert—namely, inequality. According to Rancière, "Marxist science" not only failed to transform but rather collaborated with the university as an institution set on reproducing itself as the guardian of knowledge.

The education system had been identified by Althusser as perhaps the most powerful and effective "ideological state apparatus" in France at the time. The teaching of Marxism by Althusser and his former students, including Rancière, was meant to change this. Althusser had created a theoretical edifice designed to absolve itself of accusations of vulgar Marxism while ensuring its rigorous separation from bourgeois ideology. But, Rancière argued, the radical pedagogy that emerged out of Althusser's rereading of Marx, which was meant to carry on the spirit of May '68, had become none other than the effacing of politics by the antiegalitarian discourse of the university at its most stultifying.

What is ultimately interesting about the narrative of Rancière's break from Althusser is how its consequences have unfolded over the course of Rancière's writing. It is not just a simple narrative in which the king is exposed as naked—the radical politics of the intellectual master revealed to be enhancing his own power while excluding the excluded he claimed to be speaking for. This gesture of unveiling is no more emancipatory than what it seeks to expose. Rather, Rancière's break from Althusser can be seen in retrospect to initiate a two-part discovery: (1) politics should be defined as axiomatic equality and (2) axiomatic equality is not a science but must be conceived of in relation to aesthetics. The importance of aesthetics becomes more explicit in Rancière's more recent work, but it is my contention that his disagreement with Althusser over science and politics was from the very beginning a disagreement over aesthetics. As I will demonstrate, for Rancière, thinking the interrelation of aesthetics, politics, and theory is necessary to think equality and therefore the politics of cinema.

Althusser, by largely bracketing aesthetics in the attempt to conceptualize the relation between philosophy (or theory) and politics, provided a model of reading or analysis for the politicized film theory of the late sixties and seventies that while frequently generative was bound to lead to an impasse. Rancière's work provides a way out of this impasse not through a new solution so much as a brilliant rethinking of the history of the relation between aesthetics and politics grounded in a commitment to emancipation. We must rethink theory/philosophy itself through the question of aesthetics, the ways in which the sensible is shared and divided, to offer an egalitarian approach to cinema's politics in opposition to the more hierarchical tendencies in film theory understood as ideology critique.

THE AXIOM OF EQUALITY

If, as Bergson maintained, all philosophers have only one idea, for Rancière it is contained in the following axiom: equality without conditions. His writing on cinema can be grasped as part of the intractable pursuit of this impossible idea. Rancière's vigilance about "equality without conditions" means always questioning the conditions of possibility of attempts to define politics. As he demonstrates, positions that promote what goes by the names "subversion" and "resistance," if not Rancière's preferred terms "equality," "democracy," and "emancipation," are again and again conditioned by a framework of consensus and inclusion that attempts to neutralize the radical dimension of political equality.[3] We are familiar with this insistence on the "radical" to ensure the theorist's political capital, but it has a precise meaning here as a *root* equality, an equality that grounds politics and is not an ostensible end that is dispensed with in the political process, as it is for many liberal theorists and even many "radicals." Rancière then is interested not only in criticizing conservative thinkers who denounce equality outright because it is a threat to a well-ordered society or the supposedly "natural" state of affairs that emerges from human evolution (and a market economy), but also in critics and theorists who take up progressive or radical banners to delimit what counts as seeable, sayable, and doable. The terrain of what is seeable, sayable, and doable must always be challenged by any conception of politics as axiomatic equality. Another term for the "seeable, sayable, and doable" is what Rancière has called, in his most well-known slogan, "le partage du sensible," or the distribution (both sharing and division) of the sensible. Politics, in Rancière's view, must always intervene in how the sensible is shared and divided and affirm the "anonymous capacity of anyone" to speak or make a claim. The "anyone" who speaks is the one without qualifications who assumes his or her equality without conditions.

This vigilance about equality extends from Rancière's writings on Marxism, pedagogy, and democratic theory to his work on literature, visual art, and cinema. But what is the precise relationship between political equality and the experience of art or film? One of the keys to Rancière's method is to understand that this question cannot be answered with a simple formula because, for him, it should remain a question—or rather, a site of struggle and dissensus. Equality without conditions annuls itself if it remains a mere regulative principle. Equality acquires meaning when it is instantiated or inscribed.[4] Rancière's conception of political equality is as a situated, localized intervention. How is it possible that equality can be without conditions *and* situated, rooted in the concrete material world of political struggle? We could clarify by suggesting that equality *without* conditions is in a certain sense conditioned, but only by the very conditions it breaks from. The anonymous capacity of anyone, an equality without conditions, always means inscribing something that cannot be accounted for, that both exists and does not exist, that is, in Rancière's terms, "the part of those who have no part."[5] This logic of the immanent break can be thought or imagined only through a paradoxical logic. It is in this sense that it is an impossible idea. The politics of axiomatic equality then is always a question of *aesthetics* because it always involves staging, making fictions, reframing, constructing a new mise-en-scène and montage as an intervention into "le partage du sensible,"[6] or what was once known as "the symbolic order" or "ideology."[7] Politics, in other words, has an aesthetic (and cinematic) dimension.

Correspondingly, aesthetics has a political dimension; this is what has led Rancière to investigate regimes of images and textual and artistic production as arenas where equality gets inscribed and thwarted as a counterpart to thinking through the aesthetics of politics. A painting, novel, or film, he has made clear, to many of his interlocutors' disappointment, should not be identified as a political act in itself—its very function and identification as art or entertainment that frames its legibility precludes just that—but like a theoretical essay or philosophical treatise, it constructs ways of thinking what politics might mean through new arrangements of common images and ideas. As Rancière has put it, "Art promises a political accomplishment that it cannot satisfy, and thrives on that ambiguity. That is why those who want to isolate it from politics are somewhat beside the point. It is also why those who want it to fulfill its political promise are condemned to a certain melancholy."[8] To say that the right kind of political art creates active political subjects where they did not exist before is to give up on art's capacity to be available to its spectators as equals. On the other hand, to preserve the promise that art can change the world, we have to let go of the idea that we can anticipate its effects.

This investigation into the politics of aesthetics and the aesthetics of politics has meant that Rancière has continued the project that informed sixties and seventies film theory at the same time as he has departed from it in significant ways. As discussed in the introduction, this era of theory is no longer our own. The current interest in Rancière might be seen as part of the tide that has turned away from the central concerns of sixties and seventies theory—another name to signify our suspicion of the hermeneutics of suspicion. This, for example, is how Hal Foster situates Rancière in a 2012 essay in *October*, "Post-Critical." Foster, sensitive to the appropriation of Rancière as what he takes to be the latest fashion by those who believe they have moved beyond critical theory, asserts that Rancière gives up on critique in favor of "wishful thinking," and in turn has become "the new opiate of the art world left."[9] Though I share Foster's concern about the abandonment of critical thought in contemporary writing on art, his target is misplaced. Rather, I would like to propose how Rancière's work may provide a way to start rethinking the very problems and questions about the legacy of critical theory and ideology critique that persist in contemporary cinema studies, which in turn have application for the study of art and literature. Rancière's thinking about the relation of art, theory, and politics in relation to Althusser's own thinking about that relation makes it possible to reconsider and rearrange the terms that dominate the current retreat from an Althusserian film theory that all too often amounts to a retreat from politics.

THE PARADOX OF
BRECHTIAN-ALTHUSSERIANISM

Before taking a closer look at Rancière's critique of Althusser and how this relates to his writing on cinema and more specifically his conception of the politics of cinema, I will examine a certain problem in Althusser's limited conception of aesthetics and how this problem is intrinsic to his influential understanding of the relation between politics and theory or philosophy. This limited conception of aesthetics can be seen at the root of many of the unacknowledged contradictions of the dominant operations of seventies film theory.

Althusser may have written nothing about film and little about art and aesthetics, but it is difficult to overestimate the influence his work had on the dominant currents of sixties and seventies film theory. He did, however, have an interest in Brecht, which has informed much of the uptake of Althusser in not only writings about political theater and performance but also film and literary theory. The link between Brechtian political modernism and Althusserian symptomatic reading is found both in seminal political films from the era, for example in Godard's *La Chinoise* (1967) or *Le Gai Savoir* (1969), and in many of the most referenced theoretical essays in *Screen*, *Cahiers du Cinéma*, and *Cinéthique* in the late sixties and seventies.

A significant, if not well-known, piece by Althusser from 1968 provides a remarkable illustration of the logic of Althusserianism and its impasses for thinking the political dimension of art, to which Rancière's work may be seen as providing a novel and generative solution. By following the logic of this short unfinished essay, titled "On Brecht and Marx," we can understand better why Rancière's need to rethink the relationship between philosophy and politics in Althusser's thought ultimately can be seen as leading him to rethink the meaning of aesthetics. We can also see clearly the deadlock in Althusserian aesthetics that I will show persists in modified form in many of the most influential film theory essays of the late sixties and seventies.

"On Brecht and Marx" is Althusser's most explicit attempt to think aesthetic practice as a form of politics. Brecht is offered to provide within the realm of artistic practice an analogous breakthrough to Marx's break with traditional philosophy. The analogy between Brecht and Marx is established on the ground that they both generate within their respective domains, philosophy and theater, a new kind of practice based on a knowledge of the repression of politics that founds both their practices.[10] This might be seen as an axiom of theoretical inquiry following from Althusser: everything is political, but the political dimension tends to be obscured. The form that politics takes when it is obscured is called ideology. Politics is the repressed absent cause that needs to be revealed from any given discourse. According to Althusser, Brecht and Marx are examples of an artist and a philosopher who realized this and attempted to make it intrinsic to their respective practices. Althusser makes clear that for both Brecht and Marx this new practice is less a genuinely new theater or new philosophy and more a demystification of theater or philosophy within their respective domains. Politics, which according to Althusser determines both theater and philosophy, is typically repressed in favor of enjoyment—aesthetic enjoyment or enjoyment of speculation. One must put theater and philosophy in their true places, but to do this one has to carry out a "displacement" within theater and within philosophy.[11] Through the displacement of the point of view of theater and philosophy, we can, in Althusser's words, "yield the floor to politics."[12] But we can do this only by showing that theater or philosophy is not politics and that it is only theater or philosophy. Politics in both cases is conceived as the ground of these practices, but it speaks only when its silence is revealed.

But this analogy between Brecht and Marx, Althusser suggests, can go only so far because not only is philosophy not politics and theater not politics, but theater is not philosophy. Here Althusser makes clear that he is unsatisfied with Brecht's politics of theater because the specificity of theater, its difference from philosophy, politics, science, and life, is that it shows and entertains, and yet showing and entertaining are the very things that *disguise* theater's difference from philosophy, politics, science, and life. To show what theater is, we have to betray what it is, but it must remain theater and only theater in the process without generating a new mystification. Althusser asks, how is it that theater can still provide entertainment through mere showing while also thwarting this logic at the same time? Althusser excuses Brecht for not solving the problem because he is finally a man of the theater and not a philosopher, and insists that, in the end, the true importance of Brecht is not his theory but his theatrical practice that takes ideology for its raw material.[13] But what was the answer to this question? How can theater use its own means to become political without falling into an idealistic trap of obscuring its own difference from politics? The piece remained unfinished, leaving the reader in suspense.

Nonetheless, we shouldn't imagine that Althusser had a satisfying solution to this impasse that he merely failed to get onto paper. At stake is the relation between politics, science, and aesthetics—a relation that we might say, to use a term of Althusser's, remained the "unthought" in his own theory of reading. Althusser's difficulty theorizing the politics of art and aesthetics is intrinsic to the limitations of his major works on Marx and ideology in the 1960s. The privileging of the symbolic over the imaginary—which was a central gesture of seventies film theory and had its roots in Althusser—can be accomplished only through a strict separation between theory and art.

To better understand the difficulty Althusser had in resolving Brecht's conception of the politics of theater, we can turn to what may be Althusser's most well-known piece on art. In Althusser's 1966 open letter to André Daspre, published in English as "A Letter on Art," he states that "the real difference between art and science lies in the *specific form* in which they give us the same object in quite different ways: art in the form of 'seeing' and 'perceiving' or 'feeling,' science in the form of *knowledge* (in the strict sense, by concepts)."[14] He continues, "Art makes us 'see' 'conclusions without premises,' whereas knowledge makes us penetrate into the mechanism which produces the 'conclusions' out of the 'premises.'"[15] In other words, for Althusser, art offers an immanent affective perspective on appearance, but is silent about its own conditions of possibility. Science is what gives us knowledge of causality, the mechanism that generates the logic of cause and effect. Even as Althusser's notion of "structural causality" would attempt to break from bourgeois conceptions of scientific method, his conception of the distinction between science and art still depends upon a resolutely classical bourgeois, or even Aristotelian, conception of art. Only theory (though he uses the word "philosophy" in "On Brecht and Marx") can produce knowledge of the absent cause of politics, whereas art can appeal only to our senses.

This opposition between science and art is the same one that Althusser makes between science and ideology. Ideology, he tells us, is not simply false consciousness that can be done away with. Rather, "it is a structure essential to the historical life of societies."[16] As he puts it in "Marxism and Humanism" in 1964, ideology, "while it really does designate a set of existing relations, unlike a scientific concept, it does not provide us with a means of knowing them. In a particular (ideological) mode, it designates some existents, but it does not give us their essences."[17] Ideology, like art, corresponds to the surface level of appearance but does not give us a means for knowledge.

It is this firm distinction between art/ideology and knowledge/theory that Rancière will object to, and he will propose a different conception of the politics of aesthetics. But before I get to Rancière's intervention in more detail, we first need to look at the centrality of Althusserianism in dominant modes of film theory. In French and Anglo-American film theory after 1968, from Jean-Louis Comolli to Laura Mulvey, cinema is understood as essentially ideological and as such could not be confused with theory/knowledge; and yet, at the same, time, it somehow has to be on the side of theory/knowledge to be political. We consistently see an attempt to use Althusser for a politicized film theory that failed to solve this theoretical problem.

THE ALTHUSSERIAN LEGACY IN
SEVENTIES FILM THEORY

Althusser's essay on Brecht remained unfinished, but it reveals his inability to think the relation between art and politics within the terms of his Marxian reading practice, an inability that was easily overlooked due to his relative neglect of questions of aesthetics. The paradoxical logic of Althusser's reading of Brecht can be found smoothed over in seventies film theory indebted to his Lacan-inspired definition of ideology as that which "represents the imaginary relationship of individuals to their real conditions of existence."[18] As I've proposed, Christian Metz provides us with the formula in his 1975 essay "The Imaginary Signifier": The role of film theory is "to disengage the cinema-object from the imaginary and win it for the symbolic."[19] Peter Wollen linked this logic explicitly back to Brecht to advocate for a materialist cinema that countered ideology: "Brecht wanted to find a concept of 'representation' which would account for a passage from perception/recognition to knowledge/understanding, from the imaginary to the symbolic."[20] Here we see how the Althusserian-Lacanian language is used to account for the logic that says that art, like ideology, separates us or alienates us from recognizing the material conditions that produce it. If theory can draw our attention to the symbolic dimension understood as knowledge of material conditions, art, with Brecht as the model, is also meant to perform the work of theory. Althusser, as we saw, argued that Brecht developed a practice that came close to performing the work of theory, but he also insisted that this was not fully possible. For dominant modes of film theory, however, this contradiction was ignored. Film theory used Althusserian-Lacanian language to not only supply the vocabulary for the theoretical operation that wrests the symbolic from art, but also account for the Brechtian *Verfremdungseffekt* as a solution within the artwork itself. The *Verfremdungseffekt* is the aesthetic operation that through producing distance or separation from what we are watching ruptures the initial distance that characterizes spectatorship. Whether conceived of as an immanent break within the artwork itself or through the intervention of theory, for 1970s film theory the goal is a passage or break out of appearance or sensory experience and into knowledge. In film, like theater, distance is perceived as immediacy, but once we become aware of the distance through distancing we are restored to real immediacy in the form of knowledge.

In contrast to what he saw as the insufficiently political Greenbergian modernism of the American avant-garde, Wollen insisted that for Brecht, knowledge was important because it corresponded to the "workings of society" and was not simply a matter of being aware of the "artifice of art."[21] This is what distinguished the discourse that Rodowick (following Harvey) called "political modernism" from the broader category of modernism, with its emphasis on medium specificity. Althusser's theory of ideology was mobilized to tie the awareness of the artifice of art to the mode of production.

We can see this operation at work in Jean-Louis Baudry's influential essay "Ideological Effects of the Basic Cinematographic Apparatus," published in Cinéthique in 1970. According to Baudry, the "apparatus" (cinema understood expansively as a whole network of material relations and social practices) had the effect of naturalizing and reinforcing the position of unity and mastery of the viewing subject, but since this effect was predicated on hiding its conditions of possibility, it could also be thwarted when the apparatus was exposed. As he put it, "Thus disturbing cinematic elements—similar, precisely, to those elements indicating a return of the repressed—signify without fail the arrival of the instrument 'in flesh and blood,' as in Vertov's Man with a Movie Camera. Both specular tranquility and the assurance of one's own identity collapse simultaneously with the revealing of the mechanism, that is, of the inscription of the film work."[22] The appearance of the production process within the film itself functions as an intrusion of the Real to rescue the imaginary for the symbolic. Awareness of the artifice of art directs us back to the workings of society. The "film work" or "the apparatus" was taken to be "primarily economic" and to include "the mode of production and the process of 'work' in its multiple determinations."[23]

As Jean-Louis Comolli and Jean Narboni put it in their widely cited statement of purpose "Cinema/Ideology/Criticism," first published in *Cahiers du Cinéma* in 1969, "The cinema is burdened from the very beginning . . . by the inevitability of reproducing things not as they are in their concrete reality, but as they are when refracted through ideology. . . . The most important task of the cinema, once we know that it is the nature of this system to turn it into an instrument of ideology, is therefore to question the system of representation itself: to question itself as cinema, in order to provoke a discrepancy or a rupture with its ideological function."[24] Questioning the system of representation and thereby producing knowledge was a blow to ideology and therefore a necessarily political gesture.

Philip Rosen emphasizes how this antirealism was central to the logic of film theory at this time, noting that *Screen* adopted from post-1968 *Cahiers du Cinéma* and *Cinéthique* the idea that

> the fundamental ideological power of cinema is not just its reproduction of socially dominant ideas but also in endowing these ideas with the force of reality itself. And this endowment, they asserted, operates through a tacit, generally accepted sense, among both audiences and practitioners, of what cinema itself is: a technology with a special capacity to capture reality. The theoretical and practical demystification of the filmic illusion of reality is therefore identified as a political project.[25]

In each case, we see that there was a political value attributed to knowledge or awareness in both theory and filmmaking achieved as the result of what amounted to variations of the same operation: mediation made present was to break us out of the illusion of an unmediated reality. As Althusser noted in his analysis of Brecht, this was a problematic operation for art to perform without misunderstanding its position as art and generating another mystification.

This logic, I would argue, was the dominant political pedagogy of so-called seventies film theory. To be clear, I am not accepting the description of this idea of theory as Grand Theory, in David Bordwell's terms—monolithic, totalizing, and constrained by enforced consensus. Indeed, since the term "Grand Theory" has been taken up by many theorists following Bordwell as a shorthand for this era of film theory—including in some cases theorists who are considerably more sympathetic to it than Bordwell—it is worth recognizing how the idea of Grand Theory as articulated by C. Wright Mills in *The Sociological Imagination* was distorted in Bordwell's use. Grand Theory was Mills's term for a self-contained abstract theory as epitomized by Talcott Parsons's work. Grand Theory, according to Mills, unlike Marxism, left the status quo intact, because it did not allow for critique.[26] To call Marxian critique "Grand Theory" was then an explicit reversal of Mills's concept. Of the list of five tenets that Bordwell associates with the Grand Theory of film studies, only two actually correlate with the original conception of Grand Theory—the idea that theory is "top down," and the notion that it works with abstract concepts rather than empirical testing. The additional charges that theory is really a form of hermeneutics rather than theory, that it is "associational," and that it emphasizes bricolage as a method of argumentation are all in effect counter to how Mills defined Grand Theory.[27] Bordwell is of course welcome to develop his own conception of "Grand Theory" distinct from Mills's, but my point is to emphasize how the label of Grand Theory tends to smooth over the debates within seventies film theory and repress the logic of critique that grounded its dominant operations. Unlike Grand Theory in its original conception, critique always appeals to the specific conditions of possibility of a given artwork or discourse and not to a totalizing abstract system. The incoherence of much of the discourse on Grand Theory can be further illustrated when we consider that many of the thinkers associated with it are the same ones labeled "postmodernists." Jean-François Lyotard famously defined postmodern as "incredulity toward metanarratives," or, in other words, a distrust of Grand Theories.[28]

Rosen, in his history of the influential British journal *Screen*, offers a more useful characterization of the era:

Today it is possible to identify something we can call 1970s film theory. This was a self-conscious attempt at renovation by rethinking the fundamental terms through which cinema was experienced and understood in classical film theory and in the standard modes of criticism and analysis. The term "70s film theory" is not only a periodizing label but also a collective one, because it was constituted through a tissue of intersecting, sometimes mutually contestatory arguments and discourses about cinema written by many individuals. So it was always under development. Nevertheless, its common concerns made it a recognizable intellectual constellation, which set the terms for advanced debate in film scholarship for over two decades, arguably even for those who rejected it.[29]

Rosen is right to stress that the period was a dynamic collective project, the terms of which were being contested within the project itself.

The "common concerns" might be defined by the attempt to link three questions or problems: the relation of film to the social and historical world, the internal organization or structure of the film text, and the position of the spectator in relation to the text. These three questions corresponded to three respective methodologies: historical materialism, semiotics/structuralism, and psychoanalysis. A conception of ideology critique derived from Althusser allowed for a way to link them together and in turn to show how cinema was (and was not) political.

Theory was thus defined as a form of ideology critique in which the purpose of theory was to show how art (or aesthetics) is (or fails to be) political. It did this by winning it for the symbolic. At the same time, art was expected to do this all by itself—perform the function of theory and reveal its political dimension. We can return to Comolli and Narboni's "Cinema/Ideology/Criticism" to see more closely the impasse this created for theoretical criticism. Their claim that "every film is political" derived from the same logic that allowed Althusser to argue that both art and philosophy were inherently political.[30] No film is outside politics because each film necessarily positions itself in relation to dominant ideology, which it can either conform to or disrupt. Correspondingly, theory can show how cinema is political in one of two ways: If a film is political because it conforms to the dominant ideology (which is to say, not political at all if by political we mean something positive), then theory reveals its ideological subservience. If it is political because it disrupts ideology, then it does what theory also does, which would seem to make theory's role unnecessary.

The authors of "Cinema/Ideology/Criticism" list eight possible relations that films can have to ideology, deeming two of the categories to be the essential ones—political films that disrupt the dominant ideology either through both signifier and signified or just at the level of the signifier. Comolli and Narboni write, "For Cahiers, these films ((b) and (c)) are the essence of the cinema and make up the essence of the journal."[31] These are the films that the journal says it will focus on, but of the eight categories they define, it is no accident that the descriptions of the essential ones (b and c) and of the one documentary category they endorse (category g) are the three briefest in the taxonomy. If there is a role for theoretical criticism in relation to the essential films, it was never clear what it should be. What can be said about the films that the journal agreed to focus on if the films already do what theory does? Despite their desire for the opposite to be true, in practice there was much more to say about the "bad objects," the five categories of films that were explicitly ideological. The problem was that the division of labor between the work that film did when it showed up its own work—which involved a knowledge effect—and what theory did to show you how it did it remained ambiguous. Following the terms set out by this statement of purpose, it is perhaps no wonder then that over the following decade in the pages of *Cahiers*, far fewer films were discussed than ever before.

The problem is that what exactly Althusserian "scientific criticism" might add to the disruption of ideology a film already performed was necessarily ambiguous when these critics were also working with a conception of Brechtian cinema (rewritten in Althusserian-Lacanian terms) according to which a film could pass from recognition to knowledge or from the imaginary to the symbolic.[32] As Althusser's unfinished 1968 piece on Brecht demonstrates, a closer reading of Althusser on aesthetics would only have further revealed that the problem was not solvable on the terms he offered. Art could not be called upon to do what theory does while at the same time remaining art without blurring the operations of art and theory. Meanwhile, the blurring of art and theory (and the imaginary and the symbolic) threatened the opposition between materialist criticism and ideology that needed to be maintained in order to vouchsafe Marxist theoretical practice as a subjectless science.

The Brechtian-Althusserian logic of Marxist criticism was torn between merging politics, cinema, and theory and separating them. But this logic, as Rancière has argued, was also part of the larger logic of the regime of art that emerged in modernity, the contradictions of which were constitutive of its productive operations. It was not the contradictions themselves but the formulas that sought to obscure them that led to dogma.

As Rosen points out, the didactic polemical form taken by the major essays of seventies film theory, with their emblems of political commitment and appeals to theoretical authority, did not, as Bordwell and Carroll suggested, close down the possibility for debate or innovation. The basic parameters of political modernist ideology critique were constantly being revised and rethought within a framework that allowed for it.

Laura Mulvey's "Visual Pleasure and Narrative Cinema," first published in *Screen* in 1975, is perhaps the most important example of the way a theoretical essay could remain within the basic logic of this idea of political modernism and dramatically reframe it at the same time. Nonetheless, it reveals yet again the impasse of political modernist discourse. Mulvey's essay made explicit the claim that theory as a radical "political weapon" could break us out of the unreflective pleasures of classical cinema, and like many of the other writers of *Screen* who came before her, she saw this process as part of a larger project shared with new forms of avant-garde filmmaking practice.[33] But, at the same time, she credibly argued that managing and controlling the trauma of sexual difference in a phallocentric society was not merely one among the many forms of repressed ideological work done by mainstream cinema, but was, rather, the basis for its very codes and conventions.

In Mulvey's essay, the symbolic was identified with the law and with the patriarchal language of cinema, in which "woman" is confined to the imaginary as a way of repressing the threat of castration (the Real). The image of the woman was thus both lure and threat, a way of eliciting desire and driving the narrative forward, but also of freezing desire and undermining the narrative momentum.[34] But if the role of woman in mainstream film is premised on a contradiction, as Mulvey demonstrates, so too is the theoretical apparatus that exposed the contradiction.

For Mulvey, herself a filmmaker, "a politically and aesthetically avant-garde cinema is now possible, but it can still only exist as a counterpoint."[35] New kinds of films were needed that could "free the look of the camera into its materiality in time and space and the look of the audience into dialectics, passionate detachment."[36] But we still need theory to put us on the road to a "new language of desire."[37] Why? Because we are "still caught within the language of the patriarchy. There is no way in which we can produce an alternative out of the blue, but we can begin to make a break by examining patriarchy with the tools it provides."[38] Appropriating psychoanalysis as a weapon meant strategically using the tools of the symbolic order to "challenge" the pleasure of "mainstream film" by breaking down "these cinematic codes and their relationship to formative external structures."[39] Mulvey was blunt about the costs of this approach: "It is said that analyzing pleasure, or beauty, destroys it. That is the intention of this article."[40] What we must destroy, with the cruel knowledge accorded by theory, is the "satisfaction, pleasure and privilege of the 'invisible guest'" afforded by the classical narrative cinema.[41] Here we come up against a performative contradiction: the goal of theory—breaking down and ultimately destroying the passive object of pleasure—is the very same procedure attributed to the patriarchal order that must be broken down and destroyed.

For Mulvey, active theory destroys the imaginary pleasure of the spectator very much like Jimmy Stewart's character Scotty in *Vertigo*, as she analyzes it, destroys Madeleine (Kim Novak) by revealing that, like Hollywood cinema, her lure conceals a threat. In Mulvey's reading, *Vertigo* is not only a symptomatic example of the patriarchal logic of classical Hollywood narrative cinema, but, though she does not acknowledge it, also an allegory for film theory in relation to cinephilia. As Mulvey stated in an interview published in 2008, the antagonism to the visual pleasure of Hollywood narrative cinema in the 1975 essay must be understood within the context of her own "cinephilia and . . . deep love of Hollywood."[42]

Mulvey, like Scotty, repeats the very trauma from which she wishes to free herself. As she puts it, regarding *Vertigo*, because the pleasure of voyeurism harbors the threat of castration, Scotty first forces the desired object to tell her secret through "persistent cross-questioning." This is Mulvey's own approach to the cinephilic pleasures she is now challenging. In *Vertigo*, when Scotty's interrogations do not yield the desired result, he must remake Madeleine in his image and repeat the trauma. Mulvey argues that ultimately, "repetition . . . does break her down and succeeds in exposing her guilt."[43]

This is, in effect, what Mulvey's essay itself does to classical Hollywood. Mulvey casts classical Hollywood narrative in the role of the woman that must be destroyed for the sake of liberation and theory in the place of the law that exacts the punishment. Theory is needed in addition to new forms of cinematic practice because only knowledge is thought to harbor the power of destruction, whereas imagining that a truly feminine or feminist écriture was already possible within the existing order would fall into ideology. Therefore, the only way to expose that ideology through knowledge is by appropriating that ideology, repeating it, and turning it against itself.

Mulvey effectively reframed the discourse of political modernism by implicitly revealing how, up to that point, the use of psychoanalysis for ideology critique in *Screen* had tended to repress the theory of sexual difference on which it was predicated. More significantly, she identified the overwhelming tendency of classical Hollywood narrative form to be structured on a gendered active/passive binary that reflected and reinforced the logic of a deeply patriarchal society. But the goal of passing from the imaginary to the symbolic was caught in the same contradictory logic as all Brechtian-Althusserian film theory. If Mulvey escapes incoherence, it is by acknowledging the centrality of contradiction within the project. But the powerful polemic leaves undertheorized the underlying conception of what theory could do versus what cinema could do, and the result is a fundamental ambiguity about how best to challenge patriarchal ways of seeing. *Vertigo*, like Josef Von Sternberg's fetishistic films starring Marlene Dietrich, also analyzed by Mulvey, could be seen as either exemplary instances of the insidious ideological logic of

Hollywood narrative cinema or as films that politically reveal this logic and turn it into knowledge. Meanwhile, Mulvey's own essay is vulnerable to being accused of embracing the sadistic patriarchal law in the process of exposing it in mainstream cinema. Today her essay tends to be criticized for its overreliance on psychoanalysis, but the real limitation of her brilliant essay was in reinforcing the binary opposition that dominated seventies film theory between theory as knowledge and cinema as ideology.

AFTER ALTHUSSER:
THEORY WITHOUT POLITICS

It may be claimed that this era of film theory is over because it has been discredited, but whereas the logic of seventies film theory may be out of favor, the repudiation of it is not. Indeed, what is striking today is how often the repudiation takes the form of a strict obversion of this logic. The criticism of the privileging of the symbolic as inscription of mediation gives authority to its reversal in the bodily or affective turn so prevalent in contemporary discourses on the moving image and new media over the last two decades. As Friedrich Kittler remarked in 1999, "There seem to be entire branches of scholarship today that believe they have not said anything at all if they have not said the word 'body' a hundred times."[44] Eugenie Brinkema has more recently provided a rich analysis of both the importance of the affective turn as well as how limited it has often been when it has abandoned questions of form for the sake of individual experience. She writes, "When the history of film and media theory in the 1990s and 2000s is written, it will turn out to be the long decade of the affect."[45] She adds that this new emphasis on affect has frequently been articulated as a demand to recognize what has been left out of the perceived dominant tendencies in the field understood as still derived from seventies film theory. "From the beginning of this recent turn, affect has been theorized defensively—as an omission, a forgotten underside to film and media theory. . . . The turn to affect thus has been more operation than curve, and what it has generated primarily is a series of polemics for its own tropistic gesture."[46] Sometimes anchored in a historical argument about the decline of the narrative feature film and more fluid, dispersive images in the age of the information and networks, the current emphasis in much film theory on "the body," affect, or sensation tends to take its cues from one of two sources: Gilles Deleuze (often appropriating his use of Henri Bergson) or a return to phenomenology to assert an immanent theory of film no longer conceived of as representation. As will be discussed further in the next chapter, despite many significant exceptions, this work tends too often to be a simple reversal of the Metzian dogma—theory becomes an attempt to disengage cinema from the symbolic and win it for the imaginary.

On the other hand, the "Post-Theory" position that has aligned itself with the cognitive sciences is still concerned with theory producing knowledge, but knowledge is no longer considered political. Bordwell has been one of the most influential advocates in American film studies of saving film theory from itself by advancing piecemeal theories that serve to address specific answerable questions. According to Bordwell, the ideological critiques that examine the function of race, gender, and/or class in films rarely tell us much about how films are made or the specific kinds of effects they achieve. According to Bordwell, theories "underdetermine political viewpoints."[47] Yet he implies that politics *overdetermine* certain forms of film interpretations that get called film theories, but are in fact not new theoretical inquiries at all but rather the application of theories imported from elsewhere for the purpose of finding predetermined meanings in films.[48]

The idea that theory underdetermines politics presupposes a certain conception of theory, of politics, and of the relation between the two. Since Bordwell, following Carroll, means by "politics" such examples as one's position on gun control or abortion, and means by "theories" generalizations about the principles by which films achieve specifiable effects, he is no doubt correct that no necessary correlation exists between the two. But this is an extremely narrow conception of what makes theory political. Meanwhile, that which qualifies as genuine theory, in Bordwell's terms, by definition cannot introduce supplement or lack into the distribution of the sensible. As we will see, this conception of theory provides an example of what Rancière's calls "the police"; it is a way of thinking about theory as a discourse in which both aesthetics and politics should be eliminated.

Bordwell provides one strategy for avoiding the contradictions of political modernism: to side with the separation of cinema, theory, and politics, rather than their overdetermination. Art (or film) could be understood as an object of theory in a project in which theory's operations were not to be blurred with those that it sought to explain. Meanwhile, politics could be bracketed entirely. During a period in which theory that sought to tie together politics and aesthetics was dominant, this more circumscribed results-oriented approach could not go about its business in peace and bore the brunt of undoing the knot of political modernism.

How does Bordwell justify the strict separation of theory, art, and politics? While he theorizes based on the hypothesis that theorists and filmmakers function through the same general cognitive processes—as rational actors doing problem solving—he assumes that the problems they are solving are defined by inherently different ends. Films "are designed to achieve certain effects," whereas film studies should be motivated to achieve plausible explanations of the "principles" by which films are designed to achieve those effects.[49] One cost of this approach was that the blurring of art, theory, and politics was no longer thinkable. To claim that theory itself could operate on aesthetic principles to achieve distancing effects or knowledge effects, or that a film like Godard's *Vent D'est* (1970) could, in Peter Wollen's words, "make the mechanics of the film/text visible and explicit,"[50] would only be to bring confusion to Bordwell's project of "historical poetics," which takes art and theory to be two categorically different types of intentional objects.

On the other hand, Bordwell (like Noël Carroll) has no problem with the logic of critical unveiling when it is applied to film theory itself. While the attempt to reveal the unconscious sexual, racial, and class politics of a Hollywood film is seen as an unproductive avenue for a film scholar to pursue, Slavoj Žižek can be unmasked as using "political correctness" to divert attention from close scrutiny of "strategically vague" arguments that likely conceal a view of intellectual work as "a struggle for power."[51] Bordwell and Carroll never accuse films of practicing this kind of deception because, for them, films cannot deceive—only theory can.

Nonetheless, if Rosen is able to include the 1970s work of Bordwell himself as a component of the "intellectual constellation" of seventies film theory, it is because Bordwell subscribed to at least part of the same logic of theory. Neo-formalism, to use the term claimed by Bordwell and Kristin Thompson, restricts theoretical inquiry to the aim of "produc[ing] knowledge," and in that sense it did not share all of the "common concerns" of seventies film theory evoked by Rosen, assuming we take at least one of those concerns to be radical politics. But Bordwell did subscribe to the opposition between theory and art that was shared by Metz and Althusser. Exposing the system of representation, in Comolli and Narboni's terms, or the "imaginary," meant revealing the codes and textual systems that ground the experience of film. Bordwell, and other writers often associated with the University of Wisconsin and influenced by the formalist tradition, were engaged in this practice but without the language of critical unveiling or ideological analysis. Bordwell's critiques of what he calls Grand Theory are not antitheoretical so much as concerned with advocating theoretical examinations of the codes and systems through which films achieve effects, but purged of political a prioris that followed the logic of what Paul Ricoeur famously called "the hermeneutics of suspicion"—the idea that every film was grounded, as Althusser claimed art in general was, in a politics that needed to be uncovered from an economy of pleasure that sought to repress it.

If Brechtian-Althusserian film theory wished to show up the "film work," Bordwell wishes just to show how films work. Whereas the former took politics as the motor for theory, its absent cause, and the latter saw it as noise, they both shared the desire to purge theories of aesthetics in Rancière's sense. To say that theory has an aesthetic dimension means that it is not merely explanatory but implies an "as if"; it is a contingent operation that frames a polemical world.

RANCIÈRE AND THE POLITICS
OF AESTHETICS

In opposition to not only Althusserian film theory but also Bordwellian post-theory and the affective turn, Rancière's work suggests that we need not side with the symbolic over the imaginary or affect and sensation over interpretation. The contradictory logic that Althusser found in Brecht's theory (theater must both show that it is theater and only theater but also become something other than theater) is a theoretical impasse only if we also wish to ensure that the work of art accomplishes the passage from identification to knowledge. As Rancière has proposed, this very contradictory logic, this identification of the unity of opposing terms (knowledge and sight), has been constitutive of art and the thinking of art over the last two centuries. This is what he calls "the aesthetic regime of art." In this regime, the images of cinema and art are not defined by their destiny in either the symbolic or the imaginary, thought or sensation, studium or punctum, actual or virtual, but rather invent new possibilities out of their capacity to play with and neutralize these opposing functions.

As Althusser himself recognized in the case of Brecht, this linking of art and theory in a common project of political modernism reaches an impasse unless we rethink the very relation between the imaginary and symbolic, art and philosophy. The impasse that Althusser recognized in Brecht is the same impasse Rancière recognizes in Althusser. Philosophy, art, and politics must all maintain their places to ensure the passage from ideology to knowledge effect, and yet this very passage is impossible if these places remain unmoved. For Rancière, aesthetics is a name for the blurring of these places. Aesthetics, in other words, is not the realm of the sensory or imaginary in opposition to knowledge, it is a regime of art, and a dimension of other forms of practice, that links and blurs ways of thinking with ways of doing and making.

Rancière proposes that aesthetics as a concept always concerns a relation between sense perception and intelligibility, or as he puts it "between sense and sense,"[52] and therefore undoes the false opposition between a theory that either must insulate the affective sensory dimension of art from the insult of interpretation or, on the other hand, must always save art from being lodged in a presymbolic imaginary on behalf of theoretical knowledge. As such, his work challenges Althusserian political modernism, post-theory, and many of the dominant tendencies of affect theory.

But what is political about this intervention? Or rather, what is the precise relation between politics and cinema for Rancière? In an essay, "The Politics of Literature," Rancière starts off by making clear that he is referring neither to the politics of writers nor to the representation of what is normally understood as political content. Rather, what is at stake is a politics of "literature as literature," or what is political about the literary as such. Correspondingly, if we speak of the politics of cinema, it is not meant to indicate an emphasis on the extent to which films represent the politics of their scenarists or directors. Nor does it mean a focus on films that take either social struggles or the machinations of government as their explicit subject. We should also reject the framework for the debate about a politics of cinema that ties the stakes of the discussion to whether we can affirm or deny a direct or indirect causal connection between films and changes in policy or people's attitudes or opinions about political issues. Indeed, the politics of cinema, Rancière might say, would be better sought in the "very distance" cinema takes in respect to these issues.[53]

Rancière's work argues that there is a politics of cinema as cinema because both politics and cinema are ways "of framing, among sensory data, a specific sphere of experience."[54] They are both forms of what Rancière calls "le partage du sensible," or the sharing and partition of the sensible. There is a politics of cinema because cinema (like literature and other forms of art) "is involved in this partition of the visible and the sayable, in this intertwining of being, doing and saying that frames a polemical common world."[55] We cannot say in what way a film or a work of art will directly influence political action, but we can speak of a politics or a metapolitics internal to a film. Philosophy can draw out and help articulate that internal politics as well as its relation to a "horizon of possible politics."[56]

Rancière shows that literature, like the aesthetic regime of art, is only a little more than two centuries old. The aesthetic regime of art, the regime of art from which literature and ultimately cinema emerge, is an overturning of the representational regime of art in which particular forms demanded particular contents and vice versa. Art is political within the aesthetic regime because it undoes the hierarchical logic of the representative regime; it uses sensory data to establish a community without foundation. It reframes the field of subjectivity impersonally and anonymously and therefore at a certain distance from existing communities that function through a distribution of sensory experience, while always blurring that distance at the same time. When Rancière references "literature as literature," it suggests the influential modernist concept of medium specificity, but the aesthetic regime of art allows us to rethink medium specificity. According to Rancière, literature as literature is not, as the modernist narrative would have it, merely the discovery of the materiality of the written word. In the same way, painting as painting is not merely the discovery of its own medium, the materiality of the paint and the flat surface in abstract art. Rather, what tends to get called modernism, according to Rancière, is only a small and rather limited component of the new relation between text and image in the aesthetic regime of art. The "aesthetic regime of art" is, it must be said, essentially coextensive with modernity, but it is a way of framing the questions about what qualifies art as art in the modern age that avoids some of the confusions that tend to crystallize around discourses of modernism, especially those that emphasize medium specificity. That certain modern artworks may be said to draw attention to the materiality of their specific medium is, of course, not denied by Rancière, but he reveals the extent to which this gesture has always been locked in a productive tension with its opposite, arts blurring with each other and with forms of mundane life.[57] The flatness of modernist art and the use of the page in symbolist poetry are as much about impurity as purity, an interface of painting and text in an era of commodities, design, posters, and typography in which a new link was developing between art and the everyday. Rancière states, "Such is the paradox of the aesthetic regime in the arts. It posits the radical autonomy of art, its independence of any external rule. But it posits it in the same gesture that abolishes the mimetic closure separating the rationale of fictions from that of facts, the sphere of representation from the spheres of existence."[58]

We can turn to Hegel's lectures on aesthetics from the 1820s for one example of the articulation of this transition from the representative regime to the aesthetic regime of art and the paradoxical link between autonomy and heteronomy in the aesthetic regime:

> Bondage to a particular subject-matter and a mode of portrayal suitable for this material alone are for artists today something past, and art therefore has become a free instrument which the artist can wield in proportion to his subjective skill in relation to any material of whatever kind. The artist thus stands above consecrated forms and configurations and moves freely on his own account, independent of the subject-matter and mode of conception in which the holy and eternal was previously made visible to human apprehension.[59]

In other words, once art is freed from the jurisdiction of all but its own immanent criteria, then anything can be art—both the fabric and refuse of everyday life. Art then becomes autonomous, a separate sphere, at the same time as it becomes heteronomous, linked to common forms of experience and no longer transcendent forms. In Rancière's reading, Hegel's famous "end of art" was actually, in effect, the beginning of the aesthetic regime of art. The concept of "the aesthetic regime" is intended to highlight a constructive paradox that gives meaning to the various "ends" of art in the nearly two hundred years since Hegel's lectures on aesthetics while at the same time neutralizing their polemical rhetoric of catastrophe or salvation.

POLITICS VERSUS POLICE

As I've suggested, this concept of the aesthetic regime of art for Rancière can also be seen in relation to his disagreement with Althusser over the nature of theoretical practice. For Rancière, art in the aesthetic regime is political to the extent that it is a locus for reconfiguring what he calls baldly "the police." Police means simply the framing of a common world deprived of its polemical dimension. As stated earlier, this is precisely the goal of theory for the post-theorists. Rancière's adoption of the term "police" in *La Mésentente* [Disagreement], his 1995 book that is a critique of the then revival of political theory and philosophy, can be seen as a continuation of his attempt to contest Althusserian modes of reading and analysis. At the same time, it should also be understood as a revision of Althusserianism and ideology critique, now rescued for the axiom of equality.

In Althusser's most anthologized and cited essay, "Ideology and Ideological State Apparatuses: Notes Towards an Investigation," the figure of the police is central to his illustration of the logic of ideology. Rancière's use of the same figure serves as a marker of their opposing conceptions of politics. By comparing Rancière's conception of police with Althusser's we can see how we might recognize that Rancière's own project is not a complete break with his Althusserian past but rather a way of challenging it from within. We can also see that Rancière does not abandon critique as Hal Foster contends.[60] Rather, he is rewriting the terms of ideology critique as no longer a critical unveiling that privileges the symbolic over the imaginary or theory over the sensory, but rather an attempt to reframe the partition of the sensible. This means an explicit acknowledgment of the aesthetic dimension of both theory and politics—an acknowledgment that sacrifices the attempt to preserve theory's quasi-scientific status without conceding anything to claims of postmodern pluralism or relativism. In turn, it makes thinkable the political and theoretical dimension of art and aesthetics.

In "Ideology and Ideological State Apparatuses," Althusser uses "the police" to illustrate how ideology "transforms individuals into subjects."[61] The police provide an exemplary image of what he calls "interpellation" or "hailing" by ideological state apparatuses that produce "you" as the "subject" you always already are. When you hear the police say "Hey you," you respond immediately, unconsciously identifying the "you" with yourself as a coherent subject, a sediment of identity formations that cohere to make your situation in a class-divided capitalist society seem natural.[62] Rancière takes this figure of the police and transforms it into the symbolic order as that which frames the imaginary or, in his preferred term, appearance. The police for Rancière is a metonymic term for the entire "set of procedures whereby the aggregation and consent of collectivities is achieved, the organization of powers, the distribution of places and roles, and the systems for legitimizing this distribution."[63] But rather than identify the symbolic order and mechanisms of power and order with politics, Rancière opposes them. Politics is always a threat to the police.

Police, in Rancière's polemical use of the term, is what is normally understood by the term "politics," but in actuality is the evacuation of politics. "Police," in Rancière's usage, should not evoke men with guns or batons, but rather be understood as a generic, even neutral term; it is equivalent to the symbolic order or structure. Similarly, politics should not evoke business as usual by governments and politicians, but on the contrary should be understood to be in strict opposition to that use of the term "politics." Or rather, politics is the opposite of ideology. Another word that might be substituted for "police" is "policy," which Rancière chose to use in an essay written in English, "Politics, Identification, and Subjectivization."[64] As I understand it, the word "police," like "policy," is chosen for sharing the same root as politics—*la politique* can be translated as both politics and policy—because police is always trying to define politics and politics itself always involves a disagreement over what constitutes politics. Politics proper for Rancière (though from the point of view of police politics is always improper) is reserved for what Badiou would call a "truth procedure" in that it cannot be conceived of within the existing situation or the discursive frameworks that determine the visible, sayable, and doable. Politics exposes the contingency of the police. "Police," on the other hand, encompasses business as usual, Lacan's "service des biens," including significantly everything that explicitly or implicitly goes by the name of politics but is actually about denying a meaningful space for political struggle—namely, all the modes of achieving consensus or struggling for power.

For Rancière the role of the police is not to say "Hey you" and thereby generate unified subjects of ideology. On the contrary, if we are going to anthropomorphize the symbolic order, the function of the police is to say "Move along! There is nothing to see here."[65] In this way, Rancière shows us the limits of the problematic of imaginary identification so central to Lacanian-Althusserian film theory by highlighting the centrality of appearance as a contested terrain. The police in Rancière's work shares with what Althusser calls "Ideological State Apparatuses" the function of generating identification, but Rancière uncouples the "police" from "the state" and identification from subject-formation. The police is no longer localizable to the state and its various institutions because it encompasses the entire realm of what is understood to be common sense, the unconscious rules governing the distribution of sensible and sensory experience. For Rancière, the primary function of the police today is not to instill paranoia by calling you to attention, but to return you to your place as a particular part of a whole to ensure the logic of the division of labor, as well as a broader delimitation of temporal and spatial arrangements and experiences. This is not the form of discipline analyzed by Foucault; rather, its primary technique is dispersion and generating modes of indifference, which is central to the functioning of what Deleuze calls "control," the new insidious form of power that he believed was replacing the top-down form of disciplinary power. "There is nothing to see here," the maxim of the police, does not imply a police cover-up or conspiracy, it means only that appearance is identical to itself—that there is no legitimate space for disagreement or dissensus. Move along means go about your business. There is nothing to see because everything is as it appears. All forms of revolt or critique are bound to be subsumed by the system. This means that politics concerns not unveiling appearance for deeper meanings, but challenging appearance from within appearance itself. In other words, it is an aesthetic or, we might even say, cinematic operation that insists that what we perceive is a site of contestation.

Take the increasing circulation in America in the second decade of the twenty-first century of videos shot surreptitiously by ordinary citizens of black men and women being abused or killed by police. Interpellation, as described by Althusser, gives a powerful description of the experience of increasingly advanced forms of surveillance that are directed primarily at people of color. But Rancière's conception of police and politics provides a more generative illustration of how to think about political resistance to America's racist system of mass incarceration. These videos all depict violent acts by literal police, but the police logic in Rancière's sense, is the one that denies that there is a wrong here—that says that these acts may look bad but can be explained. Indeed, in their legal interpretation of these videos—from Rodney King to Eric Garner—the courts have consistently denied that they constitute visible evidence for a wrong. The political act, on the other hand, is to construct a visibility of a wrong when consensual logic says go about your business, this is the way things are, and nothing can be done. Images are not political in themselves. The same images of police violence, if they don't generate awareness or change, can be exploitative, part of the long racist history of making the spectacle of black death available for a white libidinal economy. The political dimension concerns how these videos are framed and distributed, the constant struggle over what they mean. This is where philosophy comes in—to fight for the political over the consensual meaning.

The fight for the political meaning of these videos is being waged by the Black Lives Matter movement. First written as the Twitter hashtag #BlackLivesMatter, the slogan emerged in 2013 as a response to the new visibility of unjustified police violence against people of color in America enabled by these widely circulated videos and the simultaneous failure of the American legal system to acknowledge what these videos show us. According to Rancière, politics "means to challenge the distribution of parts, places, and competences by linking a particular wrong done to a specific group with the wrong done to anyone by the police distribution—the police's denial of the capacity of the anyone. This is what a political dissensus means."[66] The phrase "All Lives Matter," sometimes used as a response to the Black Lives Matter movement, is a perfect example of consensual police logic that says "nothing to see here." It ignores that saying "Black Lives Matter" is precisely a polemical way of stating all lives matter—a way of participating in a common world in which some lives are treated differently than others based on the color of an individual's skin. By appealing to the consensus that "all lives matter," Black Lives Matter counts the lives that have been made visible as not mattering from the point of view of the state and society. As a result, the normal distribution of lives that matter and lives that do not is disturbed. This is why philosophy is not only about the question of what is true and what is false (nobody is earnestly debating whether all lives do or do not matter), but about the reframing of the distribution of the sensible.

Whereas for Althusser the police remind you that you are a subject through identification or calling you to attention, Rancière instead associates identification with distraction and the loss of political subjectivity. For Rancière, subjectivization or becoming-subject, on the contrary, a necessity for politics, is not interpellation and identification but their failure. "Subjectivization is the formation of a one that is not a self but is the relation of a self to an other."[67] Subjectivization is a dis-identification because it posits an impossible unity, a collectivity that cannot be recognized as a part of the whole from the perspective of the police or policy. The point is not simply that the collectivity that becomes a subject *is not* recognized but rather that it *cannot* be recognized by the modes of identity that structure society. Political subjectivization is on behalf of some group denied equality—be it workers, people of color, or women—but not on behalf of the particular properties of the group or in favor of inclusion or recognition in a formal universal equality already on the books. It constructs a paradoxical logic that cannot be accommodated by commonsense understanding. In this sense, a political subjectivization always posits a virtual collectivity that cannot be counted and is necessarily aesthetic. It posits what Deleuze says cinema must posit: a people that are missing. Cinema, like all art, is not merely a machine for reproducing ideology or thwarting it by gesturing to its own conditions of production. Rather, cinema, as a way of framing aesthetic experience, can provide the resources for imagining new virtual collectivities through creating a gap in appearance.

The police may function through identification in the sense that one identifies with the way one is counted within the prevailing modes and structures of consensus, but it is an identification that is a result of a de-subjectivization. The police, according to Rancière, despite what appears to be the inescapably pejorative connotations of the term for any discourse on the left, is intended as a neutral term. The police logic is neutral and also neutralizing since it admits only what counts or what is legible and denies the existence of what is outside consensus. The "symbolic constitution of the social" must be understood as equivalent to "the distribution of the sensible." The social is symbolically constituted through the various mechanisms by which sensible experience is both shared and divided, distributed and recognized. It is then essentially aesthetic.

Rancière's conception of politics by way of aesthetics can be usefully clarified by showing how it differs from other familiar theoretical or philosophical models. By defining politics as about the contestation over the meaning of appearance, he distinguishes himself from both certain so-called poststructuralist arguments that emphasize the gap as such as a fundamental impasse, and the various discourses that see it as a false problem. For Rancière, politics as disagreement or dissensus "is not the conflict between one who says white and another who says black. It is the conflict between one who says white and another who also says white but does not understand the same thing by it or does not understand that the other is saying the same thing in the name of whiteness."[68] The disagreement between two people who both say "white" (or "police") must be distinguished from the understanding of this disagreement by some analytic or pragmatist philosophers that would see the disagreement as a question of clarity in which the differences can be elucidated through unpacking the construction and context and elucidating the misunderstanding.

On the other hand, for Rancière, the subaltern *can* and does speak. Indeed the speech of the subaltern or the speech of those who cannot speak (whose speech does not count as speech) is the basis for politics. Here I am not so much opposing Rancière's conception of politics to that of Gayatri Spivak, but rather using her famous provocation that "the subaltern cannot speak" as a way of translating Rancière for whom politics is, in effect, the speech of the one who cannot speak—as it is, in some sense, for Spivak as well.[69]

Or, if we prefer, Rancière's concept of disagreement is in disagreement with both sides of the so-called Habermas/Lyotard debate. Jean-François Lyotard's *Postmodern Condition: A Report on Knowledge* (1979) famously posited the death of metanarratives, which is to say that there were no agreed-upon forms of legitimation any more that could ground our knowledge. Jürgen Habermas countered that the enlightenment was "an unfinished project" and that we should not give up so quickly on a model for communication and debate grounded in reason. For Rancière, on the one hand, politics emerges where Habermas's model for communication is thwarted, where the framework of what constitutes communication, rationality, and validity claims is contested. On the other hand, Rancière's concept of dissensus equally rejects Lyotard's concept of the *differend*, in which the antagonism over the stakes of the common is severed in favor of the acceptance of the irreconcilability of language games.

In the *Ignorant Schoolmaster* (1983), Rancière preaches the dissemination of a message courtesy of a forgotten nineteenth-century French pedagogue, Joseph Jacotot, that intelligence ought to be defined exclusively in terms of an axiomatic equality. Intelligence becomes actualized only through the verification of the equality of intelligence. "Equality is not a goal to be attained but a point of departure, a supposition to be maintained in all circumstances."[70] The axiom of equality is an "opinion," and while it can be demonstrated or verified through the consequences of a fidelity to the axiom, it is not provable and rests on no foundation. This axiom of equality extends beyond Rancière's polemic on intelligence and education and can be seen as underlying his conception of politics.

Rancière's conception of politics as emerging from the verification of the axiom of equality should point us not toward, as some might think, a moral or ethical role in politics, but rather toward an aesthetic one. "Aesthetic," in this sense, should be understood not just in its broad, etymological sense as perceptual or sensory experience, but rather in terms of how that experience is arranged or organized. What is at stake is not so much an individual's commitment, or will toward fidelity (as we see occasionally in Badiou), but rather how we can frame a common sensible world. The axiom of equality necessarily exposes the rules governing appearance that inhibit conceiving of an equality that reality everywhere denies. The question of an aesthetics of politics is the question of the difference of the sensible from itself—the gap, in Badiou's terms, between presentation and representation or the heterogeneous sensible world and the available modes of communicating about it.

Rancière's emphasis on the sensible as the locus for the stakes of political thinking is not a simple reversal of Metz's dictum that theory is on the side of the symbolic rather than the imaginary of the phenomenological experience of cinema.[71] Police, in Rancière's sense, is a term for when the imaginary and symbolic coincide without remainder, or when one falsifies the other. Another word for police for Rancière is "saturation."[72] It is any sensorial or conceptual orientation that offers no room for supplement or lack or disagreement, no "as if" to frame a polemical world. Rancière's reading allows us to see both Metz's call for winning the imaginary for the symbolic and the reversal that claims affects and sensations must be liberated from their interpretive territorialization as but two modes of policing the uses and meanings of images.

If we continue to follow the Lacanian schema, for Rancière, politics would be on the side of the Real. But, for Rancière, the Real of politics lacks the connotations of the death drive proper to Lacanian subjective destitution or the intrusion of the impossible Thing. This distinction also separates Rancière from Žižek and other contemporary Lacanians with whom he may otherwise share a certain formal emphasis on that which is excluded from the count. The political subject is a subjectivization that interrupts identification by inscribing a subject (a part with no part) that has no place within the community's symbolic constitution. This is not a struggle for recognition or inclusion, nor is it the radicalizing of difference found in certain theoretical positions that negate the politics of disagreement in favor of an ethical conception of incommensurability. By establishing an equivalence between the singular that is not identical to any particular and the whole, a paratactical world is constructed that cannot coexist with the police logic. Politics brings into being a new world, which is incommensurable with the inegalitarian logic of the symbolic order.

Recent turns to "the body" in film and media studies are often thought to address the limitations of the Lacanian discourse that placed language as the level of materiality against the phantasmatic body of the imaginary—a discourse given an additional political valence through Althusser's use of Lacan, in which the imaginary was associated with ideology and the symbolic with politics, in an affirmative sense, as that which breaks from ideology. It is said, often with reason, that this position pitted a good modernist asceticism against emotional responses as inherently bad, and thereby sided with an elitist valorization of oblique high modernism against the unreflective pleasures of mass consumption. According to Noël Burch, "those were the halcyon days when for many scholars, including myself, identification and distanciation were like Hell and Heaven."[73] According to Burch, a formalist in the sixties who became an antiformalist (or antimodernist) Marxist in the eighties, in retrospect, this was in a reactionary Sadeian tradition that was based in contempt for the feminized masses.

While Rancière emphasizes the importance of heterogeneous appearance against the symbolic level of law and order that structures appearance, for him there is nothing necessarily political about promoting the materiality of the body against disembodied images and information. On the contrary, Rancière emphasizes how the requirement of bodily presence, from Plato through to Habermas, has been a way to ensure that certain information can be the property of only certain individuals. Rancière locates the egalitarian dimension of the aesthetic regime in the dead letter or the anonymous image. Literature is predicated on the fact that "the arrangement of words was no longer guaranteed by an ordered system of appropriateness between words and bodies."[74] As for film, this does not mean that there is anything liberating about the "imaginary identification" of disembodied cinema spectators, but only because identification is but another way of fixing the spectator to a body. "The channels for political subjectivization are not those of imaginary identification but those of 'literary' disincorporation."[75] "Disincorporation" is the putting into play of the dead letter, the establishment of a community to come, a collective body that, to borrow a phrase from Wallace Stevens favored by Badiou, is a "description without place." From this perspective, we should also be skeptical about the dire warnings about online culture that suggest that anonymity is leading to a weakening of the standards of debate. The attempt by media experts and platforms like Facebook to require that all statements be attributed to a known fixed identity is a way of ensuring a hierarchy of what speech counts and what is only noise and a way of cutting off channels for disincorporation.

Politics is a matter of inscription. It is, therefore, a matter not of refusing the symbolic, but rather of creating a gap or supplement in the symbolic order. The point is not simply to oppose the literary and poetic to rational discourse in a reversal of Jürgen Habermas's theory of communicative action. Habermas argued that a robust left-wing public sphere needed to reject the Nietzschean strain he found in certain tendencies in critical theory and poststructuralist discourses that questioned any faith in reason. Rancière rejects Habermas's firm distinction between open poetic speech acts and closed speech acts that initiate validity claims. A political statement is always both. The political construction of validity claims is also simultaneously the construction of a virtual community in which that validity claim gains its force. It is the argument for the existence of an imaginary or virtual world that eludes its symbolic constitution.

The notion of paradox so often dismissed in analytic philosophy and ordinary language philosophy after Quine must be understood in its literal sense as outside or beyond doxa. Paradox is central to ordinary language use and not some aberration from it because the ordinary is never equal to itself. Politics is paradoxical because it posits within a real material situation something that does not exist and follows through on its consequences. It is paradoxical because it introduces a supplement or lack into a situation that cannot be grasped from within that situation. Politics is beyond what can and cannot be counted within prevailing modes of discourse.

At stake for Rancière is always appearance. But he wants to say that appearance is not identical to the imaginary world of ideology in Althusser's sense. Ideology in Althusser's sense, rewritten by Rancière, might be understood as the symbolic constitution of the imaginary or appearance within the police order. What it excludes is not the real, or Marxist science, but appearance itself—appearance defined as the heterogeneous sensible that splinters reality and marks the gap between the distribution of sensible modes of being and a reality that is never equal to the sum of its parts. Hence the "loss of the real" in the so-called "society of the spectacle" in its Situationist or Baudrillardian variants, is in fact, a "loss of appearance."[76]

Rancière retains the critique of the Feuerbachian "humanism" of the early Marx and its uptake in twentieth-century Western Marxism, initiated by the Althusser-led *Reading Capital* project of which he was a part. The difference between police and politics, whatever may appear to be the connotations, is not the difference between alienation and self-consciousness. According to Althusser, the theoretical production of the Marxist theorist is not actually outside ideology, but rather is the only discourse in which one can properly say "I am in ideology." But in Rancière's reading, this is merely another twist on the discourse on alienation by drawing a distinction between good and bad forms of knowledge. For Althusser, the good Marxist no longer says, "I am outside ideology but the masses are not"; instead, he says, in effect, "We are all in ideology. The difference is I *know* it, but the masses (and the bad Marxists) do not." Knowledge as production, the symbolic, is posed against knowledge as sight, the imaginary. This is the same opposition that accounts for Althusser's distinction between science and art.

Unlike Althusser, for Rancière the dismissal of the discourse of alienation is no longer tied to the affirmation of theoretical antihumanism as the proper position of Marxist science. Indeed, Rancière's critique of Althusser is that Althusser reinscribes the binary alienation/self-consciousness he had previously dismantled when he advanced a concept of subjectless science not reducible to ideology. Politics for Rancière is not exterior to ideology (or police) but, to borrow another term from Lacan, "extimate" to it. The point is not so much that politics is irreducible to ideology, but that it is an inscription of ideology's irreducibility to itself.

With *Althusser's Lesson*, Rancière turned his back on the idea that the proletariat needs to be taught by the Marxist intellectual about his or her own exploitation. Instead, he sought to learn from the proletariat by researching workers' archives in nineteenth-century France for the book that became *Proletarian Nights* (1981). But what he found in the journals of workers was not so much an "authentic" worker's discourse that undermined the intellectual's attempt to co-opt it, but rather the refusal on the part of workers themselves of a discourse proper to the worker and another one proper to the bourgeoisie. Though, like Althusser, he rejected the humanist discourse of "alienation," when he found the discourse of "Man" in the archives of French workers in the 1830s, he decided not to read it as "the necessary subordination of the oppressed to the dominant ideology."[77] As I suggested above, Rancière's Althusserian history persists at the very least in refusing the analogy between police/politics and alienation/self-consciousness. But for that reason he also rejected the implication, found in Althusser, that humanism is itself necessarily a form of something akin to alienation. He rejects, in other words, Althusser's concept of science for its seeming return to the Feuerbachian hierarchy that Althusser had himself rejected. Rather for Rancière, the difference between police and politics is the difference between the symbolic order and that which exposes its contingency.

If the aesthetic dimension of theory means that theory, like art, takes a distance from practical politics and if it does not side with either reason and knowledge against affect, nor bodies and pleasures against the poverty of philosophy, then it may not be clear what the purpose of critical theory is for Rancière. We should start from the premise, he says, "that the incapable are capable; that there is no hidden secret of the machine that keeps them trapped in their place . . . there is no fatal mechanism transforming reality into image; no monstrous beast absorbing all desires and energies into its belly; no lost community to be restored."[78] It is statements like this that give fuel to Hal Foster's position that Rancière is "post-critical" and has abandoned critique.

But what Rancière has done is to rethink the concept of critique. His method is always about refusing to accept the consensual reading of any given situation and investigating the logic that makes it possible, which is the very definition of critique. Nor is he merely a skeptic or hysteric (to be understood in its Lacanian sense as the subject position that never accepts "yes" for an answer), as Badiou implies. His critique of critique is in favor of another kind of critique he calls dissensus. Dissensus means staging a scene that disrupts "the obviousness of what can be perceived, thought and done, and the distribution of those who are capable of perceiving, thinking and altering the coordinates of a shared world . . . to sketch a new topography of the possible."[79] So while he continues to put pressure on the idea that theory or art can ever solve the problem of inventing a formula for raising awareness in such a way as to lead directly to political action, he is decidedly not in league with the argument that critical theory cannot affect practice, which can be found in certain attacks on academic Marxism. On the contrary, he wishes to thwart the moral judgment that tends to accompany the dogmatic separation between theory and practice. To say that theory is impractical and to say that a certain political act is not properly theoretical are both ways of ignoring strategies of creating a "common polemical world."

Critical theory, if we can still call it that, from this perspective must proceed from a double refusal. It must refuse to give too much credit to the claim that the intellectual has access to something the oppressed does not—knowledge of the system—or, on the other hand, to the claim that the oppressed has access to something the intellectual does not— knowledge of the irreducible experience of being oppressed. At the same time, it must preserve a fidelity to the struggle for emancipation and equality against the division of labor and indeed, more broadly, the divisions in sense experience, the unconscious rules governing what counts as visibility, speech, and action. Marxist science and, on the other hand, the dogmatic deference to the pure speech of the oppressed can both be ways to reinforce stratification. This is a reason not to abandon theory or interpretation but to free it from its dogmatic strictures, to grant its aesthetic dimension, while still preserving a vigilance regarding the ways inequalities tend to get reaffirmed as normative even and often in discourses marked as resistant.

For Althusser, what is ignored by ideology is that it is dependent on the reproduction of the relations of production. Marxist science, in the end, is nothing other than not ignoring the relations of production and thereby "taking the point of view of the class struggle," which is also to say of history.[80] Rancière's definition of politics equates it with "class struggle" but not with *knowledge* of class struggle or solely with the analysis of class divisions from the point of view of the relations of production, that is, historical materialism. Does Rancière then take leave of Marxism by abandoning the economic base as the final instance? Rancière's intervention is not to affirm or deny the "final instance" of the economic base but to take the point of view not of the class stratification but of equality itself. The question then is not whether Althusser is right or wrong but rather what kinds of practices are made thinkable or foreclosed by a discourse that makes a distinction between "conceptual knowledge" as rendered by science (or theory or critique or philosophy) that draws our attention to the "final instance" and other forms of discourse that can at best function as symptoms by drawing our attention to the effects of a lived experience that they fail to conceptualize and therefore understand. To take the position of equality is not to ignore the reality of class stratification, but to initiate dissensus through adopting a position marked by its very distance from this reality. It is a paradoxical equality, the construction of a common stage that is at odds with the managing of common interests.

SYMPTOMATIC READING WITHOUT MASTERY (FOR AND AGAINST ALTHUSSER)

The basis for the rejection of seventies film theory in contemporary film studies tends to be the rejection of a certain logic of interpretation that is derived from Althusser. It should be clear that if Rancière too questions this logic of interpretation, it is from a perspective opposed to the one we have identified within contemporary film studies. The problem with this logic of interpretation, for Bordwell and Carroll for example, is not its equation of science and knowledge with theory, but rather the opposite—that it is not scientific enough and its deductive procedure stymies research into progressive knowledge of how film functions.[81] For Althusser himself, of course, reading was also not simply a question of right and wrong. The science he endorsed was not "bourgeois science." For Althusser, bourgeois science is "right" in the same way political economy is right but its rightness is predicated on a constitutive blind spot or unasked question.[82]

We need to look more closely at the logic of the symptomatic reading in the form endorsed by Althusser as the proper Marxist reading practice. Althusser found in Marx a way of reading that recognized in political economy a "right" answer to an unposed question.[83] The question of the value of labor power (and its corollary "surplus value") is an absent question in political economy, yet it "produces" without "seeing" the answer to this question, because this absent question is a blind spot constitutive of the text and not exterior to it. What is at stake then is not a question of right and wrong, but rather a good and bad kind of reading that correspond to two conceptions of knowledge. As Rancière describes Althusser's position, "A myopic reading corresponds to an empiricist theory of knowledge as sight, as sampling an object from the reality of vision. A symptomal reading corresponds to an idea of knowledge as production."[84] This is the meaning of Metz's dictum. The imaginary is the level that links knowledge to sight. The symbolic level is the material conditions of this "picture thinking" (*Vorstellung*) in Hegel's terms. The symptomatic (*symptomal*) reading produces knowledge by restoring a missing signifier to its place. The missing signifier stands in for an unasked question or absent cause (like the mother the child spots behind him or her in the mirror), a placeholder for the repressed subject of the enunciation and its conditions of production. The classic example in film theory is that the text of the film points to the apparatus as a constitutive absence of the film text.

The title of Rancière's statement announcing his break from Althusser was "La Leçon d'Althusser." Althusser was literally Rancière's former teacher, but even after the "break" Rancière continues to identify Althusser's work with a kind of pedagogy—a pedagogy that inverts that of the progressive educational doxa. No longer do we say that every question has a right or wrong answer but rather that every answer has a right or wrong question. The wrong question is the one the text itself asks and supplies the answer to, while the right question is produced in the margins through the constitutive absences of the stated answer. Althusser's lesson "saturates the field of the *said* like a field of proliferating answers to questions still too rare."[85] Only the notion of a collectivity defined by knowledge or know-how can support this adventure of reading that presumes the ability to identify the occluded questions from the ideological text. According to Rancière, Althusser presupposes "a certain vision of the community of knowledge [savoir], a certainty that knowledge makes community."[86] This poses a basic theoretical problem within Althusser's own discourse. The identification of the unseen or unthought in the seen or thought cannot mark an "epistemological break," as Althusser claims, because it hinges on a textual continuity that is necessary for an idea of "science as power of community."[87]

For Althusser, the Marxist intellectual's practice must be such that it cannot be confused with discourses that do not produce knowledge by returning the reader to the class struggle as the motor of all discourse. Only science can avoid this confusion and ensure transmissibility. For Rancière, literature or aesthetics is the name of this confusion. Literature is a letter without an addressee; its egalitarian basis means that there is no ground that can guarantee its transmissibility. For Rancière, the importance of the aesthetic regime of art is that it undoes this distinction between sight and knowledge. This does not mean that art is now indistinguishable from politics, science, or philosophy, but only that what makes art identifiable as art is found in its construction of a relationship to non-art that puts its own status in question.

Rancière's own pedagogy is not divorced from a kind of symptomatic reading that seeks to think constitutive absences or, in his terms, "the part with no part," but it identifies this practice no longer with production of knowledge or science but rather with a fiction, theater, montage or mise-en-scène. More provocatively, Rancière argues that symptomatic reading itself is thinkable only as the result of a new way of thinking about art in modernity. It was made possible by a poetic revolution in which literature and art of the nineteenth century overthrew the hierarchies of the representational regime of art in favor of discovering a mute speech, a world of hieroglyphs, written on the body of material things. According to Rancière, the Marxist theory of fetishism and Freudian theory of the symptom inherited this revolutionary aesthetic logic.[88] The history of theory is therefore imbricated with the history of aesthetics. In line with this aesthetic conception of anonymous speech, the "part with no part" for Rancière is not so much the "excluded" but is better conceived as the capacity or power of anything or *anyone*. It is the expression of that which has no qualification for expression.

As the theatrical metaphor often adopted by Rancière indicates, aesthetics is always central to politics, but it is an aesthetics of politics precisely opposed to the equation of spectacle and power that Benjamin grasped as the affective dimension of fascism. The aesthetics of politics affirmed by Rancière is similarly at odds with the injunction to "enjoy!" that Žižek has identified as the dominant ideology in the West today—the affirmation of bodies and pleasures.[89] Rancière's project has been to restore a dialectical relation between aesthetics and politics against the apocalyptic and utopian fantasies about aestheticized politics and politicized aesthetics. According to Rancière, this dialectical relation is at the very core of the modern regime of art whatever the attempts to divert attention away from it. Rancière's metapolitics of aesthetics is always a matter of reframing the conditions of possibility on the side of generating future possibilities for making dissensus visible and intelligible. He thereby preserves the logic of critique without privileging knowledge over sight or the symbolic over the imaginary. Indeed, he shows that critique has an aesthetic dimension and, moreover, is made possible by the aesthetic regime of art.

CINEMATIC EQUALITY

Today, as film studies has turned toward bodies and affects and away from language and subjectivity, we need to remember that the logic of critique found in Brechtian-Althusserian film theory is only one aspect of the aesthetic logic that cinema is a part of. Indeed, there is another pole of political modernism in which politics, theory, and cinema are overdetermined not by a logic of critique, but rather by a logic of sensation. As we saw, Althusser's "symptomatic reading" meant defining knowledge as production distinct from pseudo-knowledge in the form of sight. As Metz recognized, cinema from the start seemed to offer a kind of knowledge in the form of sight.[90] Benjamin gave this a name: the optical unconscious.[91] In his book *La Fable Cinématographique*, or *Film Fables*, Rancière begins with a long quotation from the filmmaker Jean Epstein written in 1921 that concludes succinctly: "Cinema is true. A story is a lie." For Epstein, cinema's essence is found in suspense and anticipation, in a pure power of the image grasped in anonymous objects—curtains, the tip of a pen, specks of dust—that narrative (or "histoire") tames and distorts. Epstein's writings in the 1920s and 1930s play an important role in Deleuze's Bergsonian taxonomy of the movement-image. According to Epstein, "There is no film that ends badly."[92] In this narrative, pure cinema, as Rancière puts it, "cannot cheat." It just records and is not about reproduction of things—likeness or similarity—because it changes "the very status of the 'real.'" It overthrows the Aristotelian model that privileges muthos over opsis. The story and its "dramatic progression" is belied by the "infinity of micromovements" captured by the machine as automaton.[93] The machine's power is not mimesis or verisimilitude but making the invisible visible. Cinema "reduces the communication of ideas and the ecstatic explosion of sensory affects to a common unit of measurement."[94] It abolishes the "problem of mimesis" so central to the historical thinking of what constitutes the arts, because as André Bazin will claim years later in a famous essay, the photographic image "is the object itself."[95] As Hugo Munsterberg's pioneering theory claimed, the mechanical eye does not reproduce but writes with matter, light, and movement and is "equivalent to mind."[96]

Rancière makes two points about this dream that cinema can break free from narrative and representation. First, this dream that was especially common in the silent era derives from a particular historical moment and a utopian vision of artistic modernity that was not restricted to cinema but was common across a range of arts. Second, it is itself a narrative or fable even as it is extolling antinarrative, the pure power of presignifying intensities. To say what cinema is, Epstein has to say what it is not. He has to extract one idea of cinema from another. It is therefore significant that the images Epstein discusses as examples of pure cinema are not from an avant-garde film but from a narrative film of an especially formulaic and melodramatic kind, William C. de Mille's *The Honor of His House* (1918). Epstein's theory is possible only through subtraction. He extracts his vision of cinema as pure intensities from a melodramatic narrative much the way Joseph Cornell would do more literally in *Rose Hobart* (1936), his reedit or remix of *East of Borneo* (1931). This defiguration, Rancière argues, is not original to cinema but has a long nineteenth-century tradition. For him, it is central to the aesthetic regime of art, which is "distributed between two extremes: a pure creative activity thenceforth thought to be without rules or models, and the pure passivity of an expressive power inscribed on the very surface of things, independently of every desire to signify or create."[97] Cinema, in effect, actualizes a dream of aesthetic modernity through the passivity of the recording device. This passivity, however, remains an empty void without the invention of operations to restore creative power to the automaton. Ironically, dominant modes of cinema thus return to the codes of the representative regime of the arts, with its focus on genres that correspond to specific narrative conventions. The pure expressive power of images that transcends representation extolled by Epstein is made visible only when contrasted with the stereotypical melodramatic devices that it is extracted from and relies on.

Cinema then emerges within what Rancière calls "the aesthetic regime of art" in which art is no longer subject to the logic of representation but rather is grasped as merging two contrary conceptions of art: (1) art's pure power lies in the surface of the external world especially at its most ordinary and indifferent; (2) art is grasped only in the pure autonomous creative act or formal gesture.[98] According to Rancière, the cinematic apparatus realizes the first pole of the aesthetic regime of art, but in effect it does it too well. Anonymous automatic speech is intrinsic to the technical apparatus of cinema, but this does not ensure an ontological grounding for its artistic possibilities. Since the automatic recording machine is itself passive, the artistic gesture of becoming passive in the face of the world is no longer readily legible.[99]

Think, for example, of the Lumière brothers' earliest films. At the time few people viewed them as art, but they can be defended as art by citing Louis Lumière's method of framing or even the choice of subject matter. But the wind in the trees seemingly unmarked and unplanned in the background of *Baby's Meal* (1895) that, like so many other incidental details in early films, fascinated many of the first viewers of moving images: is it art? And if not, what is it? Its fascination is tied to the nineteenth-century dream of art's self-effacement to yield to the expressive power of nature, but it is the new apparatus itself rather than any artist that makes this image visible. And once the novelty of the apparatus wore off, without the intervention of some legible form of framing, an image such as this would remain, as Mary Ann Doane aptly puts it, "semiotically insufficient."[100]

This is why cinema so often turns to the representative regime to thwart its powers. For the most advanced forms of art that led up to and were contemporary with cinema, the Aristotelian logic of representation or mimesis was being thwarted in numerous ways. Cinema as it developed into a mass art reversed this operation of thwarting representation shared by so-called romantic, modernist, and avant-garde aesthetics. In its most popular manifestations, it did not, as the other arts did, seek aesthetic gestures to undermine the logic of active form on passive material, but it returns to the representational logic of the conventional dramatic story or myth to thwart the aesthetic power of the pure becoming of movement-images. In Rancière's words, "The mechanic eye lends itself . . . not least to the illustration of old-fashioned stories of interest, heartbreak, and death. . . . In the age of Joyce and Virginia Woolf, of Malevich and Schoenberg, cinema arrives as if expressly designed to thwart a simple teleology of artistic modernity, to counter art's aesthetic autonomy with its old submission to the representative regime."[101]

The history of the auteur theory provides another example of how cinema seemed to be at the vanguard of twentieth-century art and yet ironically seemed to return conservative ideas of representation that predated the aesthetic regime. At the very moment that artists and literary theorists were questioning the very concept of authorship, film critics tried to claim it for the director. Cinema, the very art that seemed to do away with the old forms of authorship, becomes an art of auteurs who are "the exemplary embodiment of the author who puts his stamp on his creation."[102] Cinema, as Benjamin claimed, changed our very idea of art because there was no unique object created by a master/genius. And yet, it came to embody that idea of the creator and came to be associated with old-fashioned storytelling and mythmaking. In an essay on the "madness" of Eisenstein's *The General Line* (1929), Rancière points out how foreign and distant Eisenstein's desire for a pure language of images looks to us today. Thinking of what has become of the idea of cinema as a mass art in the late 1990s, at the time he was writing the essay and when James Cameron's *Titanic* (1997) was shattering box office records, he asks rhetorically, "what century we ourselves live in to derive so much pleasure—our Deleuzes in our pockets—from the love affair upon a sinking ship between a young woman in first class and a young man in third."[103]

But as the parenthetical reference to Deleuze indicates, *Titanic* is not the end of the story. The dream of cinema as the realization of the aesthetic regime of art persists not only in polemicists from the heyday of aesthetic modernity such as Epstein, Vertov, and Eisenstein, but also in Rancière's relative contemporaries, modernist/postmodernist figures like Gilles Deleuze and Jean-Luc Godard. If one of the interventions of Rancière's essays on cinema is to show the inconsistency of this logic that imagines that cinema can become a pure writing of sensations and affects indistinguishable from ideas as Eisenstein sought to realize, it is not to insist on the classical Hollywood model of the scripted feature film with its three- or four-act structure and typically happy ending as the inevitable destiny of cinematic production. The inconsistencies revealed by the great theorists and practitioners of so-called pure cinema do not limit cinema's potential but are the very basis for it. As Rancière states it most succinctly, "The art and the thought of images have always been nourished by all that thwarts them."[104]

Pure cinema does not exist. But that does not mean that cinema, despite what screenwriting manuals may tell us, is destined to return to classical stories in the Aristotelian tradition. The global dominance of classical Hollywood narration would seem to suggest that cinema conforms to the representative regime and not to the aesthetic regime of art. But Rancière helps us see that so-called classicism is not merely an art of representation as cognitive theories of narration like David Bordwell's tend to assume;[105] rather, as discourses on the auteur and cinephilia demonstrate, classical narration was sustained by its own potential disruption. Lines and colors, gestures and arrangements of bodies that resist the paradigm of narrative economy are intrinsic to, not aberrations from, classical narration just as attempts at pure cinema are sustained by the narrative logic they challenge from within.

Rancière suggests that there are two responses to the era of Epstein and Eisenstein in which it seemed as if cinema was poised to fulfill the utopian destiny of artistic modernity. The first is nostalgia. In this view, pure cinema was killed off by sound, Hollywood, and commercialization. We find examples of this in both Benjamin and Rudolf Arnheim.[106] And we could extend this narrative to more contemporary writers who discover the final nails in the coffin in television, video, or, later, digital and information technologies. The second response is condescension. In this view, cinema was part of a larger inconsistent utopia from approximately the 1890s to the 1920s that revolved around the dream of matter dissolving into energy. In this narrative, it is said that what Epstein welcomed about cinema not only does not exist today, but never did. Art, in this conception, is merely representation, part of the age-old tradition of storytelling, only updated with modern technology.

There is a third response to this period unmentioned by Rancière, and it is the position of much writing on new media today that I proposed would be more aptly termed Grand Theory than the political modernist and cultural studies approaches that acquired that label through Bordwell's dismissive analysis. The third position sees this period not as an inconsistent utopia or a no longer possible utopia, but rather as a genuine utopia that had yet to find or is only now finding its moment. In this narrative, we discover a link between 1895 and the twenty-first century in which much of twentieth-century film history, with its focus on classical and modernist narrative cinema, turns out to be something of a detour and a distraction. Epstein and Benjamin become theorists of the digital age by way of Deleuze and Kittler. Lumière and Méliès anticipate Bill Viola and YouTube by way of Vertov and Warhol. The reign of digital simulation and the dispersion of moving images across cell phones and museum walls freed from the ritual of the darkened theater liberates us from locating the ideological underpinnings of the apparatus in the invention of an idea of the viewing subject born in the Quattrocento, the photological ideology of actuality, the material substrate of film that creates movement out of static images and an imaginary subject that misrecognizes itself on the screen.

Rancière's proposal is significantly more modest and flexible than all three of the above. According to him, "there is no straight line running from film's technical nature to its artistic vocation."[107] The attempt to define cinematic specificity can be consistent only to the extent that it recognizes that its consistency is always built on an inconsistency. Cinema always puts into play a "thwarting logic." What this allows Rancière to do is to dispense with questions of the end of cinema or of mournful or ecstatic claims that all image production has been rendered indifferent by the age spectacle and information. Cinema will continue to be "nourished by all that thwarts" the idea of what makes cinema cinema.[108] Like Epstein finding pure cinema in a Hollywood silent melodrama, all ideas of cinema extract one idea of cinema from another or make a fable from another fable. "This particular penchant for making a fable with another is . . . a constitutive fact of the cinema as experience, art, and idea of art."[109]

CONCLUSION: AMATEUR THEORY

We have seen how Brechtian-Althusserian film theory as well as the cognitive or analytic rejection of it are sustained by ignoring the paradox of modern aesthetics. The will toward scientific criticism from Metz or Comolli meant separating theory's own operations from art. It then attributed those same theoretical operations to films when those films could be seen as thwarting the ideology of art. But there was a contradiction here that went unacknowledged so as not to threaten the power of theory. On the other hand, the critics of political modernism who call it on its incoherence attempt to isolate the empirical practices of the arts, ways of doing and making, from the discourses about them. But this is an attempt to restrict art to what it was in the "representative regime" and ignore how, for at least two hundred years, as Rancière puts it, "the simple practices of the arts cannot be separated from the discourses that define the conditions under which they can be perceived as artistic practices."[110] Art or cinema cannot be approached as just ways of doing and making, as Bordwell approaches it, without ignoring that in the regime of art in which we have lived for over two centuries, ways of doing and making are always linked to ways of thinking that make the ways of doing and making legible as forms of art or entertainment understood as a specific mode of sensible being. We are not confined to the false choice between an idea of cinema as such or cinema as only a collection of films that are defined as cinema by empirical classification or the subjective judgments of viewers. Rather, cinema emerges within a regime of art in which there is always a gap between works and the idea of art, literature, or cinema as such. Rancière's great insight is to say that it is precisely within these gaps that modern art has defined itself, found its productive operations and its politics. To think about cinema is to think within these gaps.

This is why Rancière rejects the idea of theories of cinema that are premised on ways of closing these gaps. In contrast, he poses the discourse of the amateur who circulates within these gaps without closing them:

> The amateur's position is not that of an eclectic supporting the wealth of empirical diversity against the colorless rigor of theory. Amateurism is also a theoretical and political position, one that sidelines the authority of specialists by re-examining the way the frontiers of their domains are drawn at the points where experience and knowledge intersect. Amateur politics asserts that cinema belongs to all those who have travelled, in one way or another, through the system of gaps and distances

contained in its name, and that everyone has the right to trace, between any two points in that topography, an individual route that adds to cinema treated as a world, and adds to our understanding of it.[111]

It is in the anonymous capacity of anyone without qualification to show, or make use of, how films or sequences from films thwart or disrupt the distribution of the sensible—the logic that defines the terrain of the see-able, sayable, and doable—where we can rethink a politics of cinema predicated on the axiom of equality. The axiom of equality does not mean that all opinions and ideas about cinema are equivalent; it means, rather, that ideas about film and in films can challenge hierarchies and inegalitarian forms of common sense.

It may seem as if we are not so far from Comolli and Narboni and the practice of Althusserian film theory that emphasizes the politics of aesthetics—that films and film theories should thwart ideology under-stood as both content (familiar stereotypes from the social imaginary) and form (habitual and consensual approaches to mise-en-scène and montage that define the visible and thinkable). But the goal is no longer a knowledge effect or drawing attention to the apparatus as such but finding ways that films resist these familiar formulas for political art through singular gestures and cinematic ideas.

But what does it mean for there to be ideas in films? And how do these ideas relate to ideas about films? These questions are posed explicitly by Deleuze and Badiou.

2

CINEMA'S THOUGHT

Badiou and the Philosophy of Cinema After Deleuze

G illes Deleuze's *Cinema 1: The Movement-Image* and *Cinema 2: The Time-Image* attempted to offer a new way of thinking about the relation between philosophy and cinema. Deleuze insisted that he was not writing a philosophy of or about cinema. Films, he explained, like any form of creative expression, should not be read or interpreted through the lens of philosophical systems or used to illustrate philosophical concepts or themes. Philosophy confronts cinema because films in their own fashion produce new ways of thinking that are generative for philosophy.[1]

When Deleuze's books came out in the 1980s (the original French publications were published in 1983 and 1985, the English translations followed in 1986 and 1989), they were at odds with most of what counted as serious writing about cinema at the time. They were not criticism in the conventional sense—films were not ranked or compared, and there was no attempt to make the case for or against certain films. There was cinema that mattered, that had a claim on philosophy, and then there was everything else (about which there was no need to discuss).

At the same time, he was not offering a film theory. Film theory tends to mean one of two things. It is either descriptive and offers generalizations that seek to explain specific aspects of film that can be isolated as objects of investigation, whether codes, genres, techniques, viewing practices and so on. (We could include both Bordwell and Metz in this conception of theory.) Or, as was the case with much of the most interesting theoretical writing that emerged in the late sixties and seventies that sought to frame film in explicitly political terms, it is prescriptive and reads films as signifying practices rooted in, and bearing the traces of, the larger economic, cultural, and historical context within which they are produced. Theory explains what films do or reveals what films hide, but at no point is there an encounter between film and theory in which cinema might make us rethink our ideas about conceptual thought itself.

This is where Deleuze proposes a different way of thinking about cinema. Or rather, he proposes not that we think *about* cinema but that we start from the premise that cinema is itself a form of thinking, albeit a different form of thinking from philosophy. For Deleuze, film is not an object for knowledge nor an example of ideological expression. He does not situate films in their cultural or institutional contexts or discuss them in terms of their genres, themes, or plots. Instead, he proposes that cinema is a relatively new practice of images and signs composed of movement and time that was neither a reflection of the world nor an object to be thought in relationship to the consciousness or psychology of the spectator. Cinema is, in short, a new form of thinking because it creates images that make no distinction between mental reality and material reality. But what does it mean for cinema to think and have ideas?

Alain Badiou has emerged as one of the most significant French philosophers since Deleuze, and his more recent writings on cinema might be read as a kind of dialogue with Deleuze, a sometime enemy who has deeply marked his thought.

The guiding, Deleuzian thread in his writings on cinema is the question of cinema's relation to thought. How does one understand the novelty of particular films, and of cinema in general, as both a resource for thought and a specific way of thinking? Or as Badiou poses this question in an interview with *Cahiers du Cinéma* in 1998, "What does cinema think that nothing but it can think?"[2]

The interview was conducted in a special issue of *Cahiers du Cinéma* devoted to the thirtieth anniversary of May '68. Badiou was featured as a central figure who both lived through this era and still sought to emphasize its importance following the increasing backlash among French intellectuals against its supposed excesses.[3] Keeping this in mind, it is notable that in the years immediately following 1968, the question about cinema's relation to thought is one that the influential French journal would have found hopelessly idealist. In the era of Althusserian film criticism (as laid out in Comolli and Narboni's "Cinema/Ideology/ Criticism") film was to be read as a necessarily ideological and symptomatic means of meaning making within a capitalist society. In the 1970s, not only in France but in Britain and the United States as well, a desire for a more rigorous film theory, even when not explicitly politically oriented, sought to purge itself of any romantic conception of art as well as the more poetic or metaphysical trappings that had often accompanied early attempts to think the uncanny power of moving images.

Today, by contrast, we are told that films not only think but also feel; they have bodies and minds. New philosophical inquiries have renewed interest in writings on cinema by a range of different historical figures from Hugo Munsterberg, Jean Epstein, and Maurice Merleau-Ponty up through Stanley Cavell. But if there is a single person who has been most frequently used to give authority to many of the most interesting new forms of film-philosophy (as well as some of the worst), it is Deleuze.

The question we will return to is this: what happens to politics in this philosophical turn? "Theory" in the post-'68 era often served as a code word for Marxist political theory, and, as we have discussed, Althusserian ideology critique often served as the ground for reading films politically. We have seen how Rancière helps us rethink the terms of "film theory" as it developed in the late sixties and seventies out of an Althusserian conception of theory as producing a "knowledge effect" that gets wrested from film conceived of as ideology. For Badiou, another former Althusserian but with a different relation to his former master than Rancière, the terms of thinking cinema's potential are emphatically those of philosophy rather than "theory." (The latter might be assimilated with what he calls anti-philosophy.)[4] In this, Badiou follows Deleuze despite what is often taken to be his adversarial relationship with the thinker he once referred to ironically as "Saint Gilles."[5] While much of the recent philosophical turn has served to depoliticize film theory, I argue that Badiou, through philosophy, reconceptualizes the politics of cinema in a way that shares a great deal with Deleuze and helps us rethink the use of Deleuze in film studies. At the same time, Badiou offers new resources for thinking about cinema that have remained largely unexplored. And, like Rancière, he helps us rethink what it means to understand cinema's relation to politics today.

Deleuze concludes *Cinema 2* with the statement: "There is always a time, midday-midnight, when we must no longer ask ourselves 'What is cinema?' but 'What is philosophy?' Cinema itself is a new practice of images and signs, whose theory philosophy must produce as conceptual practice. For no technical determination, whether applied (psychoanalysis, linguistic) or reflexive, is sufficient to constitute the concepts of cinema itself."[6] If theories of film typically seek to explain or analyze it, or aspects of it, philosophy for Deleuze as for Badiou doesn't explain cinema but is *conditioned by it.* According to Badiou, the thought of cinema begins in the shadow of Deleuze. As he puts it, "Today, which is to say 'after Deleuze' there is a clear requisitioning of philosophy by cinema—or of cinema by philosophy."[7]

AXIOMATICS OF CINEMA

What does it mean for philosophy to be conditioned by cinema? In a chapter on cinema in *Handbook of Inaesthetics,* Badiou identifies two ordinary ways of talking about film. The first is our immediate, stupid (in Lacan's sense) reaction, which Badiou calls the "indistinct judgment." "I liked it," "I was bored," and so on. *This is how it made me feel*—the realm of affect and opinions. The stars, the plot, or perhaps the most striking aspects of the spectacle (the display of what money and technology are capable of) are focused on. Meanwhile, the norm of judgment is obscured.[8] According to Badiou, this kind of talk is an important and necessary part of cinema as cultural ritual, but it is not in itself a philosophical approach.

The second way of talking about film attempts to preserve something that gets lost in the immediacy of the indistinct judgment, to rescue our pleasure from the lazy habits of consumption and give it lasting value. Here, we propose a norm and a system of evaluation. Filmmakers are emphasized rather than actors, plot, or isolated effects—the name of the auteur providing an emblem of the effect of a certain style. Badiou calls this the "diacritical judgment,"[9] and by it he means to include the history of sophisticated film criticism. This way of thinking is also outside the realm of philosophy.

What both these two ways share is that they are judgments and presume the necessity of evaluation. Therefore, Badiou proposes that the link between film and philosophy should be pursued through a path that is indifferent to judgment and is not normative. Badiou does not here acknowledge that much academic writing also tends to avoid evaluative distinctions, but he would see this academic tendency as part of what Lacan calls "the discourse of the university," which holds that everything can be counted or categorized. Such academic discourse is able to dispense with evaluation because it says that there is only knowledge and not truth. Much of what gets called film theory, as distinct from the philosopher's approach, would fall into this category.

According to Badiou, philosophy, and indeed thought more generally, has a meaning only because something other than just "bodies and languages" exists.[10] Adapting Badiou's language to that of today's digital capitalism, we might add that there exists something other than information and networks. The philosopher, in one sense, shares the dominant ideology, what Badiou calls "democratic materialism," that insists that all that exists is individuals and communities or bodies and languages. But he adds that there are exceptions, which while materially composed of language and bodies cannot be deduced from them or reduced to them. An exception is what he calls a "truth," a word that when presented in this affirmative form would make many aligned with the theoretical tradition blush. One legacy of theory that has bled into mainstream common sense takes "truth" to be a word always requiring scare quotes, a dubious aspiration inseparable from a will to power that it seeks to obscure. For Badiou, an essential purpose of philosophy is to reject this undermining of truth. If film has meaning for philosophy, it is because it is an arena where truths are possible. This means that film cannot be grasped only in terms of its effects on bodies and languages but must construct a new relation (or non-relation) between bodies and languages by way of the fragile consistency of a subject.[11]

As I have suggested, a recent trend in film studies has been to correct the attempt to privilege film's symbolic dimension (and the assumption that it is the locus of subjectivity) by insisting on the importance of the body and the spectator's emotional or cognitive response. Badiou's philosophy suggests that both the symbolic and affective are always crucial in art, but truth cannot come from only one or the other. Truth, according to Badiou, is not substantive; rather, it is what punctures a hole in knowledge or sense. Truth cannot be fixed or eternal because that would make it indistinguishable from knowledge. The "classical" link between art and philosophy developed by Aristotle, what Badiou calls "aesthetic regionalism," and continued in academic scholarship may eliminate evaluation, but only because evaluation is considered too subjective and therefore has no place in a normative mode of classification.[12]

Badiou proposes a way of thinking or talking about film that avoids all opinion (the indistinct judgment) and evaluation (the diacritical judgment), as well as the converting of all the effects of cinema into objects of knowledge. Rather than knowledge, philosophy is concerned with the effects of films on thinking the exception to dominant regimes of sense. He calls it "axiomatic." This position "asks what are the effects for thought of such and such a film."[13] This is a way of conceiving of film as a mode of thought, which is to say not that it demonstrates already existing theoretical concepts, but that it produces its own new constellations or operations that can lead to the generation of new concepts.

If there is a work that could be seen as a model for the axiomatics of cinema, as Badiou calls for it, it is none other than Deleuze's two-volume *Cinema* (1983/85). So before we look more closely at Badiou's writings on art and cinema, we will take a closer look at Deleuze's writings on cinema—their novelty and ambiguity and what separates them not only from the tradition of seventies film theory, but also from some of the writings that have taken Deleuze as an inspiration and have helped shaped the recent field of film-philosophy. From there, we will show how Badiou understands art as a distinct mode of truth and then cinema as a form of art that challenges his conception of both art and truth. In the conclusion to this chapter, we will look at how we might bring Deleuze, Badiou, and Rancière together to rethink film-philosophy as both a rejection of aspects of "film theory" but also a continuation of the political tradition of seventies film theory in a way that separates it from some of the newer forms of film-philosophy.

DELEUZE: CINEMA'S THOUGHT AS RESISTANCE TO CONTROL

From the point of view of debates in academic film studies in the 1980s and 1990s, the arrival of Deleuze's two books on cinema seemed to be of no help to anyone. Offering a complex engagement with the history of Western film theory, his books nonetheless rejected the terminology that defined the central concerns of film theory at the time—dismissing all manner of Saussurean semiological approaches, psychoanalysis, and the language of ideology critique. At the same time, Deleuze's project was implicitly even more antagonistic to any form of cultural studies, on the one hand, or the kind of piecemeal descriptive theory of the sort promoted by the so-called post-theorists.

It is worth recalling how long it took Deleuze to make his way into Anglo-American film studies. Two examples should suffice. Contributors to *Post-Theory* in 1996, edited by Bordwell and Carroll, could have treated Deleuze as either a tactical ally of a sort for his opposition to linguistic and psychoanalytic approaches or (more likely) as a new antagonist—yet another French master thinker adopted uncritically as an absolute authority in opposition to careful scholarship. But there is not a single reference to Deleuze's books on cinema in the volume.[14] Meanwhile, in 2000, a book titled *Reinventing Film Studies*, edited by Christine Gledhill and Linda Williams, was presented as an attempt to ask: where is film studies now? Situating itself, unlike post-theory, as not

strictly anti-theory, it nonetheless saw its mission as arising from the belief that "film theory can no longer be the kind of overarching grand
theory that flourished in the 70s."[15] Featuring a wide range of inquiries
about the current status of film studies by twenty-four major scholars
in the field, the book contains not a single reference to Deleuze.

But despite the lag in the reception of Deleuze in Anglo-American
film studies, in the twenty-first century he has rapidly become among
the most referenced, if not *the* most referenced, figure in academic writing on cinema. As I am writing this, in the last two decades, there have
been twenty English-language books devoted exclusively to Deleuze and
cinema, eighteen of which came out in the last decade and twelve in the
last three years.[16] While the consensus seemed to be that we were post-
theory and post–cultural studies, it seems as if not everyone was satis-
fied with the reinvention of film studies along the lines of cognitivism
or historicism; Deleuze belatedly seemed to fill the gap for a desire for
something else. What was key was that while he was another French
master thinker, the use of Deleuze was seen not as a return to seventies
film theory, but as a new kind of philosophical approach.

Deleuze's *Cinema* books were often presented as a new way to approach film because they reject outright two of the three theoretical
traditions that had most shaped seventies film theory: psychoanalysis
and semiology in the Saussurean tradition. (If the third most central theoretical tradition, Marxist analysis, was not directly rejected by Deleuze,
it was notably absent from his approach to cinema.) The eschewal of
these traditions is no doubt significant. But I would suggest that the
more substantial challenge Deleuze poses to the film theory that was
dominant from the 1970s through the 1990s is a new conceptualization
of the relation between cinema and theory—the attempt to submit philosophy or theory to the conditions of cinema. Deleuze proposes a reversal of the traditional relation between film and theory. The attempt
is not to think a theory of film but instead to think of film as theory—to
think of how film itself is creative and can give rise to the creation of
new concepts within philosophy.

Beginning most explicitly in *Difference and Repetition* (1968) and con-
tinuing most influentially in *Anti-Oedipus* (1972), written with Félix

Guattari, Deleuze has attempted to construct an "image of thought" that inverts the basic methodology of much Freudo-Marxism, as well as French structuralist and poststructuralist theory, by proposing that the "critique of representation" already gives priority to representation over the singularities that representation appropriates. "Schizoanalysis," as proposed by Deleuze and Guattari, starts with desire and affect as forms of production and not with the modes of power and dominance that thwart them. Schizoanalysis is the "war-machine" of a new philosophical ethics posed against a psychoanalysis that provides a diagnosis of the repressive mechanisms of power at the same time as it derives its explanatory power from the assumption of the inevitability of Oedipal triangulation. Deleuze and Guattari's intervention provides an antidote to Laura Mulvey's provocative assertion, so influential in film studies, that theory was a weapon necessarily destructive of pleasure because it exposed the mechanisms of power on which our pleasure was predicated.[17]

But schizoanalysis does not mean anything goes. The seemingly anarchic ethos, and what may seem like a celebration of madness, should not obscure the recognition that schizoanalysis, like psychoanalysis, is working toward a form of organization. Art for Deleuze is not, as is sometimes suggested, equivalent to unmediated affect and sensation, a purely anarchic schizoid intervention; rather, the link between art and hysteria or schizophrenia is a complex one that needs to be grasped in relation to a concept of individuation and not asserted in some pretheoretical affirmation. And while Deleuze is often used as an antidote to a psychoanalytic tradition of film theory believed to be overly punitive, he does not come to the rescue of all the pleasures that seventies film theory had rejected. He does not take the democratic position that all pleasure and emotion is good in itself. "Desire," which for him is primary in *Anti-Oedipus*, should not be mistaken for the "visual pleasure" of narrative cinema. Though he approaches cinema from a different direction, Deleuze, no less than Mulvey, is interested in thinking about the ways cinema separates itself from the reactionary habits and desires that get recycled and renewed by a medium given over to the laws of commodification.

Far from developing the possibilities opened up by Deleuze's axiomatics of cinema, the dominant tendency in American academic theory that seeks authority in Deleuze, Bergson or, in a related but separate move, phenomenology, and places its emphasis on affect or "the body" might be said to be an attempt to debunk what Badiou calls the diacritical judgment, in favor of the indistinct judgment now recuperated for the discourse of the university. As Brinkema states bluntly about contemporary affect theory, "Affect is taken as always being, in the end, *for us*. The theoretical consequence of this assumption is an approach to writing theory that emphasizes the personal experience of the spectator."[18] In other words, the tendency in affect theory is to use what Badiou calls the indistinct judgment associated with one's individual affective response to critique the normative traditions of film criticism and film theory. Deleuze, I will argue, should lead us not in this direction but toward a different philosophical way of thinking that is conditioned by cinema. His writings on cinema should not be perceived as an absolute rejection of seventies film theory, but, on the contrary, can help us return to what was most valuable in it. The project of seventies film theory is not saturated as long as it takes a lesson from Deleuze and does not use films and filmmakers as substitutable pretexts to illustrate theory's concepts. To approach cinema in a way that makes it a condition for thought means affects/bodies and form/structure are not mutually exclusive. The philosopher must think both of these to think the new forms of thought that are not found in either form or affect alone, but the new cinematic ideas that always concern a relationship between the two.

It will be objected that my claim that recent film-philosophy has reversed the tendency in seventies film theory to privilege the signifier over the realm of the imaginary is to presume in advance the efficacy of the Lacanian triad—Imaginary, Symbolic, and Real. Readers of Deleuze will be quick to point out that mapping these terms onto Deleuze's work or equating the imaginary with affect or sensation is not so easily maintained without distortion. There is some truth to this objection, but a closer look at Deleuze will show that things are more complicated than they may first appear.

For Deleuze, cinema, as a relatively new practice of images composed of movement and time, is neither a reflection of the world nor an object to be thought in relationship to the consciousness or psychology of the spectator. It is, in short, a new form of thinking because it creates images that make no distinction between mental reality and material reality. It actualizes, in other words, the concept of the image that Deleuze found so important in Henri Bergson's *Matter and Memory*, published in 1896, almost at the very moment of the birth of cinema. Cinema was a modern art to correspond to a modern thought no longer based on representation and the Cartesian dualism it implied. By affirming Bergson's identification of image and matter and offering cinema as, contra Bergson, the actualization of this identification, Deleuze treats the problematic of representation that much of seventies film theory revolved around as a false problem. Philosophy's role, for Deleuze, then, is not to explain cinema in terms of anything exterior to it, but to produce and classify concepts that grasp the immanent aconceptual material that compose the ideas of cinema's great authors.

For seventies film theorists, the field of the symbolic, of signifiers, that needed to be wrested from the imaginary was understood as a locus for grasping the reproduction of the relations of production. To win the cinematic object for the symbolic was to restore to cinema its absent causes and conditions of possibility. The assumption was that the image was whole only because of a hole. Lacan's 1949 essay "The Mirror Stage as Formative of the *I* Function as Revealed in Psychoanalytic Experience," the basic tenets of which were often rehearsed in *Screen* and other film theoretical journals of the sixties, seventies, and eighties, offered "the imaginary" as a relation of a subject to the image that was central to the formation of the bodily ego. This was a relation defined by transparency and identity that is, at the same time, a misrecognition (*méconnaissance*), a relation that misses its mark. Before Metz identified the cinema as composed of imaginary signifiers, the imaginary in Lacan was already cinematic. Film gives us an image of gestalt or "good form" like the child in the mirror who sees himself as whole only at the cost of identifying himself with his image. The child's "mirror stage," Lacan claims, is more than a developmental phase; it remains the formative prototype of the ego or "I function" as a necessarily regressive and rigid structure in which a primary identification with an imaginary signifier undergirds all future identifications. As Lacan says, "It suffices to understand the mirror stage . . . *as an identification*, in the full sense that analysis gives to the term: namely, the transformation that takes place in the subject when he assumes [assume] an image."[19] Once Althusser used Lacan's concept of the imaginary to define the subject's "relation" to his or her "real conditions of existence" as represented by ideology, Marxist critical theory could be rewritten in structuralist language that offered cinema, the so-called first mass art, as a privileged locus for ideology critique.

As discussed in chapter 1, in this narrative, the experience of cinema as cinema was predicated on the effacement of what produced the image that manifested itself in various forms: the properties of the apparatus itself and modes of perception embedded in it, the material substrate of the film, the photogram, the subject of enunciation, and finally history itself. The heterogeneity of this list made for numerous arguments and sometimes slippages about what constituted materialism in cinema. Was what Jean-Louis Baudry called "the revealing of the mechanism" or the "inscription of the film work"[20] better sought in an agit-prop anti-imperialist call for revolution like Octavio Getino and Fernando Solanas's *Hour of the Furnaces* (1968) or in a structural materialist provocation like Tony Conrad's *Flicker* (1965)? Should a Marxist French film journal after May '68 be writing about *Méditerranée* (1963) or *The Battle of Algiers* (1966)?[21] Even if there was no unanimity in the response to these questions, there was at least a framework for debate that presumed that there was nothing natural about cinema or narrative conventions and both film theory and the new waves and avant-gardes needed to rescue cinema from the illusion of transparency.

Turning our attention to these effaced mechanisms—be it through breaking down the illusion of movement, the return of sprocket holes, or the return of the gaze—is of no interest to Deleuze, because for Deleuze nothing has been effaced. Deleuze announces in the introduction to *Cinema 1: The Movement-Image* that "cinema is always as perfect as it can be."[22] The identification of matter and image is also an identification of matter and its movement and temporality, being and becoming.

As Agamben suggests, Deleuze grasps that the movement-image undoes the distinction between psychical and physical reality.[23] There are no components of the movement-image that can be isolated to reveal how cinema works because "cinema begins with the movement-image—not with any 'relation' between image and movement even: cinema creates a self-moving image."[24] Deleuze takes the famous maxim of Husserl's phenomenology that "consciousness is always consciousness of something" and argues that Bergson goes further by proposing that "consciousness is something."[25] Hence an image, as a form of consciousness, has an autonomy and materiality that is only obscured by bringing in questions about a "subject of enunciation."

To claim, as I have, that cinema for Deleuze actualizes the identity of matter and image may seem paradoxical since the identity of matter and image is neither an identity nor actual in Deleuze's terms. The image is rather "virtual" in Deleuze's sense—an immanent plane of fields of potentiation that create signs out of blocks and movement and time. It is a grin without a cat, an event-sensation without body or object.[26] To preserve the creative power of the new sign grasped as image, Deleuze rejects the Saussurean distinction between signifier and signified, which means he also rejects the distinction between imaginary and the symbolic. Deleuze's natural history of signs forms something like what Charles Sanders Peirce calls "pure grammar." Deleuze has claimed, pitting Peirce against Saussure, that he is interested in a "semiotics," not a "semiology," of signs,[27] but it should be added that he is primarily interested in the first of Peirce's three branches of semiotics and on principle pays far less attention to what Peirce calls object or interpretant. In other words, to read Deleuze on cinema is to learn to think about cinema by thinking about the image as such while suspending any interest in the represented (the profilmic) or the position of the spectator.

If Brecht was the model for political art for the Althusserian reading of film in so-called *Screen* theory, the Deleuzian reading might be understood in terms of another major figure of modernist theater, Antonin Artaud. Like Brecht, Artaud, who wrote some suggestive short pieces on cinema, offered a method for breaking from the representational logic of more traditional theater. Yet he did so through an inverse process.

Rather than creating distance or separation between the audience or spectator, Artaud sought to eliminate it. Brecht's "A Short Organum for the Theater" prescribes techniques of distancing "designed to free socially-conditioned phenomena from that stamp of familiarity which protects them against our grasp today."[28] Artaud similarly appealed to "unhabitual ideas" in order to rescue theater from "psychology and 'human interest'"[29] or "the present and its events," but he demanded immediacy rather than techniques of alienation, in order to eliminate the familiar artificial distance that already separates the spectator from the stage (or screen).[30] As he put it, "Between life and theater, there will be no distinct division, but instead a continuity. Anyone who has watched a scene of any movie being filmed will understand exactly what we mean."[31]

The axiom of art and philosophy, in other words, is what Deleuze calls *immanence*. Indeed, the *Cinema* books repeat Deleuze's philosophical project more generally. Jean-Luc Nancy draws out the deep connection between cinema and philosophy in Deleuze's work as a whole. "Deleuze's interest in the cinema is not just appended to his work: it is at the center, in the projective principle of this thought. It is a cinema-thought, in the sense of having its own order and screen, a singular place of presentation and construction, of displacements and dramatization of concepts (the word 'concept' means this for Deleuze—making cinematic.)"[32] Cinema does not precisely produce concepts in Deleuze's terms, but what Nancy exposes is that cinema does appear to realize the image of thought that Deleuze requires of philosophy. Using Deleuze's terms, the screen is "the plane of immanence" from which haecceities emerge. According to Nancy, Deleuze's philosophy is "a philosophy of nomination not of discourse. . . . The point is not to signify things but to index by means of proper names the elements of a virtual universe."[33] This is why his work is a taxonomy, not a history nor even a theory. This is also why auteurism is intrinsic to his philosophy. The virtual universe is, as Deleuze says, "a metacinema."[34] Philosophy is still needed for the creative power of nomination.

If Deleuze's *Cinema* books do not constitute a history, they are organized around two modes of images—the movement-image and time-image—that are divided by a historical break located at World War II. And the argument made for Deleuze's analysis of cinema and the corresponding abandonment of seventies film theory is often given a historical justification. Deleuze's *Cinema* books are thought to speak to the contemporary moment in a way that the film theory of Metz, Baudry, Mulvey, and Heath that came to dominate the American academy does not. Part of the appeal of Deleuze for film theorists at the beginning of the twenty-first century surely came from a desire to distance themselves from a discourse that, once provocative and new, had been codified and assumed an orthodoxy in the academy and film journals. Deleuze offered a vocabulary for ways of thinking about cinematic images that was not only largely free from the Althusserian-Lacanian language of the era of burgeoning film theory, but also did not fall back on the language of other disciplines or the vocabulary of more traditional film studies that focus on the techniques, technology, and formal conventions that have been applied to generate successful conventional products and acceptable deviations. Indeed the explicit repudiation of psychoanalysis and any structural-linguistic-inspired semiotics to read cinema as "representation" is repeated in most of the earlier English-language Deleuzian-inspired books about moving images before that second claim is made about Deleuze's relevance for popular cinema in the digital age.[35] What tends to get critiqued, dismissed, or ignored is what Deleuze shares with the sixties and seventies French film theory (which he is well versed in and influenced by, despite the marked differences), and that is a shared canon of auteurs that frames his analysis. He is then not only auteurist—the names of directors provide the site of the production of specific kinds of images—but also modernist—the time-image that realizes the virtual essence of cinema is identified in a series of postwar mostly European and American auteurs who break from the classical mode of narration constructed around the action of a protagonist toward a free indirect discourse that liberates time from what Deleuze following Bergson calls the sensory-motor schema.

One explanation for these dimensions of Deleuze's work is that he was writing at a specific time and did not live to see full-blown postmodernism. This is, of course, in part what authorizes many of these recent books and essays that take Deleuze as a starting point. According to this logic, we have Deleuze himself on Hitchcock, Godard, or Antonioni, but are still in need of the Deleuzian analysis of Mathew Barney, the Wachowskis, David Fincher, or whomever.[36] In András Bálint Kovács's words, "Ultimately Deleuze's insight suggests how narrative develops from classical to modern to postmodern cinema and digital culture. The concrete historical contribution of Deleuze's approach is a new analysis of modern cinema whereby the latter is shown as a transitional stage between prewar cinematic art and the aesthetic possibilities offered by a subsequently evolving digital audiovisual form of communication."[37]

My claim is that one should be skeptical about the hasty adaptation of Deleuze as someone who offered a way of thinking that is readily adaptable to affirmation of the potential of cinema as digital art, or post-cinema, as it is sometimes called. I do not wish to question the value of Deleuze today, nor would I argue that he cannot be used to talk about objects he himself might not have recognized as relevant to his project. But I do wish to suggest that by highlighting certain ambiguities and overlooked dimensions in Deleuze's thought on cinema we can restore certain problems and questions about how we might most productively think about how images are political today. These are questions and problems that are too often elided by certain trends in contemporary film and media theory that seek an authoritative ally in Deleuze.

My skepticism about using Deleuze for a theory of digital media derives first of all from Deleuze's own skepticism about art's relation to electronic media and computers. In his "Letter to Serge Daney," Deleuze reflects on Daney's work to elaborate three ages of the cinematic image, rather than the two that we find in the *Cinema* books. He bases these on Alois Reigl's chronological categorization of tendencies in the artwork: the embellishment of nature, the spiritualization of nature, and the rivalry with nature.[38] This involves transposing a classical and romantic history onto the twentieth century, which already seems to pose a problem for linking Deleuze's ages of cinema to twentieth- and twenty-first-century stages of capitalism. The first two phases correspond with Deleuze's movement-image and time-image. The first is the cinema of montage and the "encyclopedia of the world" in which the movement-image dominated and cinema was, through various national configurations, thought to grasp the open whole. The second era is the post–World War II "writing of disaster"—Blanchot's phrase adopted by Deleuze—in which the whole is no longer accessible, narrative structure collapses, and movement becomes subordinated to time rather than the other way around.[39] This is cinema's version of the Kantian revolution in philosophy in which the problem of time emerges as central and thereby questions cinema's very foundation. This period therefore demands a new "pedagogy of the image."[40] The third era, according to Deleuze, is when the image becomes mere information, a cinema for the society of control in which pedagogy gives way to "professional training of the eye."[41] Let's call this the "data-image."[42]

Like Daney then, Deleuze writing in the eighties, without being nostalgic or elegiac, still views the essence of cinema to lie within the second age. There is no sense that the time-image will exhaust itself. The resistance from film within the "society of control" is what Daney calls "mannerism."[43] In the age of control, cinema's history as a medium that explores beauty and thought confronts the purely social function of television giving birth to a new pop expressionism. We get then De Palma instead of Hitchcock or Peckinpah and Leone instead of Ford. The classical elements still present in an earlier generation of modernist auteurs are now subtracted in favor of a heightened visual expressivity that is now drawn out and emphasized; meanwhile, classical elements return only to be falsified in the iteration of clichés in what Deleuze calls "the power of the false."[44] Despite Deleuze's lack of interest in television as medium, he suggests that new cinema—Hans-Jürgen Syberberg is offered as a prime example—is situated within the battlefield of film and television. As he put it in 1986, "Television is the form in which the new powers of 'control' become most immediate and direct."[45] Deleuze's favorite example was the game show, as it merges business and entertainment and is a testament to the society of control's logic of endless assessment and "healthy" competition.[46]

The internet, smartphone, and social media serve this function in even more powerful and pervasive forms now. Today, we must extend

Deleuze's observations about cinema in the age of television to include all the modes of image dissemination and information processing that go under the banner of "new media," from streaming to smartphones, the latest video games, and the internet.[47] Already with TV, Deleuze proposed that the screen was no longer a window or a frame (as it was in classical and modernist cinema respectively) but "a computer screen on which images as 'data' slip around."[48]

We find an analogous three-part periodization in *What Is Philosophy?* (1991), written with Guattari, in this case with regard to philosophy itself. In the introduction, Deleuze and Guattari announce three "ages of the concept" that correspond precisely to the ages of cinema found in the "Letter to Daney." Again, it is clear that Deleuze privileges the second age for its power of resistance against the leveling of creativity with instrumentality and consumer capitalism. "If the three ages of the concept are the encyclopedia, pedagogy, and commercial professional training, only the second can safeguard us from falling from the heights of the first into the disaster of the third—an absolute disaster for thought, whatever its benefits might be, of course, from the viewpoint of universal capitalism."[49] In other words, for Deleuze, it would seem that the "society of control" does not mean we have arrived in an era in which we are required to embrace the concept or image as pure information or the philosophy of proliferating language games or the montage of postmodern pastiche, but, rather, we still need to reinvent the pedagogical image and concept.

In the "Conclusions" section of *Cinema 2*, Deleuze points in the direction of what would be a *Cinema 3*—an analysis of the "electronic image" of TV and video that he says would be "beyond our aims."[50] The images in the third age, images as data, are "worthless . . . if not put to the service of a powerful, obscure, condensed will to art." What might this new will to art be? Deleuze leaves open whether it would be "based on still another will to art, or on as yet unknown aspects of the time-image."[51] Either way, the new forms of such a will to art must be found in new modes of cinema themselves. These new cinematic forms will be unpredictable, but what is clear is that they will challenge the logic of

control or the data-image as a means for commercial professional training. To recognize them and the concepts they give rise to is the task of
the Deleuzian film critic-theorist today.

There are many attempts to seriously pursue this project, but if we re-
move all elements of dissensus and pedagogy, then Deleuze's claim that
cinema is "always as perfect as it can be" is readily adapted to something
called "filmosophy," a concept introduced by Daniel Frampton. Frampton's ambitious 2006 book *Filmosophy* demonstrates the impasse that
arises with respect to film theory or philosophy's role once it has shaken
off the shackles of any form of hermeneutics, historicization, or ideology critique. The concept of "filmosophy" is meant to be a way of writing
about film as a purely immanent thinking and feeling. No source, no
outside, no recourse to a "language of representation" or to filmmaker or
spectator needs to be appealed to in order to speak of the cinema-
effect. Each film is its own perfect cybernetic machine. Cinema for
Frampton cannot be thought of as reflexive or in terms of excess, supplement, void, or lack because all these concepts betray the film's own
immanent expression. Therefore, the language of production and technology adopted by film studies is also seen as taking what a film does or
is and recoding it in a language of representation that refers only to how
it was made. "We should not be taught to see 'zooms' and 'tracking shots,'
but led to understand intensities and movements of feeling and thinking."[52] An apparent resonance with Deleuzian (and Lyotardian) concepts
betrays on closer examination a confusion about cinema's relationship
to philosophy. What does it mean to be "led to understand" something
that Frampton claims we already understand? In his own words, "We
do not need instruction in how to 'read' film, we only need a better language of those moving sound-images—we are already well suited to understanding film."[53] Ultimately, Frampton's argument can only affirm a
kind of transparency of images in the pure self-sufficiency of what he
calls the "filmind." But then why do we need a language for these images at all if language applies a representational over-coding to images
that are always already their own "filmosophy"?

To get out of this tautology that would seem to negate the need for
his own project, Frampton affirms a poetics of interpretation. "The

film (through its affective forms) might be said to be crying in empathy, sweating out loud, feeling pain for the character. (The concept of the filmind should provoke these kinds of interpretations.)"[54] Deleuze attempts to create a semiotics of moving images that presupposes an importance for philosophy as a creative practice separate from cinema; Frampton's Deleuzian reading anchored in a new age of information and fluid digital images is finally interested only in a descriptive language (generously termed poetic) that is still analogical and vague. Before we start "sweating out loud," this "better language" can be deferred in favor of a back-and-forth between speculative utopian claims that consciously echo writings of the 1920s (by Munsterberg and others) about film's equivalence to mind and a repetitive insistence on the way academic "film theory" reterritorializes the immanent singularities or intensities of film's own creative power.

This is why I claim that, following Badiou and Rancière, we need to insist on a concept of *impurity* in relation to cinema that makes the idea of cinematic thought possible if we are to stave off the disaster of the reduction of the image to techniques of control or advertising for advertising's sake.

Rancière observes a shift from a dialectical to a symbolist relation in contemporary art in which consensus replaces dissensus, which we could loosely connect to what is often theorized as the shift between modernism and postmodernism or indeed the "time-image" to the "data-image." In the "symbolist" mode that has succeeded the "dialectical" mode, differentiated spheres, heterogeneous elements, high and low, art and politics, art and commodity still get juxtaposed in the name of artistic gesture and provocation, but the meaning of this juxtaposition has been transformed. It marks no longer an unveiling or even a tension, but rather the "mystery of co-presence" in which the meaning of the juxtaposition hovers in a state of undecidability, or what Rancière calls "mystery."[55] This is perhaps a more contemporary corollary to what Daney in the seventies and early eighties called mannerism in which art retains the reworking of the classical or representational arts characteristic of so-called avant-garde, critical or pedagogical arts of the past, while subtracting their political dimension in favor of a new aesthetic rendering of consensus.

When Deleuze speaks of "pure images," the purity is tied to an essential impurity. When Deleuze refers to "pure optical and sound situations," he is attempting to describe limit-situations in which something unbearable is gestured toward. Here he can be seen to be within the romantic discourse that Rancière highlights as a component of "the aesthetic regime of art." This is not a question of shocking imagery or exhibitionist display but more often than not a kind of subtraction or emptiness. We find these limit situations in Ozu, Rossellini, or Akerman and not in the flirtation with the pornographic. The intolerable is not the extreme in a sense that would register for the MPAA Rating Board but rather the quotidian and diurnal—as Deleuze makes clear, the affliction of pure time comes from an inhibition of movement. The so-called pure time images are not pure in the sense of autonomous or without relation to context or the history of visual representation. On the contrary, they are operations deriving from a subtraction or torsion of dominant modes. The time-image in Deleuze still bears the marks of what Rancière calls a "dialectical" relation to heterogeneous elements. That is, its goal is dissensus.

So Deleuze is closer to the project of seventies film theory than he may at first appear. Deleuze's objection to Metz, and semiology more generally, is that it subordinates movement-images to narrative and structure. Deleuze acknowledges that cinema contains narrative and has structure, but he argues that movement-images are primary and make narrative possible. By emphasizing narrative, structure, and the level of enunciation as primary, Metz and other film theorists treat cinematic images as utterances. According to Deleuze, to make cinema into images composed of utterances is to "immobilize the image."[56] This must be avoided because movement is intrinsic to cinema as such. And yet, at the same time, we learn in *Cinema 2* that the pedagogical time-image itself reveals movement to be "false movement." In other words, despite warning the reader to not eliminate movement from our conception of cinema, he tells us that the essence of cinema is discovered once movement is subordinated to time and not the other way around.[57]

Deleuze's project in the *Cinema* books is no less redemptive than those of Bazin or Kracauer or Metz. The motive force is ambiguously located between an emphasis on the creative production of new images and a restoration of perception and affection to a world from which they have been obscured. Deleuze makes this most explicit when he starts to speak of digital and electronic images. "Redemption, art beyond knowledge, is also creation beyond information." What is needed, according to Deleuze, is a pedagogy that works against informatics by setting up "the question that goes beyond it, that of the source and its addressee."[58] What is "the source and addressee" but the use of information theory to reinvent the question posed by seventies film theory in linguistic or psychoanalytic terms of the subject of the enunciation (the utterance) and the subject of the text, which Deleuze so explicitly rejects? What is this but the basic Lacanian insistence on the fissure marked by the object-cause that breaks the symbolic order, an order that, as Kittler has emphasized, was described by Lacan as early as the 1950s, not in terms of language as understood by linguistics, but in terms of signifiers understood as information, as ones and zeros, through his reading and critique of cybernetics?[59]

This should turn us toward an ambiguity in Deleuze often ignored by his commentators. The cinema that gives us a direct movement-image is cinema as art. Not every film is composed of movement-images, only specific films that qualify as creative acts. Deleuze seems to be arguing at first that cinema technology gives us a new kind of image, but he soon makes clear that the technology is not sufficient. These images must be created. He excuses Bergson's misreading of cinema in terms of "natural perception" by acknowledging that the origins of cinema disguised its true novelty by aligning the screen with a view. According to Deleuze, movement in the earliest films does not inhere in the image as such. It was only with the development of montage and the mobile camera that we got not images in movement but movement-images. Until then, we could not yet identify films as artworks. It is only when cinema can be attached to the name of an auteur that cinema can be cinema. Deleuze's auteurism tends to be overlooked by writers eager to authorize a rejection of seventies film theory (still disingenuously labeled as dominant) in favor of a rhetoric of subversive flows, bodies, and sensations affirmed through a patchwork of Deleuzian concepts and neologisms and illustrated more often than not by examples from contemporary Hollywood films. Auteurism, it is sometimes claimed, is an elitist and conservative practice of cinephiles since it amounts to a list of great names and separates cinema from its more immanent pleasures, which are connected to what makes it popular. But if cinema is an art in Deleuze's sense, then it must "stand up on its own,"[60] which means that there must be names attached to the signs it produces. His use of auteurs is not diacritical because the names are not tied to individuals so much as they are signifiers for singular modes of creative production. The name of the auteur is the name of an individuation that is better conceived of as an event or an ascesis than a subjectivity. As he puts it, "The proper name . . . is precisely not a reference to a particular person as author or subject of enunciation; it refers to one or several assemblages."[61]

If the assemblages of art are capable of creating genuinely new relations that challenge the logic of information, communication, and control, then names are needed for the singularity of these assemblages. The rejection of auteurism, according to Deleuze, is an attempt "to deny any distinction between the commercial and the creative."[62] It is a falsely democratic move that places all authority in the hands of the theorist. To understand Deleuze's *Cinema* books we must understand his auteurism not only because it allows for thinking what constitutes art for Deleuze but also because the logic of his thought implies that the specific proper names that he is invested in form the basis of his philosophical concepts.

Cinema as art should not be tied to the "natural perception" of early cinema; nor should it be tied to the "information table" of TV or digital cinema.[63] The cinema privileged by Deleuze, the cinema of the time-image, is a cinema between ordinary or natural perception and information table.[64] The cinema of the time-image is the immobilization of the direct movement-image. It is the place of the "in between" that for Deleuze is always the source of art, philosophy, and science. The place of the "in between" is what makes possible what he calls "resistance to the present."[65]

It is here that we can understand the sense in which cinema and the philosophy of cinema is political for Deleuze. Art is affirmative and creative but also "in between," which means that it is a form of resistance. According to Deleuze, all art is resistance. "It resists death, slavery, infamy, shame...."[66] Like Foucault, he does not want to conceive of resistance as reactive. According to Deleuze, Foucault understood that "resistance comes first."[67] In other words, power is the reactive force, always seeking to appropriate resistance for its own purposes. Nonetheless, the implication is that creative acts cannot ignore power. As resistance, they always constitute responses to dominant forms of power even if they are affirmative and not merely reactive. For Badiou, as we will see, this complicated position is important as well. It is not that films are merely critical of dominant ideology but they that they create something new out of their transformation of dominant forms.

Cinema, in the age of control, must resist the "disaster" that is the universal market and the reduction of cinema to information. In 1987, three years before publishing "Postscript on Control Societies," Deleuze discussed control in a lecture delivered at La Fémis, a film school in Paris. In this lecture, which has been published under the title "What Is a Creative Act?" he explained that creation is irreducible to communication, which is defined as "the transmission and propagation of information."[68] With the breakdown of sites of confinement—Deleuze's reference is Foucault's disciplinary society, but we could just as easily think of Althusser's "ideological state apparatuses"—we arrive at a new form of power called "control." "People," he explains, "can travel infinitely and 'freely' without being confined while being perfectly controlled. That is our future."[69] Control names a capitalist world in which the logic of business permeates all forms of life and corresponds to the digital logic of the image as information. Cinema challenges control, he argues, by appealing to a people that does not yet exist, a virtual community that is at odds with any actual community who might receive the film as a form of training in how to keep up with the contemporary world.

To get beyond the indistinct and diacritical judgments to an axiomatic philosophical approach to cinema does not mean an end to the questions of representation and ideology critique that dominated seventies film theory, but it does mean a different approach to these questions. As we will see, it is Badiou, perhaps more than anyone else, who has continued this Deleuzian project in the twenty-first century. What is the political importance of cinema as a nonconceptual mode of thought today? For Badiou, like Deleuze, to ask this question means we first have to work through art's relation to philosophy and cinema's relation to art. Badiou is at odds with Deleuze in his answers to these questions, but in the end is more faithful than many Deleuzians in challenging us to think through the questions posed by Deleuze: How does cinema think? And how does cinematic thinking today resist control?

BADIOU ON ART

As was true for Deleuze, Badiou's conception of cinema as a way of thought and a form of politics must be understood in relation to his conception of philosophy and its relation to art. Like Rancière, Badiou approaches film by way of the broader question of artistic configurations, but whereas Rancière's method is to interrogate how art is grasped as art during different historical periods, Badiou attempts to delimit precisely how we can think art as an exception to the distribution of the sensible. If we can use Rancière's vocabulary to define Badiou's project, it is because there is a distinct overlap to their conception of art. But there exists a significant divergence too: whereas Rancière focuses on the conditions of possibility of thinking art's operations, Badiou's philosophical position, closer to Deleuze, takes art as a distinct mode of truth or rather an affirmation of a possibility. Rancière's thinking on art and cinema can be identified with critique; that is, he identifies the conditions of possibility for modes of thought, rather than emphatically affirm a conception of truth, as does Badiou. For Badiou, like Deleuze, art is a place not for blurring preexisting categories but for the creation of something truly new. Therefore, before we examine Badiou on cinema in more detail, we must first understand how art conditions Badiou's philosophy.

"Something else is possible." For Badiou, this is what art today must say.[70]

What is at stake in asserting that an indefinite thing that is not has the possibility of being? Why is this the domain of art?

The reader of Badiou will need to entertain, if provisionally, the project of what Badiou calls philosophy—in his definition "thought thinking itself"—and take seriously the question of "what is possible" in relation to "what is." For Badiou, this is the question of how to think an *event* in relation to *being*. Badiou rehearses two alternative responses that he views as symptomatic of the refusal to really confront the question of what is possible. The first alternative is *everything is possible*. This position sees no limit to what can be expressed or imagined today. Not content with a mere "something else," this position embraces the open, unequivocal affirmation of unlimited possibility.

The second alternative is an inversion of the first: *everything is impossible*. This position responds to our distance from this sort of abstract speculation by suggesting that we turn our backs on the seductive but illusory gesture of trying to think that which is not, and declare once and for all that there's nothing beyond our finite experience. In his reflections on art, Badiou suggests that both claims, although they seemingly contradict one another, are simultaneously behind most artistic production today and, what's more, that they are the same claim.[71] Together they announce a world of progress and a world without events: the desire for infinite innovation within an essentially closed world. To say that everything is possible—there is no end to novelty, variation, the realization of latent consumer fantasies, or infinite self-improvement— means only that everything is impossible—there is no new thing that is not made up of a series of effects that cannot be calculated or assimilated to a certain conception of the world that remains fundamentally unaltered. Philosophy, in contrast, exists to say "something else" is possible. As with Deleuze, this ties together the need for creation with "resistance to the present."

Mallarmé, in a letter explaining his refusal to write an introduction for a friend's book, explains that art cannot tolerate introductions. Art, he claims, arouses "love at first sight, as a woman does in her lover, without the assistance of a third party, the husband."[72] What Mallarmé calls art serves as an excellent illustration of Badiou's conception of "the event," and it is fitting that the event take the form of art through the metaphor of love, as art and love are two of the four loci of events for Badiou, which include the additional realms of science and politics. No husbands needed—no intermediaries, no witnesses who represent institutional authority—but are we left then with something that has no ramifications outside the finite experience of a single individual— the woman, the reader of the poem? If we must lean on something, it can only be, to use a phrase by Paul Celan favored by Badiou, "on inconsistencies."[73]

Badiou's philosophy proceeds from two disjunctive fidelities. He insists on the adherence to the conception of the event as that which is subtracted from the third party, any and all places of support. In other words, the event and its truth, like Rancière's conception of equality or Deleuze's idea of creation, is that "something else" that cannot be subsumed under any of the figures of what we could call husbandry: namely, according to Badiou, any form of historicism, contextualization, or categorization. At the same time, however, Badiou insists upon the importance of maintaining the third party despite everything. So what is this third party, free of all foundation, but keeping vital watch over its own uselessness? The third party is what Badiou calls "philosophy."

While philosophy's existence, for Badiou, is dependent on the existence of truths, philosophy itself does not produce truths. Philosophy is thinking the mutual but disjunctive construction of truths, which fall under four "procedures" of which philosophy itself is not one. By Badiou's standards the test of philosophy's own legitimacy should come under these four headings. That is, the test is not within the four procedures themselves, nor in philosophy itself as a truth procedure, but in philosophy's relation, or in Lacan's sense "non-relation," to the four procedures of truth.

According to Badiou, to say that there are truths also means that there is something other than just "bodies and languages." "Democratic materialism," Badiou's term for what he takes to be dominant ideology today in our so-called post-ideological era, insists, contrary to any notion of religious transcendence, that all that exists are individual singularities (bodies) and cultural constructions (languages). In other words, something else is not possible. This "axiom of contemporary conviction" does, according to Badiou, accurately refer to "what there is," but it denies the possibility of truths.[74] Truths today are "exceptions" to what is recognized by democratic materialism. These exceptions, while materially composed of bodies and languages, cannot be deduced from them or reduced to them. They come in four forms that Badiou calls "truth procedures": science, art, politics, and love. These are philosophy's "conditions," and the original ideas or events emerging from these four realms transform philosophy and make it what it is: a servant to these semiautonomous practices, which make life worth living. Philosophy, like life itself, has purpose only because of these realms beyond "bodies and languages." Without science, art, politics, and love, according to Badiou (riffing on Plato), the human being is no more than a "'biped without feathers' whose charms are not obvious."[75]

For Badiou, philosophy then exists to challenge business as usual, to be faithful to events that have changed the terrain of the possible in the past and to preserve the possibility of new events in the future. Philosophy is not explanatory; it does not produce knowledge or understanding but tries to think the points at which they fail to explain events in the world. Indeed, he insists that philosophy exists when or because things are not functioning smoothly or do not add up.[76] Philosophy is not seen as a creative practice, as it is for Deleuze. Rather, it offers a new relation like a radical form of montage linking irreconcilable elements, not for a vague pluralism but to arrive at a point of affirmation.

Badiou proceeds axiomatically, seeking to articulate the stakes of a philosophical problem and clarify a choice to be made, one that falls on the side of what he calls "truth." Truth is an exception, something that emerges from an event that, if acknowledged, creates a new situation or world that cannot persist simultaneously with the old one. To use Rancière's terms, truth is what the police order denies when it says "go about your business, there's nothing to see here." Since a truth is not a fact whose existence can be pointed to for proof, to insist on truths means to initiate dissensus.

This is what it means to say that, for Badiou (and Deleuze), cinema is a condition for thought. Cinema is a condition for thought because philosophy asks what it means to think in the contemporary world. Thinking in the emphatic sense used by Badiou and Deleuze does not concern eternal verities but is a response to the world as it is and ultimately a way of resisting that world. Cinema as a new form of thinking emblematic of life in the twentieth and twenty-first centuries demands a response from philosophy.

Of Badiou's "generic procedures," his philosophy of art has received the least attention from critics. Like any contemporary philosopher who receives a degree of name recognition, Badiou has found a receptive audience in the art world, but this has not meant that his "inaesthetics" have been frequently analyzed or understood very deeply. Many of the more sophisticated commentaries on Badiou have, for obvious reasons, focused on his more provocative "fidelities": his identification of ontology with mathematics, his unrepentant Maoism and political militancy, and his striking inclusion of love as one of the specific conditions of philosophy. Perhaps Badiou's understanding of art has received less engagement, because what Peter Hallward calls "his broadly modernist conception of art" may appear relatively familiar when compared to the other three procedures.[77] Moreover, though Badiou's use of certain poets remains a consistent motif throughout his writing, the sense that art as a procedure of truth is ancillary to the other procedures, if not to philosophy itself, may derive from the sense that when Badiou "summons" the events constituted by the generic procedure of art, the truths are most often utilized for thinking philosophy itself, and more specifically the philosophical problem known as "the event," rather than art.

Badiou warns against collapsing art and philosophy, though he does insist on knots, imitation, and sharing. To look then at the encounter between philosophy and art in Badiou's thinking, we cannot simply bracket the other procedures, nor can we work by analogy, but rather we must think the two together. "Thinking the two" evokes the project of the truth procedure of love, but here the two in question are not like two lovers who cannot be thought from the position of a third party; philosophy itself is the third party. Thinking philosophy and art is like thinking both a star and its constellation.

THE INTRAPHILOSOPHICAL
EFFECTS OF ART

Badiou's insistence on the necessity of philosophy to retain what we could call a hard notion of truth, provocative as it may be, is a more immediately comprehensible intervention than understanding what precisely philosophy's relationship to truth ultimately is. Badiou's attacks on the various proclamations of the end of philosophy or the reduction of philosophy to a matter of relativism or pragmatism (for him amounting to the same thing) are centered around a Platonic conception of truth as radically heterogeneous to fact, knowledge, common sense, understanding, and opinion.

Badiou's "return to philosophy" may have seemed a provocation in the 1980s, during the height of poststructuralism, but the last decade has seen a renewed emphasis on ontology and metaphysics in both continental thought and among Anglo-American thinkers in the continental tradition. It must be noted however that this recent "ontological turn" in continental philosophy and theory, whatever role Badiou himself might have played in it, would also fall outside the domain of what Badiou sees as the central project of philosophy since it tends to focus on "what is" or Being and not "what is possible" or the event and the corresponding existence of truths.

But while for Badiou philosophy exists to preserve the possibility of truth, it cannot itself produce truth and its role is also significantly not the production of knowledge. So what does philosophy do? "Philosophy is the locus of thinking wherein the 'there are' truths is stated, along with their compossibility."[78] The *il y a* highlighted by Badiou is to insist that philosophy involves an affirmative practice. It is a place for not equivocation, but axiomatic expounding. The word "compossibility," derived from Leibniz, suggests that the philosopher is something like a nondialectical mediator. In other words, the four types of truth are placed in what Deleuze might call an "inclusive disjunctive synthesis"; the task is to think them together in their mutual coexistence, while at the same time preserving their autonomy. Given this claim, it may come as some

surprise that Badiou also insists that philosophy is fictional and its relation to the other truth procedures is one of imitation. "As a fiction of
knowledge, philosophy imitates the matheme. As a fiction of art, it imitates the poem . . . it is like love without an object . . . political strategy
without any stakes in power."[79] This is evocative of Lacan's "analytic discourse" in which the analyst assumes the locus of the object cause of
desire, which is a matter of the excess or the place of the void where truth
emerges of the form of a fiction, but not from the analyst himself. Truth
must emerge from the analysand, or in the case of philosophy, from lovers, artists, scientists, or political activists. Philosophy is, then, like psychoanalysis for Lacan, a matter of ethics: staving off the sophist who is
always in service to his own self-interest and refuses to recognize any
affirmative truth, yet simultaneously "staving off disaster," which means
not doing away with the sophist by assuming truth is substantial and
can be produced by the philosopher herself.[80]

Badiou has repeatedly acknowledged (and both Deleuze and Rancière would agree) that to do art or cinema one does not need philosophy. If philosophy's role is seizing the truth of these procedures, it is
decidedly not doing the procedures. This is to say not that a philosopher cannot, as Badiou himself has done, write plays and novels (as of
this writing, his filmmaking aspirations have yet to be realized),[81] but
only that when writing a play, he is no longer a philosopher or, for that
matter, a political activist, mathematician, or lover. Hence, Badiou's
philosophical reflections on politics he calls "metapolitics" and his reflections on art, "inaesthetics." Inaesthetics "describes the strictly in-
traphilosophical effects produced by the independent existence of some
works of art."[82] We should understand by this not the description of the
effects of the works of art themselves, but a description of the "intraphi-
losophical effects," which insofar as art is concerned is a matter of "localized prescription, not description."[83] (In his *Ethics* he claims there is
no "ethics in general," and indeed it would seem that for him there is no
aesthetics in general.) This is primarily a matter of making any aesthetic reflection a matter of what Badiou calls situation. "Every philosophical enterprise turns back towards its temporal conditions in order
to treat their compossibility at a conceptual level."[84] Philosophy is then

a matter of the historicity of the relationship to the generic procedures themselves.

DESUTURING PHILOSOPHY AND THE POEM: HISTORICITY VERSUS ACT

The sophistic position of anti-philosophy exists either as the refusal of the possibility of truth *tout court* or as a blockage caused by the handover of truth to some other generic procedure. This last is what Badiou calls, using Jacques Alain-Miller's term derived from Lacan, "suturing." The question of compossibility is then a matter of desuturing. We must separate Badiou's position from the more familiar insistence that despite the claims of the various postmodernisms or poststructuralisms, one must maintain the status of the Kantian diremption model or the semi-autonomy of art's claim to truth production in relation to politics or philosophy.

For this reason we must look at why Badiou rejects this model as his own. Unlike Rancière, for example, Badiou does not see the question about the relative autonomy of artistic truth as an inheritance of modernity, but instead views it as a classical question. Badiou's separation from this aspect of Kantian aesthetics is evident in his rejection of Aristotle's conception of art. Badiou provides three models for understanding philosophy's relation to art. The models emerged with the inception of philosophy, but he sees them as carrying over into the twentieth century. This, again, separates him from Rancière, for whom the distinct regimes of art have a history. "Three possible relations of philosophy (as thought) to the poem are *identifying rivalry* [Parmenides], *argumentative distance* [Plato] and *aesthetic regionality* [Aristotle]. In the first case philosophy wants the poem; in the second, it excludes it; and in the third, it categorizes it."[85] It should come as no surprise to anyone familiar with Badiou's insistent fidelity to Plato (in part a tactical gesture stemming from a rivalry with Nietzsche, Heidegger, and Deleuze over the stakes of philosophy) that while not sanctioning it, Badiou finds more philosophical purchase in Plato's ban on poetry than Aristotle's categorizing of it:

> For Aristotle—as little a poet as is possible in his technique of exposition (Plato, on the other hand, and he recognizes it, is at every moment sensible to the charm he excludes)—the Poem is no longer anything but a particular object proposed to the disposition of knowledge. . . . With Aristotle, the foundational debate is finished, and philosophy, stabilized in connection to its parts, no longer turns back dramatically on what conditions it.[86]

Here Badiou condemns Aristotle for not recognizing art as a singular form of truth.

Hence, Badiou's philosophy of/on art is significantly not an aesthetic philosophy if we understand aesthetics not as Rancière does, but in the more traditional sense of a "science of art" as a separate sphere. According to Badiou an aesthetic model leads to what Lacan calls "the discourse of the university," which is strictly opposed to Badiou's own conception of philosophical thinking. Philosophy's role is not interpretive—it is not about making "sense" of the four generic procedures. On the contrary, philosophy's role is "founding a unique place in which, under the contemporary conditions of these procedures, it may be stated how and why a truth is not a sense, being rather a *hole in sense*."[87] Philosophy, like Badiou's four truth procedures, subtracts itself from both sense making and sensual experience. "How" and "why" must be stated through reason. "Philosophy is an insensate act, and by this very fact rational."[88] Badiou therefore has no interest in the philosophy of art insofar as it is aesthetic or poetic, or a matter of making sense of art by understanding it, categorizing it, or defining its parameters. Philosophy is restricted to the "rational act" of seizing the truths of art.

Badiou identifies several suturings that have historically blocked the practice of philosophy. Positivism sutured philosophy to science. Certain versions of Marxism sutured philosophy to the political in fidelity to Marx's famous claim that concludes his "Theses on Feuerbach" that philosophy's role is no longer to "interpret" but rather to "change" the world.[89] (Such a charge could indeed be made about Badiou's own writings in his more explicitly Maoist period preceding *Being and Event*.)

If there is a particular sophist that is situated as the enemy when it comes to the relation of philosophy and artistic truths, it is Heidegger. Heidegger, according to Badiou, sutured philosophy to the poem.[90] Nonetheless, Heidegger remains a great sophist, and in regard to philosophy's relationship to the poem, he cannot be ignored. Badiou sees Heidegger's act of suturing as, on the one hand, a failure in regard to philosophy, but as, on the other hand, possessing a saving grace that endows it with a "ground of historicity" since Heidegger rightly identified the "Age of Poets."[91] Badiou grants that an "Age of Poets," spanning from Hölderlin to Paul Celan, marked not so much the death of philosophy, but a historical sequence in which philosophy lost its "free play" and poetry became the "locus" of enacting the truth of "being and time."[92] This epoch, characterized by "inconsistency and disorientation," was articulated in a kind of subtractive metaphysical poetry: "The scintillating dryness of these poems cut open a space . . . within historical pathos."[93] Heidegger's work, despite its failure, grasped the event. "The reformulation of that which both joins together and separates the poem and philosophical discursivity is an imperative which, thanks to Heidegger, we are obliged to submit ourselves to."[94]

Heidegger is, then, the end of aesthetics as a branch of philosophy, though not the end of the coexistence of art and philosophy. "Until today, Heidegger's thinking has owed its persuasive power to having been the only one to pick up what was at stake in the poem, namely the destitution of object fetishism, the opposition of truth and knowledge and lastly the essential disorientation of our epoch."[95] Still, because Heidegger failed to grasp the matheme, he turned artistic truth into something sacred. Objecting to Heidegger's claim of an "original indistinction" between the poem and the logos, Badiou claims that Parmenides is "not yet philosophy." Badiou continues, "For every truth that accepts its dependence in regard to narrative and revelation is still detained in mystery; philosophy exists solely through its desire to tear the latter's veil."[96] If philosophy exists as a certain desacralization and denarrativization, these turn out to be precisely true of artistic truth as well. That is, art, while having access to narrative and the iconography of the image, finds its truth in an immanent interruption with "the sacred authority of the image or the story."[97] This paradox in which art is both tied to the sacred and at the same time a form of desacralization, as we will see in the next chapter, is present too in Agamben's writings that are strongly marked by Heidegger.

Badiou's situating of both narrative and the image as heterogeneous to the rational and the capacity for truth evokes Lacan's distrust of the imaginary. In order to desuture philosophy or the poem from narrativization, both must borrow from another truth procedure: mathematics. As we've seen, compossibility means we can't think of these procedures in isolation. It is a matter of nondialectical relationality. Badiou is adamant about not confusing different procedures and claims that any given truth procedure itself involves a process of purification. Still, the purification is never complete; every procedure will remain permeated by the other procedures. Badiou freely acknowledges that each procedure will find reason to borrow from the others and occasionally they will get tied in knots. Indeed, philosophy's role as thinking compossibility would lose its force if the autonomy of each procedure could be delineated in advance of any event within one of the procedures. This is central to Badiou's philosophical project in its relation to the different procedures—a denial of rivalry, an assertion of independence, and yet an acknowledgment of an ever renewed tension or conflict between the procedures that demands a subtle and cutting precision to renew the integrity and vitality of each procedure and of the philosophical project more generally.

So, for example, fidelity to mathematical truth is not restricted to the domain of mathematics. Not only philosophical but also poetic, political and indeed amorous practice (thanks to Lacan) must be presented from an "imperative of consistency . . . which turns out to be incompatible with any legitimation by narrative, or by the initiated status of the subject of enunciation."[98] This is, of course, adamantly not a version of positivism. In *Being and Event*, Badiou constructs an ontology on the basis of a decision to accept the unprovable axiom "The one is not."[99] Badiou finds in figures like Kurt Gödel, Georg Cantor, and Paul Cohen a way to think inconsistency as that which under-lies consistency, a foundationless foundation. Mathematics, in Badiou's use of it, allows for being to be separated from any romantic, vitalist, or humanist trappings. Identifying ontology with mathematics allows Badiou to in some sense dispose of ontology, to render it empty. Being as such, inconsistent multiplicity, is logically meaningful but not experienced directly. Mathematics allows us to think a genuinely an-tihumanist ontology in which the event is, in a philosophical sense, primary.

WOUNDS, KNOTS, AND THE LAW

As we've seen, Badiou's attack on the poetic suture concedes quite a bit to Heidegger, which means not the end of philosophy but the end of aes-thetics. Aesthetic reflection as a productive discipline, he seems to be saying—despite the indication that he would never have endorsed the Aristotelian model—comes to an end with Heidegger. It is striking that, despite all the persuasive attacks Badiou makes on what he calls the so-phistic position that holds that the traumas of the twentieth century have put an end to philosophy, he clearly supports the notion that mo-dernity has seen an end to both moral and aesthetic philosophy, and even to ontology insofar as it is to be thought as within the domain of phi-losophy. It makes one wonder whether the return to philosophy isn't to a rather impoverished form. And indeed Badiou makes such a claim: "Philosophy is under the conditions of art, science, politics and love, but it is always damaged, wounded, serrated by the evental and singular character of these conditions. Nothing of this contingent occurrence pleases it."[100] All the procedures of truth not only condition philosophy but also call it into question. Plato, he suggests, recognized that philos-ophy suffers from the "wound" of art to the concept. Badiou insists that all the conditions of philosophy are also its wounds. "Poem, matheme, politics and love at once condition and insult philosophy. Condition and insult: that's the way it is."[101]

When philosophy's role cannot be interpretative, journalistic, or literary and cannot be reduced to the status of algebra, it may seem unclear what language philosophy is written in. Badiou's answer is that while philosophy maintains its distance from the generic procedures, it must have recourse to the effects of their truths. While philosophy desutures, it preserves and even engenders tangles. So philosophy does not place a ban on art even within philosophy itself. What saves philosophy from becoming art is a matter of jurisdiction. This is the position that might lend credence to Deleuze's alleged accusation that Badiou is a secret Kantian.[102] Maintaining the category of truth seems to necessitate the adherence to an impersonal law, one determined by reason or rationality as distinct from sense or understanding. Badiou says this about "occurrences of the literary" in philosophy: they "are placed under the jurisdiction of a principle of thought that they do not constitute. They are *localized* in points at which—in order to complete the establishment of the place in which why and how a truth hollows sense and escapes interpretation is stated—one must precisely through a paradox of exposition, propose a fable, an image or a fiction to interpretation itself."[103] This claim is striking as a weak point in Badiou's philosophy not because philosophy should not have recourse to the literary, but rather in the broader sense of what is meant by compossibility. It reads as a rather strained attempt to smuggle literary devices back into philosophy without conceding anything to so-called anti-philosophy.

Beyond this "paradox of exposition," poetry plays another more specific and more necessary role in philosophy. The nomination of an event "is *always* poetic."[104] When philosophy attempts to present what in the poem constitutes its truth, what he calls "truth's proving of itself" within the poem, it "falls under the imperative of having to propose to sense and to interpretation the latent void. . . . This presentation of the unpresentable void requires the deployment within language of the latter's literary resources; but under the condition that it occur at this very point; thus under the general jurisdiction of an entirely different style, that of argumentation, of conceptual liaison, or of the Idea."[105] The act of naming the void so central to Badiou's conception of the philosophy is itself literary, but in such a way as to be marked as a gesture that refers back to another authority.

Philosophy is therefore knotted up with art, but it must rigorously subtract itself from art's aim. Philosophy's duty to art is to "envisage . . . the poem as truth of sensible presence deposited in rhythm and image, but without the corporeal captation by this rhythm and this image."[106] It reduces the material of representation to nothing, leaving only presentation. The impoverishment of philosophy is that it must seize the truth of art (and each of the other procedures) but without the jouissance attached to them. Philosophy is characterized by simultaneous impoverishment and excess—deprived of the power to create truth while granted jurisdiction over all truth.

As for philosophy relinquishing the jouissance of art, it is not clear to what extent art itself has access to this jouissance. "Imaginary captation" is hardly prescribed to art by Badiou.[107] On the contrary, it is precisely what needs to be subtracted. Rhythm and image seem ultimately to have a similar role in art to the one they have in philosophy—extrinsic to truth, they subsist as only residue or the site of deposition. And if, as we saw earlier, while philosophy may "imitate" art, in a peculiar reversal, artistic truth must subtract itself from all fictional or mimetic aspects. Like philosophy, both anemic and revitalized, Badiou characterizes poetic truth alternately by lack and excess, as figured correspondingly by Mallarmé and Pessoa.[108] "Excess," of course, is not the discourse of the university, universality as encyclopedic, but rather an inverse method of breaking from particularity toward the impersonal through a kind of infinite dispersion. We could think of Beckett's distinction between himself and Joyce: "He was always adding . . . I realized that my own way was in impoverishment, in lack of knowledge and in taking away, in subtracting rather than adding."[109] The cinematic equivalent to Mallarmé and Pessoa, or Beckett and Joyce, might be Bresson and Godard.

The emphasis on impersonality and abstraction may corroborate Hallward's claim that Badiou does not distinguish his ideas on art from the familiar tenets of modernism. And excluding his writings on cinema, Badiou's canon, if we can call it that, or the names that recur as emblems of artistic truths are largely still within the framework and period of the so-called Age of Poets. Common examples for him in realms of music and painting include Schoenberg and Malevich, both of whom exemplify subtractive aesthetics. He also has suggested that dance and cinema are the two key arts of the twentieth century, and his cinephilia has been central to his thinking and writing in general throughout his career even if, as we will see, cinema for him poses a complication for his conception of art.[110] He has insisted that there is a "plurality of arts" and "there is no imaginable way of totalizing this plurality."[111] In addition to an argument against the Wagnerian "total work of art" as a necessarily anti-subtractive conception that would ignore the necessity of the void intrinsic to any truth (a false "excess") or indeed its contemporary variant in the will toward an all-encompassing virtual reality or multimedia experience, we can see Badiou here making an argument against the suturing of the truth of art to any particular form of art, despite the privilege he sometimes seems to give to poetry.

He also sees truth as historically defined. Given Badiou's classicism and anti-historicism, as well as the fact that his examples tend to come from an earlier era of aesthetic modernity, it is important to note his insistence on the situatedness of every philosophical project. This goes for art as for the rest. In Badiou's "Fifteen Theses on Contemporary Art," the word "contemporary" is essential, and it is especially crucial for his conception of cinema, which as a "mass art" has a special role in relation to the present. Badiou's foundationless ontology allows for a conception of the universal and eternal that is inseparable from a confrontation with the historical moment.

The subject to an artistic truth is a configuration that ruptures the regime of some particular form of art. As with Deleuze, this may seem to reproduce a familiar, conservative approach to art that emphasizes the works of great masters, leaving everything else in the dustbin. While Badiou does at times seem to conform to this tendency, it is worth noting that his "auteurism," like that of Deleuze, is somewhat more complicated. The configuration that is the subject to an artistic truth, he tells us, should not be equated with either a great work or a great artist. Badiou insists that neither single artworks nor the names of artists are equivalent to events. The single work subject to a truth remains for Badiou a "finite fragment."[112] As for the artist, she may lend her name to the event constituted by her formal invention, but the subject to the truth is composed of the works (always multiple) themselves and not the individuals who were instruments of their creation. Indeed, the artist is "finally, what disappears in art."[113] Badiou is proposing an ethic radically antagonistic to the cult of the artist in which the artist is identified with the work and subsequently rewarded. For him there is a kind of martyrdom to artistic creation. He claims the ethic of art is "desperation."[114] We must separate this ethic from its simulacrum, the fake martyrdom of the romantic artist. Of course, the "desperation" should not be marketable, but nor should we be seduced by more subtle variations in which the apparent disappearance of the artist as creator draws only more attention to the elusive figure behind the work, rather than to the work itself.

PRESCRIPTION AND DIAGNOSIS

All of Badiou's philosophical prescriptions emerge out of a diagnosis. If artistic or aesthetic production is to be within a truth procedure, it must say something other than what counts as art within the art world, the accepted discourses surrounding contemporary aesthetic production and the culture at large. The diagnosis identifies what gets counted as art—call it art's illness. He provides two dominant tendencies for art and calls them "romanticism" and "formalism."[115] In art, romanticism and formalism can be seen as the corollaries of what he calls "bodies and languages"—that which the dominant ideology recognizes as existent.

What Badiou identifies as romanticism, a tendency that he claims still dominates artistic production, is itself a kind of subtractive aesthetic that purports to find truth in abjection—exposing the finitude of the body and sexuality. It is not hard to think of many acclaimed artworks in different media that in the guise of provocation offer up the body as the limit of experience.[116] According to Badiou, this is "only the reversal of the ideology of happiness" and is but another figure for resignation.[117]

In other words, the ever-present reminder from consumer culture that happiness and fulfillment are within our grasp, as figured in the still-powerful, if dated, tradition of the "Hollywood ending," only finds corroboration in the romantic gesture that seeks to expose mortality as the final word on human experience. In Badiou's view, dominant practice, obsessed with finitude as the marker of substantial truth, places infinity on the side of formal innovation. Badiou makes it clear that he believes art will inevitably create new forms, but as a motivation for art, this drive is only a kind of complicity with capitalist progress. In this sense, he is decidedly not modernist as the term is usually construed.

Cinema too must avoid the tendency of artistic practices to seek their truth in either the gesture of some formal or technical innovation or, on the other hand, in sex, death, and the exhibition of the erotic or suffering body. Likewise, film theory and criticism should no longer anchor their own operations in seeking the truth of films in bodies or languages. From structural linguistics and semiotics to neo-formalism, film theory has long sought legitimacy through versions of formal analysis. In recent decades this tendency has been countered by an emphasis on the sensorial—the bodily or affective, the haptic or tactile. Thus a brief history of the last half century of film theory: from discourse to figure, from language to mind and body. Badiou cuts through this simple binary to propose that we must think instead the exceptions—the singular effects for thought found in specific films.

Despite art's autonomy from politics, it nonetheless has an explicitly political importance. According to Badiou, art or cinema is political because its purpose is to resist the new sensible relations to the world proposed by global capital and to provide a "proposition about a new definition of what is our sensible relation to the world."[118] Indeed, this is quite close to Deleuze, who argues that philosophy, science, and art are "all related insofar as they must counter the introduction of a cultural space of markets and conformity."[119] For Deleuze, art is distinct from philosophy and science because it does this through using percepts and affects. In Badiou's terms, art concerns the creation of different sensible relations to the world. According to Badiou, art's value today is about political emancipation because "without art, without artistic creation, the triumph of the forced universality of money and power is a real possibility."[120] The "something else" posited by an artwork must be other than what is allowed or understood not only by the art world but by capitalist experience more broadly. The singular subtracted from any particularity is the only meaning of universal address for Badiou. Badiou is, of course, well aware that what gets called globalization or empire comes with its own form of universalism. His proposal is that whereas the representation of the particular—be it a group or community or some form of so-called personal expression—might be conceived of as one form of opposition to this "abstract universality of money and power,"[121] what we need is a different form of abstract universality that emerges from a concrete or singular creation.

For Badiou abstract art is the evacuation not of content, but of particularity. Art for him is a matter of pure presence, and this is what links it to political equality: it does not "distinguish between kinds of people."[122] Badiou opposes the notion of art as ever being a matter of asserting the truth of any particular subject position. This has significant ramifications for his conception of the politics of art, which has so often been associated with questions of the representation of identity. Art as presentation but not representation should intervene at the edge of the void of the situation, which means, for Badiou, not being able to be included in the meta-structure or state of the situation. All art is like Mallarmé's book: "Impersonalized . . . without any human accessories, it takes place all alone."[123] For Badiou, Mallarmé's seemingly extreme assertion of art's autonomy means that the event constituted by an artwork is that part of the artwork that cannot be counted or claimed. What has been called Mallarmé's hermeticism is for Badiou precisely his universalism. Mallarmé's book is a figure for democracy, though one contrary to any notion of consensus or the common denominator. That which is addressed to everyone equally will, like a star, necessarily seem elevated, distant, and ungraspable, qualities that should not be mistaken for hermeticism or elitism.

In one of his fifteen theses on contemporary art offered in 2003, Badiou states, "Non-imperial art must be as rigorous as a mathematical demonstration, as surprising as an ambush in the night, and as elevated as a star."[124] Here we see the analogy to the other procedures—their sharing or imitation. We can also see Badiou's localized use of the literary for philosophical purposes. Art is informed by the other procedures with which it must be made compossible. From mathematics it borrows rigor and consistency as well as a certain irreducibility. The ambush evokes surprise and political risk, and the star suggests both distance and authority, a sensual aura and material reality but one untouched by worldly interests. All three may indicate the "new," whose importance Badiou maintains in what could be considered a modernist vein. But again we must recognize that he is not referring to new forms per se. He says art must "create a new possibility," not, however, in order to "realize" it: again, an art that desires to realize new forms would be complicit with a philosophy of the market, for which there are infinite possibilities, infinite solutions to invented consumer problems, within our finite world.[125] Instead, art should say "something else" is possible. Dominant art insists that all is possible because all is impossible. That is, within our closed, globalized, liberal, capitalist world innovation is infinite, but no real alternative is thinkable. For Badiou, art should on the contrary refuse innovation but say that another world is possible. Art should render visible "that which, as far as Empire is concerned, doesn't exist." This is another way of stating Deleuze's proposition that cinema should address a people that are "missing" or do not yet exist.

Using the set-theory-inspired language of *Being and Event*, Empire is the state of the situation, but not the situation itself.[126] The gesture of art is to present that which Empire cannot count, or, to use Rancière's language, "the part of those who have no part." From this vantage point we can understand Badiou's insistence on singularity over particularity. The assertion of the particularity of a specific group is a matter of making it countable within the state.[127] If the group is oppressed, the oppression is ignored by the state and must be made visible by subtracting the particularity on which the state relies. Art is always giving form to the void of the current configuration of sensible experience or more specifically what passes for artistic production. Badiou reverses what he takes to be Wittgenstein's anti-philosophical claim that "whereof one cannot speak, thereof one must be silent."[128] For

Badiou, only what cannot be said clearly must be given expression through art.

We see in Badiou's theses on art the way in which diagnosis is followed by prescription, but in way that may not immediately seem obvious. The diagnosis merely marks the empty space for what is missing that an artistic configuration that can constitute an event would offer. If Badiou, like Deleuze, is proposing a kind of aesthetics of resistance, it cannot be a simple matter of reversal or inversion of dominant forms or mere avoidance of the symptoms. The prescription must involve some element of what he calls "forcing."[129] Here we can appreciate the philosophical importance of the void in Badiou's work. It marks a place for resistance both immanent to dominant and oppressive practice, but also necessarily unacceptable to it and unanticipated by it. Subtraction is the elimination of the terrain of the opposition, but it must be a rigorous and rational procedure and not the sort of confident indifference that more often than not repeats what it sought to ignore. While Deleuze himself would agree, this is a point that sharply separates Badiou from the strain of post-Deleuzian aesthetics that seeks justification for artworks based on the notion that they exhibit unconstrained raw affect.

What makes art its own generic procedure, what gives it its "evental and singular character," is that it is the truth of sense or, as Badiou says, "of the sensible." Since as we saw all truth is a matter of making a hole in sense, rupturing the regime of sense making, art has the peculiar position of presenting the truth of that which truth itself interrupts. Sensual or sensory material is reduced to its "minimal image." Art is then the self-negation of its own material, a breaking of its own mirror. As Badiou says, "The very act of the poem consists in bringing about the emergence of an object (swan, star, rose . . .) an object whose arrival imposes its own termination."[130] Inaesthetics is then not simply meta-aesthetics but, as Rancière has countered, closer to anti-aesthetics. It is this that allows Badiou to claim that art is pure presence. Art is the assertion of the existence of a "formless form." As pure presence, an immanent singularity, art is indifferent to differences, which connects it to a conception of political equality. Like politics, art "must be received . . . in the egalitarian anonymity of its presentation as such."[131]

CINEMA: THE PLUS-ONE OF THE ARTS

This may seem to leave few opportunities for cinema beyond perhaps certain avant-garde gestures, but for Badiou, surprisingly, "pure" cinema in the avant-garde tradition is unceremoniously rejected: "Pure cinema does not exist, except in the dead end vision of avant-garde formalism."[132] Rather, cinema turns out to be a supplement to Badiou's inaesthetics that threatens the logic of his conception of art. If art is a condition and insult to philosophy, cinema is a condition and insult to art. Cinema is, according to Badiou, not one art among many but the "plus-one of the arts."

The notion that cinema is an impure art that combines the other arts is not a new idea. Badiou points to the influence of Bazin, but it can be found at least as far back as Vachel Lindsay's 1915 *The Art of the Moving Picture*. But the term "plus-one" suggests that cinema is not a proper art so much as a supplement to the very division of arts. For Badiou, cinema does not totalize the plurality of arts but is conditioned by them, patrolling their borders, subjecting them to its impure operations. Contaminated by the other arts, cinema is also contaminated by non-art and the realm of what he calls "the indistinct judgment." It is in this relation to everyday life where we can locate cinema's politics. Badiou states, "This is . . . what politicizes cinema: it operates on a junction between ordinary opinions and the work of thought."[133] Cinema's relation to politics is also a relation to theory or ideology critique. Cinema performs work on the common and ordinary. Cinema is then not pure presentation like Mallarmé's book, and which Badiou claims is true for all art. What Badiou calls the "proletarian aristocratism" of art—"Art is made, and says what it does, according to its own discipline, and without considering anybody's interests"[134]—is undercut by cinema, which Badiou sees as both a democratic and mass art. The other arts as truth procedures are indifferent to "commercial laws of circulation and democratic laws of communication,"[135] and rather necessitate a "differential education" and preserve a "proximity to the history of the art concerned and the vicissitudes of its grammar."[136] Cinema is the opposite in that it addresses itself to a "generic humanity" unconcerned with the logic of artistic truth only with a shared sensible world.

This is not to say cinema's truths can be simply judged in terms of their mass appeal, but rather that cinema must engage in a rigorous subtractive mode with the "vulgar" productions of the culture industry or "ideological indicators of the epoch."[137] Though he does not use the language of ideological critique as it is typically formulated, Badiou seeks to isolate the dominant tendencies that serve to block genuinely new cinematic forms from emerging, but which might themselves be possible sites of intervention since they constitute the raw materials that make a film contemporary.

In Badiou's view, unlike the other arts, cinema is not indifferent to the culture of consumption. In an essay from 1999 titled "Considerations on the Current State of Cinema and on the Ways of Thinking This State Without Having to Conclude That Cinema Is Dead or Dying," Badiou proposes that one direction of the purification process of cinematic truth should be aimed at the ways desire, sex, and bodies feature in mainstream visual culture. Adorno and Horkheimer once referred to the Hollywood film as both "pornographic and prudish" to describe how exhibitionism and prurience coexisted with conservative moralism and the repression of actual sex.[138] It could be argued that Hollywood has since become less prudish, but as Badiou points out, it was the proscriptions of the Hays Code that led to the use of metonymic images for desire in classical Hollywood, its saving grace, but a practice that has become saturated through Empire's progressive ban on censorship. Since the classical period, the culture industry has taken the direction of explicit use of "extreme violence, cruelty" and "the motif of erogenous nudity" while remaining as prudish as ever in regard to desire.[139] These images of sex and violence constitute raw material that need to be submitted to artistic purification. The non-art of the times, namely "pornographic nudity, the cataclysmic special effect, the intimacy of the couple, social melodrama, and pathological cruelty," are purified by cinema.[140] This process should be directed "not through an aggressive posture with respect to inherited forms, but through mechanisms that arrange these forms at the edge of the void, in a network of cuts and disappearances."[141] These operations lead to "the passage of the idea."[142]

We can see how prescription and diagnosis work with cinema in an explicitly political way. Cinema is directly concerned with the non-art of the times. According to Badiou, a goal of contemporary cinema should be to perform work on the tropes that are part of our common audiovisual language. A work of art, like any truth, is composed of bodies and languages of our world, but it introduces a bit of resistance such that it is available to another world. This is one way of thinking about what a cinematic idea consists of for Badiou. It is also what makes a film political, for to create a new idea in cinema is to affirm that another world is possible.

For Badiou, cinema ideas pass through the purification of cinema's non-artistic character and its relation to the other arts. The idea of "impurity" in Badiou means two things. Cinema is impure in relation to what he calls non-art, which is literally all that falls outside the realm of art, the chaos and banality of everyday life as well as all that counts as art and entertainment but offers no new gesture or idea.

It is impure in relation to non-art in three ways: (1) how it is experienced (whether on a Friday night date or a lazy Sunday afternoon, cinema is not often felt to be an event so much as an escape and a source for gossip and the exchange of opinions); (2) how it is produced (as a collaborative medium within an industry dependent on capital, cinema is never the sole product of a single author; as Badiou has insisted, "The cinema is first and foremost an industry");[143] and (3) in terms of its content (the moving indexical image always contains an excess or infinity of information and the genre clichés that compose cinema's stories are a necessary part of it as a mass art). Even the greatest films, Badiou is fond of saying, contain worthless material, and every film is at war with the non-art of the times (the dominant forms of spectacle, the sensory overload of information, all the cultural detritus and popular manifestations of ideology that we live with on a daily basis). If victorious, a worthy film salvages something from the worst of this sensible infinity of the contemporary world. Cinema starts not from the void (the blank page of Mallarmé), but from the chaos "of the non-art of its times" that it seeks to purify.[144]

Cinema is also impure in relation to the other arts. In 1952 André Bazin wrote an essay titled "Pour un cinéma Impur: Défense de L'Adaptation" (given the unfortunate title "In Defense of Mixed Cinema" in Hugh Gray's standard English translation) that claimed that cinema was not opposed to theater or literature and could be more faithful to its own potential when it sought to serve the other arts rather than making them "cinematic."[145] This went against a certain modernist conception that any given art finds its destiny in how the specific material of the medium is distinct from other arts with which it may seem to share certain superficial properties. In a twist on the concept of "medium specificity," for Badiou this impurity is in some sense the specificity of cinema, although it is a paradoxical specificity. This is why he calls cinema not the seventh art but "the plus-one" of the arts. Cinema is a supplement to the division of arts; contaminated by them, it subjects them to its impure operations, finding in them what is most accessible or universal.

The purification of non-art and the making universal or accessible of the other arts may seem in opposition to one another. When Badiou gives specific examples of purifying operations such as Godard's use of "dirty sound" or how Goethe's *Wilhelm Meister's Apprenticeship* is transformed by Wenders's *The Wrong Move* (1975) and so on, they often seem to be highlighting the critical dimension of cinema's operations and therefore might be seen to place Badiou's ideas about cinema in the venerable Brechtian-Althusserian tradition of affirming "counter-cinema" or the operations constitutive of a familiar idea of political modernism. That cinema's ideas operate on vulgar forms and on the other arts are two compelling ways to conceptualize cinema's specificity. On the one hand, elite forms of art are made accessible. On the other hand, accessible forms are made strange. Both touch on cinema's significance as what he calls a "mass art," but also seemingly emphasize marginal and oppositional films and not necessarily those that can be said to have mass audiences.

But Badiou's conception of cinema as a mass art has another sense. In an echo of Benjamin, the capacity for genuine mass appeal intersecting with great art is summoned to isolate the specific potential of cinema: "An art is a 'mass art' if the masterpieces, the artistic productions that the erudite (or dominant, whatever) culture declares incontestable, are seen and liked by millions of people from all social groups at the very moment of their creation."[146] Appealing to attempts to address "generic humanity" in the 1920s from Eisenstein to Chaplin's tramp, Badiou has less convincingly suggested that more contemporary films in what he calls a "neo-classical" mold like *Titanic* and certain films directed by Clint Eastwood (he has written about *Perfect World* [1993] and *Bridges of Madison County* [1995]) continue this legacy of making good on cinema's potential as a mass art.

The very idea of mass art is paradoxical according to Badiou. The paradoxical dimension is that cinema combines an aristocratic category (art) with a political and democratic one (mass).[147] And perhaps the paradox is meant to account for a never fully addressed tension between two ideas of what the art and politics of cinema are capable of. For Badiou, cinema is torn between the possibility of creating new ideas by undermining dominant forms and dividing its viewers (Godard, Wenders, Straub/Huillet, Debord, Oliveira, Antonioni are the subjects for some of his finest writings on film) and of producing new potential for the immediate engagement of an anonymous collective by elevating genre tropes to popular myths. He has called cinema

> an art grounded in the fondness of all classes, ages and peoples for an important man being doused with liquid manure by a tramp, of an enormous sinking ship, of a terrible monster suddenly emerging from the bowels of the earth, of the good guy, after many setbacks, finally killing the bad guy at high noon, of the policeman detective tracking down the Mafioso-thief, of the strange customs of foreigners, and of horses in a field, and of brotherly warriors, and of the romantic drama, and of the naked woman torn by love.[148]

Badiou's acknowledgment that "mass art" is itself a paradoxical idea and his insistence on cinema's "impurity" allow for a dialectic between these two possibilities—classicism and modernism.

Badiou has also consistently highlighted two additional philosophical arenas within which cinema operates: as an ontological art and as an art of time. As an ontological art, cinema becomes an arena in which the relation being and appearance gets played out. This, for example, is why Badiou has a qualified appreciation for the Platonism of *The Matrix* (1999), explaining, "The question of challenging the image on the basis of the image itself, in the direction of its foundational beyond, is the very question of cinema."[149] "Foundational beyond" refers to the Platonic question of what lies beyond appearance or the image. Cinema, Badiou argues, is "the height of the old art of the image."[150] Capable of seemingly capturing an "integral reality," as Bazin once put it, as well as being capable of the height of artifice, cinema more than other arts can exhibit fables that become a place in which the difference between the real and the imaginary gets played with. Similarly, despite his criticisms of forms of multimedia sensory overload, he has noted the significance for ontological art in new forms of digital cinema:

> Following on the heels of cinema (the greatest artistic invention of the past century), new possibilities are springing up, without their exploration having, as yet, produced a decisive shift towards a fundamental reorganization of the classification and hierarchy of artistic activities. The advent of virtual images or images without any referent undoubtedly opens up a new stage of questions of representation.[151]

Since philosophy is conditioned by art and cinema and not the other way around, it is only by looking at what has been created with new technology that we can discover the events that allow for rethinking the relation between being and appearance. In the meantime, while it is not yet clear what major new arts if any will emerge out of the possibilities of convergence, social media, infinitely manipulable digital worlds, virtual reality, and other new cultural forms tied to new technologies, cinema, he points out, is already "multimedia" and can allow us to think about new syntheses that help us think our shared "social imaginary" in the twenty-first century.[152]

In conjunction with cinema as an ontological art, Badiou, following Deleuze, emphasizes that cinema is an art of time, which offers time in the form of a perception or "the most powerful becoming visible of time."[153] Unlike Deleuze, Badiou suggests that the image need not be the central category in understanding cinema, but he sees cinema as always in time, its ideas always in the form of visitation, conveyed in movement or passage and infected by the vagaries of memory. And while Deleuze sees cinema as offering an image of time in a pure state—not as a representation but as a qualitative time understood in the manner of Bergson's conception of duration—Badiou emphasizes instead cinema's capacity to combine a sense of both continuous and discontinuous time. This is still, as we find in Deleuze, a making time visible, allowing for the perception of time as such, but in keeping with the concept of impurity, Badiou emphasizes time in cinema as a paradoxical representation, a new kind of synthesis between continuity and discontinuity or between time as preserved and time as ephemeral or lost. As Bazin noted, cinematic time is always paradoxical: it mummifies the passage of time and in the process makes the irreducibly contingent past eternal. In an explicit repudiation of Deleuze, Badiou states, "But cinema's greatness doesn't lie in reproducing Bergson's division between constructed time and pure duration; it lies in showing us that a synthesis between the two is possible."[154] Cinema, the impure art, includes both the constructed time theorized by Eisenstein as montage and the affliction of duration in real time in Akerman's *Jeanne Dielman, 23 quai du Commerce, 1080 Bruxelles* (1975). These are not two regimes of images divided by a historical break, but two forms of time brought together in a medium that according to Badiou undermines the metaphysical dualism of Bergson.

CINEMA AS ART'S RELATION TO NON-ART

Both Deleuze and Badiou believe it is necessary to affirm cinema as art before we are able to consider cinema's link to philosophy or theory. Benjamin, when declaring cinema's destiny was found in politics, proposed that this was not because cinema was not art, but because cinema was the evidence that art is no longer what it used to be. For Deleuze and

Badiou, philosophy's approach to art wrests art from the consideration of cultural practices and ideology. Art, unlike ideology, is the concern of philosophy because it is a specific creative mode of thinking. Both Badiou and Deleuze get subsumed into the tradition of "theory" against philosophy, but it could be said that one of the things that marks them as philosophers is their belief that art is irreducible to one signifying practice among many.

Deleuze and Badiou both see art as a locus for production that gives rise to concepts. These concepts belong neither to art nor to philosophy. Art cannot create concepts, and philosophy when thinking about art cannot apply its concepts to art. Philosophy when thinking about what art thinks about creates the concept that it derives from art's sensual and sensible production. For Badiou, philosophy seizes hold of or submits itself to the conditions of art's truths. For Deleuze, philosophy's creative practice lends the consistency of the concept to art's logic of sensation. Both Badiou and Deleuze thereby seek to get beyond the binary in which the work of art is either ungraspable by theory or a mere instrument for theory's purposes. For Badiou and Deleuze, philosophy's relation to art is not a respect for the work's autonomy or a subsumption of the one by the other, but a non-relation, because artworks are the real and not an effect or performance of the real.

But we should not take for granted the affirmation of cinema as art, nor indeed art's separation from culture, opinion, and ideology. As Benjamin observed, cinema becomes a locus for evaluating the boundaries of these very categories. For Benjamin, photography and cinema open up the possibilities for thinking about artistic production as being less about having a specific learned skill that puts the artist in a tradition associated with her medium and more about having a perspective on the shared perceptible world that is revealed by selecting, arranging, or sampling from it. Indeed, for Badiou himself, cinema's relation to art is a precarious one. The autonomy of cinema is inextricable from its heteronomy. As he claims, the singularity of the cinematographic procedure is tied to its essential impurity; what is intrinsic to cinema is that it bears the traces of non-art as well as all the other arts; again, not the seventh art, but the plus-one of the arts.[155]

Like Benjamin and Adorno, Badiou's skepticism about cinema as an art like all the others derives from identifying in it a social function that cannot be evacuated from its aesthetic dimension. As Adorno claimed, "There can be no aesthetics of cinema . . . which would not include the sociology of the cinema."[156] For Badiou this means that a cinematic truth procedure, unlike Mallarmé's book, cannot exist in itself, but must perform its operation as an intervention into dominant tendencies in the circulation of moving images. This impurity is double in relation both to non-art and to the other arts. Cinema cannot completely purify itself of its history as mode of communication and as a recording device that can function in the absence of an author's will to art. At the same time it subsumes all the other arts.

As an example, we can think of Dziga Vertov's attempt at creating a sui generis language of images. *Man with a Movie Camera* opens with the following statement:

> The film Man with a Movie Camera represents AN EXPERIMENT IN THE VISUAL TRANSMISSION Of visual phenomena WITHOUT THE USE OF INTERTITLES (a film without intertitles) WITHOUT THE HELP OF A SCRIPT (a film without script) WITHOUT THE HELP OF A THEATER (without actors, without sets, etc.) This new experimentation work by Kino-Eye is directed toward the creation of an authentically international absolute language of cinema— ABSOLUTE KINOGRAPHY—on the basis of its compete separation from the language of theater and literature.

But does *Man with a Movie Camera* effectively purge itself of the other arts? We can see in the case of Vertov how the subtraction of any leaning on the literary, theatrical, or painterly is possible only through the creation of a rhythmic montage that ultimately finds recourse to music as an analogue for cinematic language.[157] In another turn of the screw, Lev Manovich will show at the end of the twentieth century how Vertov had anticipated the language of new media by grasping the logic of networks and computation in his database cinema.[158] If Vertov did create new cinematic ideas in Badiou's sense, it was not by inventing a pure language of cinema but by revealing the explosive power of cinema's impurity. As we saw, Deleuze arrives at this same point. The new ideas cinema creates involve thwarting its own powers.

So we should not pass lightly over this peculiar role that Badiou assigns to cinema. He wishes to preserve its status as art, as capable of immanent singularities, but immanent singularities are for Badiou, as they are for Deleuze, dependent on the claim that there is something proper to art and to each art, whereas what is proper to cinema is precisely its impropriety. As Badiou is aware, preserving the distinction between art and philosophy is something Deleuze struggles with as well. He must keep reminding us, and himself, that what Mallarmé does is not the same as what Nietzsche does—a sensation of the concept is distinguishable from the concept of a sensation.

The subtraction of art from ideology in Badiou finds a limit in cinema. Therefore, for Badiou, cinema brings us back in touch with the sociological, cultural, and ideological functions of entertainment and cultural consumption because its function as art is to make visible art's relation to non-art or ideology today. This makes cinema very explicitly political since its social function—its work on the ideological content of everyday life—is central to its artistic function. Deleuze, as we saw, seems to reject any concern for culture and ideology in his conception of cinema, but he ultimately sees cinema as a form of resistance to the logic of control, commercialization, and the reduction of everything to information.

Badiou's thesis that cinema is the plus-one of the arts should not be isolated from Benjamin's recognition in the 1930s that all arts are now under the condition of cinema; that is, cinema is symptomatic of a particular moment in the decline of art's ability to mark its separation from non-art. Hence Benjamin's claim that cinema realized for art what dada anticipated. Cinema's impurity should be seen in the context of the intrinsic impurity of all the arts in what Rancière has called "the aesthetic regime of art." Badiou's tendency, like Adorno's, to find the truth of all art in a subtractive poetics evacuated of rhythm and image may come from the refusal to fully accept the truth content of cinema in the other arts. Inversely, for Deleuze, as Nancy suggested, philosophy itself becomes cinematic. What's left of this project in certain Deleuzian writing on film is—through a disavowal of the symbolic—a return to that obscure ontological background that Pasolini declared is film theory's role to cut through.

RANCIÈRE AND BADIOU: ROMANTICISM VERSUS MODERNISM

Rancière's concept of the aesthetic regime of art is a polemical or pedagogical intervention. One of the primary assumptions guiding it is that the persistent discourses about "modernism" obscure our ability to think about the future of art. Many histories and theories of modern art identify its emergence with a new kind of art that, in Rancière's words, "turns its attention away from the content of common experience and . . . directs it towards the means of its practice."[159] As Rancière argues, this familiar narrative of modernism misses what is essential about a new regime of art that emerges at the beginning of the nineteenth century and makes this modernist doxa possible. This conception of modernism— perhaps most directly associated with Clement Greenberg—is thinkable only by siding with one pole of a new dual image function that emerges in the nineteenth century. It is an attempt to save art from contamination by the commodity form through effecting a realization of an idea of art that cannot be realized without our losing the ability to identify it as art in the first place.

Following Badiou, but keeping within the general thrust of Rancière's discourse, we might recognize in modernist practices a "passion for the real" enacted through "operations of purification."[160] Badiou rarely speaks of "modernism," but the artists on which his philosophy most consistently leans—Mallarmé, Celan, Pessoa, Malevich, Schoenberg— are all figures that could be tied to what Rancière calls "the inconsistent utopia" of aesthetic modernity in the late nineteenth and early to mid- twentieth century, or witnesses to its failure. Badiou's emphasis on poetry indifferent to, in Mallarmé's words, "universal reportage" and his claim that no art production at all is preferable to participation in art that can be recognized by the language of commodity exchange put him, as Rancière suggests, in "the anti-aesthetic consensus" that is often used to characterize high modernism.[161]

Badiou refers to certain truth procedures as "saturated," which means that they have become consistent with the regime of sense. It is from the point of view of an event, emerging out of the process of purification, that this saturation comes to light, inaugurating a break or rupture within the history of artistic practice—for instance, after Schoenberg, classical music is no longer a viable truth procedure. The question of saturation should probably be interrogated further however, since it seems that all art for Badiou is itself a kind of high modernist art of exhaustion, exposing the saturation of dominant regimes of sense by pushing the sensible to its limits. Cinema forces Badiou to go beyond the art of exhaustion and impersonality in a way that the other arts do not.

If Badiou's inaesthetics sometimes seems trapped in a modernist framework, Rancière's concept of "the aesthetic regime of art" is arguably even more anachronistic to the degree that it suggests that we have never left the era of romanticism. Yet Rancière's romanticism bears little resemblance to the romantic disposition attacked by Badiou, which, as we saw above, is a synonym of the belief in finitude. What is important for Rancière about German romantic philosophy on art is the inauguration of an egalitarian principle at the core of aesthetic thinking.

Both Rancière and Badiou seek ways of thinking an immanent break from an always inconsistent situation that determines what counts as art or politics. Both view the axiom of equality as the political principle that ties the singular to the universal. But for Badiou the emphasis on the event and its truth sutured to a subjective fidelity emanates from an imperative of consistency and a cold distance from the ordinary practices of business as usual. Rancière, on the contrary, is invested in gestures that reframe the ordinary itself, in the blurring of borders that opens up the conditions of possibility of thinking the common, precisely not in Badiou's affirmation of the new whose singularity safeguards its appropriation by critical thought.

Both Rancière and Badiou have sought a path that keeps faith with an experience of '68 that put each of them at a certain distance from his Althusserian background, which came to be associated with the revisionism of the Communist Party. For Badiou, Althusser's belief in science was not the problem; the challenge was rather how to think art, science, politics, and sexuality together without making all truth a matter of one of these four arenas. He found in Lacan the beginnings of research into the use of mathematics, specifically set theory, to construct a nonromantic concept of the subject to provide the link between an ontology based on an unprovable axiom affirming inconsistent multiplicity—the one is not—and the thinking of the new, of change, or what he calls "the event."

Rancière for his part has remained on the terrain of aesthetics and politics. To draw out the aesthetic or literary dimension of both politics and philosophy was a way of upsetting the assumptions behind dominant political theories of art. This was not a handover of truth to art, as Badiou accuses Heidegger, but something more like a handover of philosophy to aesthetics. Aesthetics, for Rancière, is first of all a regime of art, but it is a regime of art in which art itself thinks about what makes art, art. It thus ties art to philosophy and politics because art in the aesthetic regime calls into question art's relation to non-art, the very fabric of what gets called life—either ordinary or extraordinary—and constructs a community in response. Politics and philosophy are aesthetic to the extent that they too are free from foundation and must find the means for generating their own unstable consistency. But if cinema's specificity is precisely its *impurity*, its subsumption of the other arts, and its proximity to non-art, as Badiou claims, then how do we square this with Rancière's claim that this paradoxical meaning of cinema was already contained in the very definition of art given by Hegel, Schelling, and Schiller that preceded cinema by nearly a century?

Rancière and Badiou are both guided by an egalitarian principle that is not progressive but a priori and, in Badiou's sense, "generic." For Badiou this principle demands an affirmative and prescriptive militancy. For Rancière, it means rather a minor philosophy that occupies spaces in between discourses. Rancière is then a kind of restrained and ironic anarchist: as Badiou puts it, there is "a brilliant hysteria to Rancière" that submits the philosopher-master to "the local expressions of non-mastery of the dominated who contradict, at each and every moment, the guarantees of the master's existence."[162] For Badiou, Rancière remains too lodged in an aesthetic paradigm, in what he sees as the powerful but ultimately confused "poetico-political" avant-gardism that belonged to many of the most creative figures of the twentieth century for whom the word "politics" "dilates to the point of vaguely designating every radical break, every escape from consensus."[163] What Rancière's work fails to think within Badiou's framework is militancy and the matheme. According to Rancière's philosophical project, on the other hand, Badiou's anchoring of truth in a concept of militant fidelity directed at the rarity of events could be viewed as risking becoming yet another way of policing what counts as thought versus what is deemed to be the mere chatter of the mob.

CONCLUSION: CINEMA'S IMPURE POLITICS

It is the claim of this book that Rancière and Badiou help us preserve something from the axiomatics of Deleuze's natural history or taxonomy of cinematic signs and at the same time remain faithful to the political critique of representation in seventies film theory, but only by forcing us to rethink both of these projects.

Without minimizing the differences between Deleuze, Badiou, and Rancière, it is my contention that they find a meeting point in cinema. Cinema for each one becomes a site of ambiguity in their larger philosophical projects. For Deleuze, cinema actualizes his theory of perception and affection, yet its essence is realized in a moment of crisis when this theory undergoes a kind of involution. Deleuze tends to be posed as an answer to Althusserian and Lacanian film theory because he reverses its central move. Deleuzian film theory announces immanence rather than distance or separation as cinema's vocation. Once again a modernist theater tradition provides the missing link between philosophical thought and aesthetic practice. Against a Brechtian cinema of alienation, Artaud offers a model of a cinema that *erases* rather than increases the distance between the spectator and the screen. But immersion like alienation is not a solution to political art. It can function only as a way of challenging and resisting dominant forms of representation. When Deleuze describes the politics of cinema today as resistance to control, he makes it clear that a philosophy of immanence does not mean we can completely escape the problems of political cinema posed by Brechtian-Althusserian film theory.

For Rancière, cinema's technological means realize "the aesthetic regime of art," but only at the cost of erasing the tension in it that made art possible; therefore, cinema tends to return to the outmoded representative regime of art to develop its aesthetic possibilities. For Badiou, cinema incorporates all the arts and therefore is not capable of truth in quite the way of the other arts; rather it patrols the border of art and non-art. For Deleuze, cinema is pedagogical. For Badiou, cinema is impure. For Rancière, it always puts into play a "thwarting logic."

What unites them finally is a way of preserving the idea of cinema as political and as a way of thwarting ideology while breaking from the tradition of political film theory that sees this politics in terms of exposing the level of mediation and the film's conditions of production. Indeed as conditions of production change and the raw material of cinema takes on new forms in the age of the digital, there may still be ways of exposing the apparatus that have a political valence. Whether this modernist operation is saturated remains to be challenged by new individual examples. But cinema becomes political not because it becomes symbolic but rather because it creates a new relation between the symbolic and imaginary. It becomes political because it creates a new configuration of the sensible that challenges the distribution of the sensible as defined by what Badiou would call the contemporary ideological indicators of our epoch. The political dimension of cinema is found in all the ways that films propose that "something else is possible" by evoking a people, a collectivity, that does not yet exist.

A young Badiou wrote an important essay in 1966, "The Autonomy of the Aesthetic" (quoted in Godard's *La Chinoise* no less), that already rejected the idea that art could be reduced to ideology or politics. As he articulated it years later, as someone who remained faithful to May '68, he never accepted the slogan of the era that "everything is political." Art was in a certain sense autonomous from politics, and this claim was necessary to recognize in what sense art could be substantively political or metapolitical. As Deleuze and Rancière would both agree, "subjecting aesthetic production to political imperatives" is actually a way of depoliticizing art because it means conforming to what Badiou calls a "statist imperative."[164] The political dimension of cinema that philosophy can explore is found rather in its own immanent criteria. Cinema plays with the raw material of the shared sensible world, and in the process posits the possibility of a different world. This is what makes it capable of thought.

But if philosophy's response to cinema must be driven by resistance to the contemporary moment, as Deleuze and Badiou insist, then it must also think about new mutations in cinema. Both Deleuze and Badiou point in this direction, but their models largely remain either the classical feature of the movement-image or the modernist time-image. Agamben's thought about cinema takes us further in this respect—not by analyzing new media but by looking backward to a project begun by Benjamin who sought to understand cinema's uncanny relation to history and memory.

3

CINEMA AS EMERGENCY BRAKE

Agamben and the Philosophy of Media After Benjamin

On June 4, 2007, the *Guardian*'s website posted a short piece by the great American filmmaker and fabulator Kenneth Anger. The occasion was ostensibly a commentary on the then-current blockbuster *Spider-Man 3*—"the biggest spider turd that ever dropped from the great big spider web in the sky," Anger called it, claiming he saw the film with two psychiatrists who were there to restrain him with handcuffs if he lunged at the screen out of sheer rage. The short piece ends with Anger revealing a "secret." Hollywood, he explains, attempts to "flimflam" the public about time and aging because it is ignorant of the magic formula that only Merlin, Shakespeare, and Anger himself are aware of. The secret comes by way of Hotspur's dying words in *Henry IV*, "*Time must have a stop.*"[1]

What does Anger mean by this? By time's "stop" not only is he referring to the fact of death, which Hollywood disavows or sentimentalizes, but in evoking a "magic formula," the secret "that you can do something through sheer force of human will to twist time upside-down and tear its heart out," he is also suggesting a capacity of cinema that has gone unexplored. The comments section following an online article may not be the best way to gauge the full range of responses to it, but it is amusing if perhaps not entirely surprising to see how much indignation Anger's alternately crude and cryptic screed inspired: *How could the*

Guardian *publish this nonsense?* Among the commenters, Anger's lone defender tells us it is all a joke and we are not meant to take the revelation of his "secret" the slightest bit seriously.

One person who would have understood the secret and taken it seriously is Italian philosopher Giorgio Agamben. The stoppage of time, according to Agamben, is one of the "transcendentals" of cinema.[2] It is also, as he might point out, the meaning of revolution for Walter Benjamin. In his late meditation on the philosophy of history, Benjamin writes, "Marx says that revolutions are the locomotive of world history. But perhaps it is quite otherwise. Perhaps revolutions are an attempt by the passengers on this train—namely, the human race—to activate the emergency brake."[3] For Deleuze, cinema offers (in a line borrowed from Proust) "a little time in its pure state."[4] For Agamben, like Anger, what is key is the *interruption* of time, an impossible operation made possible by cinema and intimately linked to time's repetition, pulling the emergency brake on the locomotive of world history and wresting a new potential from the past. For Agamben, the stoppage and repetition of time goes by another name: gesture.

Let's continue with two claims:

1. "The element of cinema is gesture and not image."[5]
2. Cinema "belongs essentially to the realm of ethics and politics (and not simply to that of aesthetics)."[6]

These suggestive propositions are offered in a short essay by Agamben called "Notes on Gesture" written in 1992 and later appended to his book *Infancy and History: On the Destruction of Experience*, originally written in 1977. For Agamben, the second claim derives from the first, because "an ethical life" is one that "accepts putting itself into play in its gestures."[7] And politics is "the sphere of pure means, that is, of the absolute and complete gesturality of human beings."[8] Man, therefore, Agamben will argue in a later essay, can be defined as "a moviegoing animal."[9] Finally, we should add that gesture binds cinema's aesthetics not only to ethics and politics but also to philosophy because a philosophical idea is a constellation in which "phenomena are composed in a gesture."[10] Or as he puts it in "For an Ethics of Cinema," published the same year as "Notes on Gesture," cinema "gets to the crux of our metaphysical tradition, namely to the ontological consistency of human existence, to its *way of being*."[11]

I described these cryptic propositions as suggestive. "Suggestive" may sound like a noncommittal adjective, but in the case of Agamben, I think it touches on something specific to his discourse or what, following Guy Debord, we could call his "strategy." A strategy of suggestion. Suggestion has the same Latin root as gesture, *gerere*, which means to bear, bring, support, or carry. Suggestion means to bear or bring (or gesture) from below. Suggestively, we might add that suggestion is a prepsychoanalytic method of psychotherapy that works at a level more immanent to the unconscious than the logos-directed talking cure and it is a word that is often used when describing the potentially dangerous effects of cinema. Cinema as gesture is a dangerous art of the unconscious for its capacity both to control subjectivity but also to interrupt the logic that Deleuze called control.

If we stick to Agamben's strategy, these suggestive claims need not be left in a state of undecidability, but can be "studied" or "played with"— not to unlock their secret but to activate the space in Agamben's discourse between what he says and what can be said. When writing on a philosophy that prescribes "profanation" (a central concept for Agamben to which we will return), we need to reach a point in which the letter of the text is found to violate what may seem to be its spirit. So what do we make of these suggestive claims: that the cinema's element is gesture, which is to say *pure means*, and that it is therefore a matter of ethics, politics and philosophy?

Agamben's collected published writing explicitly on cinema would scarcely fill thirty pages. Meanwhile, his often-noted appearance when he was a twenty-two-year-old graduate student, as the apostle Philip in Pier Paolo Pasolini's *Gospel According to St. Matthew* (1964), amounts only to a few fleeting seconds, and its resonance with his mature work is perhaps best not overanalyzed and left suggestive. Nonetheless, the claims he makes on cinema's behalf reveal that it has a greater significance for him than the limited quantity of text may imply. And whatever importance we decide to give to it within his larger project, he offers an original intervention within this history of the politics of film theory and philosophy.

As I will argue, Agamben allows for a way of conceiving of cinema as both political and critical that is in certain respects very different both from the political modernist tradition of seventies film theory and from that of his contemporaries discussed in this book—Rancière and Badiou. For Agamben, cinema is both the apparatus that captures life and converts it to spectacle, and the pharmakon that redeems life from that capture. By hacking spectacle, by pulling the emergency brake on the religion of late capitalism, cinema has a weak messianic power.[12]

As discussed in chapter 1, the seventies tradition read Brecht through Althusser and Lacan and privileged the symbolic over the imaginary. This was largely based on a somewhat limited reading of Brecht that emphasized the *Verfremdungseffekt* (or, as it gets variously translated, the alienation, estrangement, or distancing effect) as any technique that draws attention to the cinematic apparatus as such. Given far less attention by film theory was Brecht's conception of *Gestus*, which would have complicated the simple binary that privileged the cinema of the symbolic associated with awareness of the conditions of production over the ideological cinema of imaginary captivation. Agamben's theses on cinema do not derive directly from the tradition of seventies film theory insofar as its central theoretical ground can be found in Althusser and Lacan, but he can help us reread it by revitalizing some of its key questions through a new light; namely, Agamben asks us to consider the politics of cinema through the question of gesture in relation to cinema as an apparatus for the capture of forms of life. Indeed, gesture, as we will see, refers precisely to mediality, the presence of the medium, and through the figure of gesture, Agamben provides a way to rethink the concept of the apparatus that was central to the theories of Baudry, Metz, and Comolli, among others.

Nonetheless, these figures are not central reference points for Agamben. Rather, we can illuminate Agamben's theses by putting them in the context of the thought of Walter Benjamin, Gilles Deleuze, and Guy Debord. By looking at Agamben's project in relation to these figures, we can also open up new possibilities for using them today that may take us away from how they have traditionally fit into histories of film theory while also allowing us to rethink the politics of film theory in the Lacanian-Althusserian mode.[13]

Benjamin, Deleuze, and Debord are not commonly aligned or easily assimilated with one another, and their grouping here is due less to any prior affinities than to those constructed by Agamben's discourse. Still, each has served as privileged objects of transference for writers who are not seeking to understand films as merely forms of art or leisure, nor objects in need of technical specification or interpretation, but rather to grasp *cinema* as a dispositif connected to the historicity of our perception, experience, and thought, what Agamben calls our "way of being," or, following Wittgenstein, "forms of life."[14]

Agamben's work shares with Deleuze, Badiou, and Rancière the idea that we should reverse the traditional logic of film theory. Film is not an independent object that theory or philosophy can then examine; rather, the question should be, what does philosophy itself become in a world where there is cinema? As Badiou puts it, philosophy is *conditioned* by cinema. For Badiou, however, philosophy is conditioned primarily by contemporary events found in specific works of film and media. For Agamben too, philosophy must be a response to exigencies of the current moment, but he is less concerned with marking new events as signed by specific auteurs than in the potential of the medium grasped for its untimeliness. Like Benjamin, he asks us to think more in terms of cinema's capacities as opposed to the actualization of new cinematic ideas as we find emphasized in Deleuze or Badiou.

Deleuze, according to Agamben, has shown that cinema wipes out "the fallacious psychological distinction between image as psychic reality and movement as physical reality."[15] As discussed in the last chapter, Deleuze is not a thinker who privileges the bodily and affective as is sometimes implied by new Deleuzian film and media theorists. He is better read as a thinker who develops an image of thought that attempts to overcome the binary separation between matter and spirit, mind and body—the logic of what Deleuze calls "representation," or what has recently been dubbed "correlationism" in an influential book-length essay by Badiou protégé Quentin Meillassoux.[16] In Deleuze's Bergsonian reading of cinema, moving images are not images of movement or indeed images of any *thing*, object, or model but movement-images grasped as blocks of sensation that free the image from its dependence on the archetype or the eternal pose. Gestures are precisely these affects, percepts, and optical or audible signs that emerge from movement-duration images that are grounded in what Deleuze calls any-instant-whatever rather than archetypes.

Nonetheless, if Agamben's reading of cinema may be seen as Deleuzian in many respects, he also draws out aspects of cinema's potential that remain unexplored by Deleuze. He helps us shift our understanding of what can be done with the medium toward new possibilities that may even be foreclosed by Deleuze's focus on the creation of time-images and movement-images. Like Badiou, but unlike Deleuze, Agamben's approach to cinema allows us to think about cinema philosophically in relation to cultural detritus and the commodity form, which for Agamben are embodied in advertising and pornography—two sides of a coin, each the not-so-secret meaning of the other. For Deleuze, cinema as art is indifferent to its debasement in commercial forms. But Agamben, like Badiou and like many theorists of the seventies, asks us to think of cinema's potential in relation to critique. To combat dominant forms, cinema must use them and repurpose them. Cinema, when accessing its potential, becomes a counter-dispositif within the larger dispositifs called media and spectacle. It is within this context that we should understand Agamben's approach, which is not interested in a taxonomy of images (as was Deleuze), but instead turns to the concept of gesture to understand the specificity of cinema both as an apparatus of capture and as harboring a redemptive potential.

GESTURE

So what is this sphere of action named by the word "gesture" that is the essential element of cinema? The emphasis on gesture in relation to cinema has a long history, but it was perhaps most prominent in the silent era when an extra burden was placed on bodily gestures to signify the action in the absence of audible speech. Indeed, what came to look like the excessive gesturing and gesticulating in many silent films seemed dated to audiences in the 1930s after the sound cinema became the standard. But thinkers with a specific sensitivity to the originality of the silent film as art lamented the loss of this gestural cinema. To be precise, the problem was not sound as such, which was always present in the theatrical presentation of so-called silent film, but rather the arrival of "the talkies." According to Rudolf Arnheim, speech makes gestures redundant and therefore less legible, noting, "If, however, the words are omitted, the spectator surrenders entirely to the expressive power of the gestures."[17] The sound film endangered what film had made possible: the ability to make gestures visible in a way that they never had been before.

This is precisely what was revolutionary about cinema for Béla Balázs, the Hungarian critic who along with Arnheim was one of the most influential thinkers of the silent film. Perhaps no major film theorist before Agamben had given gesture as central a role as Balázs, who saw film as an art that made visible what he called "inner man." In other words, film offered the inscription of interiority, the mark of the inside in appearance, and the name for that inscription was gesture. In *Theory of the Film: Character and Growth of a New Art*, he writes: "It is the expressive movement, the gesture, that is the aboriginal mother-tongue of the human race."[18] But if gesture as such was the ur-language of humanity, Balázs also recognized film could contribute to the development and spread of gestures—to their mimetic or, as we might say today, memetic power. Gestures may emerge from specific groups, but once inscribed on film and distributed widely, they would be learned by individuals to whom they were not indigenous. In other words, gestures on film form a language that exposes a complex local cultural means of communication through shared conventions of bodily expression, but through this new art of mechanical reproduction, Balázs thought they would also transcend cultural boundaries. Just as Plato saw writing contaminating speech by allowing it to get into anyone's hands, film contaminates gesture with the tendency toward its universalization and homogenization. According to Balázs, this was because gestures activated the mimetic power of identification: "If we look at and understand each other's faces and gestures, we not only understand, we also learn to feel each other's emotions."[19] As Balázs recognized, the film industry was less interested in showing difference than in encouraging homogeneity: "The laws of the film market permit only universally comprehensible facial expressions and gestures, every nuance of which is understood by princess and working girl alike from San Francisco to Smyrna."[20]

This "leveling of gesturology [*Mienenlehre*]," as he called it, could help create an "international human type."[21] These claims, included in his 1948 *Theory of the Film*, were reworked from his 1924 *Visible Man*, but the earlier work included explicitly racialized material that he later removed. As he argued in 1924, "The cinematograph is a machine that will in its own way create a living, concrete internationalism: *the unique, shared psyche of the white man*."[22] Balázs was an advocate of this grotesque idea, inadvertently exposing the violent racist dimension of capitalism's universalizing of gesture through the mass media. Though he later censored his claim that the cinema was a useful viral agent of racist social Darwinist ideology, the early writings have the virtue of making the politics of gesture explicit. For Balázs, gesture could touch on something singular that might otherwise be snuffed out: as he put it, "The language of the gestures is far more individual and personal than the language of words."[23] At the same time, however, film was an agent in the individuation of the human species and could capture these singularities as part of the mission of cultural imperialism. Though he does not draw out the racial and imperialist dimensions, this is precisely what is at stake for Agamben: wresting gesture from its capture by capital to save heterogeneity and singularity. The moving image becomes the battleground.

But what is gesture precisely? It is in the nature of the concept of gesture and its relation to linguistic communication, as understood by Agamben, that offering an explicit definition would be problematic. Indeed, as a rule, definitions are resisted by Agamben, whose method allows us to see how concepts crystalize as they get reconfigured across a series of historical examples. Nonetheless, we might turn to media theorist Vilem Flusser for a useful starting point. Flusser defines gesture as "a movement of the body or of a tool connected to the body for which there is no satisfactory causal explanation" and in another context states that "gestures are movements of the body that express being."[24] Though not directly referenced by Agamben, Flusser's definition resonates with Agamben's conception of "gesture," as a bodily expression that is not clearly motivated or explicit in its intentions and yet *expresses being as such*. For Agamben, gesture is tied to being because it puts the logic of cause and effect into question. It is therefore a means of expression that is not directly translatable into words, which is why it eludes a concise dictionary definition. (It also puts both narrative and theory into question if we understand narrative and theory as defined by a relationship between cause and effect.) Nonetheless, for Agamben, gesture should not be placed in opposition to verbal language. Gesture, according to Agamben, should not be thought of as prelinguistic, a more primitive, primal mode of communication as it was for Balázs. It is intimately connected to the symbolic and yet it is mute. It is language without speech or a "speechless dwelling in language,"[25] while cinema is defined by "an essential muteness, that has nothing to do with the presence or absence of a soundtrack."[26]

We have called gesture, following Flusser, a means of expression, but there is something inexpressive about it as well. Agamben describes gesture as if it is suspended between expression and lack of expression. Jean-Louis Schefer has written about cinema in a way that touches on the sense implied by Agamben's claim that cinema is mute. As Schefer puts it, cinema "make[s] an immediate pact . . . with a part of ourselves that lives without expression; a part given over to silence and relative aphasia as if it were the ultimate secret of our lives."[27] Cinema is not purely imaginary and outside the symbolic, but for cinema the symbolic or the law is suspended. Cinema has been widely compared to dreams, but "the problem with dreams," as a character in Godard's *Sauve Qui Peut (La Vie)* says, is that "in them we are still searching for solutions." As Kenneth Anger believed, we might be better off finding the potential of cinema not in dreams but in magic. Magic, as described by Agamben, is the only way to true happiness because it is outside the realm of merit. True happiness, he argues, is never earned or deserved; it gives the lie to the protestant work ethic and official morality.[28] In the magic land of cinema, gestures replace names. Theory and philosophy then seek not to rescue the imaginary for the symbolic, but rather grasp the specific medium in which there is "a sublime breach between the sensible and the intelligible, between copy and reality, between a memory and a hope."[29]

Gesture in Agamben is then deeply bound up with his thinking about language and humanity's capacity both to make meaning and to fail to do so—an important chapter of which is the invention of cinema and mass media. "Gesture is the communication of a potential to be communicated. In itself it has nothing to say, because what it shows is the being-in-language of human beings as a pure potential for mediation."[30] Or rather, gesture is "what remains unexpressed in each expressive act."[31] A gesture is an enigmatic signifier, the mark of meaning to mean.[32] We can say that gestures have been "captured," and cease to be gestures as such in Agamben's sense, when they become equivalent to a meaning that has been realized or actualized in a completed act or statement, when they become communication or information. This is key for the political dimension of gesture: as a realm of action that does not reduce everything to quantifiable information, it harbors a political potential.

Agamben explains the specific form of action signified by "gesture" with reference to the Roman scholar Varro, who, writing in the first century AD, defined a sphere of action that was neither doing/making (facere) nor acting (agere):

> A person can make [*facere*] something and not enact [*agere*] it, as when a poet makes a play, but does not act it [*agere* in the sense of playing a part]; on the other hand, the actor acts the play but does not make it. So the play is made [*fit*] by the poet, but not acted [*agitur*] by him; it is acted by the actor, but not made by him. Whereas the *imperator* (the magistrate in whom supreme power is invested) of whom the expression *res gerere* is used (to carry something out, in the sense of taking it

upon oneself, assuming total responsibility for it), neither makes nor acts, but takes charge, in other words bears the burden of it [*sustinet*].[33]

Agamben connects *agere* and *facere* in Varro to Aristotle's *praxis* and *poiesis*: the latter a means to an end and the former an end in itself. What makes gesture different is that it is purely immanent, a displaying of means themselves without regard to the ends they serve. It is therefore the realm of human expression that resists the economy of means and ends. It opens up a different conception of use outside the logic of utilitarianism and yet is connected to a more profound sense of responsibility or bearing.

As with so many of the concepts that are central to Agamben's inquiries, we can trace his use of the term "gesture" back to Benjamin. Benjamin was deeply influenced by Brecht's concept of *Gestus*, though he also made it his own. In "A Short Organum for the Theater," Brecht defines *Gestus* as "the realm of attitudes adopted by the characters towards one another." For Brecht this included "physical attitude, tone of voice and facial expression."[34] Ultimately what was at stake for Brecht was when a particular gesture took on an allegorical function or become exemplary in some way—this is what he called "social Gestus," distinguishing it at times from a broader category of gesture. Brecht developed the concept of *Gestus* in relation to the theater, but repeatedly appealed to cinema to illuminate it. His cinematic examples came primarily from silent film and Chaplin in particular. A useful example of what Brecht meant by *Getsus* comes from a line he takes from Charles Laughton in response to why he became an actor: "Because people don't know what they are like but I believe I'm able to show them."[35] This ability to typify social behavior and make it visible is what Benjamin, in his reading of Brecht, will call its "quotability."[36] Gestures cease to be particular and become available for repetition and use in other contexts.

But Benjamin adds an extra twist to Laughton's statement by making explicit a point often found in Brecht, that showing people what they are like is not a simple case of recognition but produces an estrangement-effect. In Benjamin's 1934 essay "Kafka: On the Tenth Anniversary of His Death," he declares that the gesture or *Gestus* in Kafka is that which

Kafka could "fathom least of all" and yet at the same time remained "decisive."[37] In the essay, Benjamin evokes cinema to explain the uncanny dimension of the gesture as that which is both proximate and distant, a profound expression of being and yet also alien and in need of decipherment:

> The invention of motion pictures and the phonograph came in an age of maximum alienation of men from one another, of unpredictably intervening relationships which have become their only ones. Experiments have proved that a man does not recognize his own gait on film or his own voice on the phonograph. The situation of the subject in such experiments is Kafka's situation; this is what leads him to study, where he may encounter fragments of his own existence.[38]

Benjamin understood Kafka as a writer for the age of cinema and the phonograph. And while for Agamben, following Benjamin, gesture is also an important concept in twentieth-century literature and theater, cinema is the art that would make gesture its primary element.

Benjamin is an essential link between Brecht's concept of *Gestus* and Agamben's use of the term "gesture" because he makes explicit the connection between gesture and the arts of mechanical reproduction and cinema in particular. The objective form of memory made possible by modern technology allows us to study ourselves for all our strangeness. The gesture can be understood as these fragments of existence captured by film that we do not recognize but are nonetheless the nearest to us of all (what Benjamin elsewhere famously referred to as the "optical unconscious"). We encounter the medium itself and human potential in the same moment as a failure of recognition. This is not what Lacan identified as the misrecognition of the imago as the ego that occurs during the mirror stage and that undergirds the logic of identification harnessed by Hollywood cinema and taken a primary target of much seventies film theory—but on the contrary, the encounter with the part object that disrupts the unity of the transcendental perceiving subject, associated with the Real. For Brecht, *Gestus* in epic theater was opposed to the logic of identification because it opened up to the realm of the social. It was therefore not imaginary identification, but a distancing encounter with ourselves as something other.

Gesture might be usefully grasped as the virtual potential in the image. Agamben ultimately associates gesture with "imagelessness" because, if we translate it into Lacanian language, it is no longer imaginary (the realm of the image) but the mark of the Real that escapes the imaginary, which is also to say the place where the symbolic fails. As Agamben puts it, gesture "grasps the real that is always in the process of being lost, in order to render it possible again."[39] Gesture cannot be appropriated by the traditional realm of aesthetics, beautiful semblance; nor can it be understood within the broader realm of appearance that can be grasped phenomenologically.

It is important to note that Agamben's claims contain a historical argument. Gestures take on a new meaning in the age of mass media and modern capitalism. Gestures, according to Agamben, were lost by the bourgeoisie sometime in the late nineteenth century, and yet for this very reason, they are always seeking to reclaim them. In cinema, "a society that has lost its gestures seeks to reappropriate what it has lost while simultaneously recording that loss."[40] According to Agamben, the "too late" awareness of the loss of gestures spurs attempts to recuperate them—the evidence for which he sees in Proust as well as "in the most exemplary fashion, silent film."[41] And this can lead to the encounter with fragments of one's own existence—the fated sense of (non)recognition of one's own unconscious that Benjamin tied to film as well as to Kafka's writing. As Agamben puts it, "An epoch that has lost its gestures is, by the same token, obsessed by them; for men from whom all authenticity has been taken, gesture becomes destiny."[42]

In Agamben's narrative, there exists a kind of prelapsarian moment when the bourgeoisie was still in control of its gestures evident only decades before the birth of cinema, for example, when Balzac wrote his essay "Théorie de la demarche" (Theory of Bearing), on the meaning of human movement in 1833.[43] We have reason to be suspicious of this firm division into before and after. Agamben asserts that gestures in the 1830s were still symbols and could be subject to a hermeneutics that provided a key. But we might better see this era, which corresponded to the age of the birth of photography as well as pseudo-sciences like phrenology, as one when gestures are already being captured and controlled as a response to their emergent disappearance. Either way, like "aura" for Benjamin, it is clear that "gesture" takes on its philosophical importance for Agamben at moment of its fading, at the very point at which gestures begin to seem inaccessible. It is as if this prehistory of gestures when they were still legible symbols and not yet enigmatic signifiers is interesting only retroactively. That cinema was invented in the last decade of the nineteenth century, the same decade that Freud discovered psychoanalysis, is thus no accident. It is a moment when the bourgeoisie "succumbs to interiority" and forms of expression are no longer decipherable.[44] According to Agamben, it was during this period of Western culture that a split in subjectivity occurred and we get the sense that man's true nature is unconscious and must be encountered in exceptional moments. Agamben argues that, for example, Nietzsche's theory of eternal return, also from the late nineteenth century, was one attempt to resolve this split— looking to theater to make indiscernible "power and act, naturalness and manner, contingency and necessity."[45] Gesture names the liminal space where these oppositions get blurred and cinema works on theatrical gesture in a new way by mediating it. Nietzsche's "eternal return," like Freud's "unconscious," is a concept that attempts to solve a problem of subjectivity in modernity that gets exhibited by cinema.

The significance of the gesture in the case of film is that it gives form to the gesture as other. The gesture is a sign produced by humans that because it gets seized in a repeatable image can be encountered and studied. In films, according to Agamben, the gesture withdraws from presence. As Badiou argues in less explicitly Heideggerian terms, "It is of absolute importance that the flowers cinema displays (as in one of Visconti's sequences) be Mallarméan flowers, that they be absent from every bouquet."[46] In Agamben's terms, the gesture exhibits the image *as image* by allowing for the appearance of imagelessness. The gesture is then wrested from the image, even as the image seeks to claim the gesture. The image then is animated by an antinomy: on the one hand it is "the reification and effacement of a gesture (the *imago* either as symbol or as the wax mask of the corpse); on the other it maintains *dynamis*,"[47] which is to say the potential of what Deleuze called any-instant-whatever. It is the latter aspect of the image that Benjamin, inspired by Proust and Freud, called "involuntary memory" and saw as having a messianic power that he associated with historical materialism in opposition to teleological history. Cinema can wrest gesture from the image by deactivating it. How does it do this? What are the specific means available to cinema?

REPETITION AND STOPPAGE

Gestures in Kafka, according to Benjamin, "had no definite symbolic meaning for the author from the outset; rather, the author tried to derive such a meaning from them in ever-changing contexts and experimental groupings."[48] Though Benjamin links this to the theater, these "ever-changing contexts and experimental groupings" suggest the resources of montage that Agamben calls "repetition" and "stoppage"— the two operations that he attributes to cinema as a philosophical machine. These operations become ways of creating a new meaning out of forms of expression that both imply communicability but have, in the age of commodity and spectacle, been rendered enigmatic.

Agamben proposed these concepts—repetition and stoppage—in a 1995 lecture on Debord, the Situationist founder and author, most famously of *The Society of the Spectacle* (1967). After "Notes on Gesture," the reflections on Debord compose Agamben's next most substantial engagement with cinema. While the essay bears the Deleuzian title "Difference and Repetition" and has Debord as its occasion, Benjamin again remains a central, albeit largely implicit, reference in the piece. Here the word "gesture" is not used; rather cinema is tied to messianic history. Repetition and stoppage, the transcendentals of montage, introduced in this essay may be understood as techniques for deactivating or "decreating" (to use a term Agamben borrows from Simone Weil) the image to grasp fragments of the past that invest the present with a new potential.[49] While not articulated as such in the essay, these fragments are what Agamben has elsewhere called gestures.

Thinking of repetition and stoppage as ways of decreating or deactivating can help further reveal Agamben's differences from Deleuze, who otherwise deeply influenced Agamben's understanding of cinema as a specific mode of thought and his conception of repetition as difference. Their differing conceptions of cinema can be understood first of all in their differing conceptions of philosophy itself. Philosophy for Agamben is not, as it is for Deleuze, the creation of new concepts, and cinema, correspondingly, is not the creation of blocks of movement and time. Rather, both philosophy and cinema are about what Agamben calls "decreation," the hesitation or stutter that evokes a sphere of action through which a purely immanent creative potential or creaturely being is disclosed. Decreation refers then not to new images or signs but to the capacity for images and signs to be invested with potential, which is bound up with thinking cinema less in terms of art than as a history and memory machine. In an essay titled "Bartleby, or On Contingency," Agamben explains that in decreation "what happened and what did not happen are returned to their originary unity in the mind of God, while what could have not been but was becomes indistinguishable from what could have been but was not."[50] Decreation then takes on a specific meaning in terms of cinema's relation to history and memory, because cinema bears the indexical trace of duration and yet has the capacity to stop, repeat, and recontextualize it as a way of restoring potential to the past.

Decreation is, in many respects, proximate to what Deleuze calls the virtual—in effect, it is an operation that makes the actual virtual, mobilizing what Deleuze following Nietzsche calls "the powers of the false." Deleuze (along with Kierkegaard, Nietzsche, and Heidegger) becomes one of the central thinkers for thinking a concept of repetition as potentiality that Agamben will apply to cinema. As Agamben puts it, "What returns returns as possible. Hence the proximity of repetition to memory: a memory is a return of what was, qua possible. Repetition, for its part, is the memory of that which was not. This is also the definition of cinema: the memory of that which was not."[51]

Repetition and stoppage are two intertwined ways to redeem the dynamic potential in danger of being assimilated by the image within the linear time of progress. The redemptive power of repetition and stoppage in the service of messianic history should not be mistaken for the testimonies to the unspeakable so often mobilized in photographs or moving images of atrocities that have been linked to the medium's indexical dimension. Indeed we might say that for Agamben the gesture is predicated on indexicality, but by grasping something contingent that is wrested from the continuum of time, it takes on a generic function. The gesture indexes finally not a moment fatally stamped by time but only itself and the potential of what was not and what could have been. Writing of certain photographs, he says that they "contain an unmistakable historical index, an indelible date, and yet, thanks to the special power of the gesture, this index now refers to another time, more actual and more urgent than any chronological time."[52] The gesture as what remains unexpressed in each expressive act is a kind of political unconscious shot through with what Agamben, following Aristotle, calls potentiality.

If this all sounds rather cryptic, it may help to tie it back to a fundamental antinomy grasped in one of the most influential essays in the history of film theory. André Bazin's "The Ontology of the Photographic Image" (1946) attributed to the photograph the capacity to strip "the object of habits and preconceived notions, of all the spiritual detritus that my perception has wrapped it in" and "offer it up unsullied to my attention and thus to my love."[53] This power that Bazin grants to the objective lens has often been taken to be an idealist fantasy, but he was making visible the antinomic structure underlying the specific power of what Agamben calls "gesture"—namely, the way that the photographic arts, by removing the motivated event (for cinema, always in duration, it is no longer an "object" but an "event") from time, make the singular generic, the contingent necessary and show it to us as if for the first time. The photograph, according to Bazin, interrupts habit and everyday phenomenological experience, to exhibit a gesture.

Interruption, like deactivation, is another word for stoppage. As Benjamin suggested in his analysis of Brecht, gesture cannot be a matter of performance in the traditional sense because it always concerns an encounter with something not consciously motivated. As he argues, "The more frequently we interrupt someone engaged in acting, the more gestures result."[54] This is attested to by so many of the viral videos and GIFs that have withstood endless repetition and become part of a new symbolic vernacular in the last decade. These are new forms of making gestures into information and commodities. In epic theater the actor mobilizes repetition to make his own gestures quotable. In cinema, as the GIF attests, this quotability is the condition of the medium itself, because repetition is built into it. Readers of Benjamin have tended to follow the emphasis found in the title of his famous essay "The Work of Art in the Age of Its Technical Reproducibility" on the *reproducibility* of film prints (never original at least not in quite the same way as a painting), but perhaps more significant, if not unrelated, is the *repeatability* that is a condition of the indexical moving image as such—its combination of temporal uniqueness and timelessness. Repetition has a double meaning—film images are on the one hand always already repetitions, or come bearing an intrinsic repeatability, but Agamben's concept also points to forms of appropriation, in which images from one context are repeated in another.

Any strip of film repeats a profilmic event, the singular moment of time that transpired in front of the camera lens. A film like one of Debord's, which uses and transforms the meanings of sequences from advertisements or Hollywood films, however, repeats what Étienne Souriau called a "filmographic reality." Souriau—who also introduced the better known term "profilmic"—used "filmographic" to refer to the concrete material of a given film, the semiotic meaning of which is tied to its context within a given fictional film, itself a historical cultural object, rather than the profilmic reality when it was being shot.[55] Any serious analysis of montage as repetition must keep in mind both the profilmic and filmographic levels as two distinct forms of repetition that can interrelate in complex ways.

"Stoppage" can also be read more specifically and more broadly. On the one hand, Agamben is referring to literal ways of arresting the movement and time of the image—the freeze frame, slow motion, or the pause—which may return to our awareness the photogram that would otherwise be lost in the flow of images. Bazin was writing about the ontology of the *photographic* image and emphasized how the photograph arrests time. But it is only with cinema and its images of time and movement that the power of stoppage takes on a more profound function—because it allows for both flow/duration *and* its interruption.

More broadly, we can connect the operation of "stoppage" to the sense in which the gestural dimension of the image can be tied to what Benjamin called "the dialectical image" or "dialectics at a standstill." Agamben quotes Benjamin's definition of image: "It is not that what is past casts its light on what is present, or what is present its light on what is past; rather, image is that wherein what has been comes together in a flash with the now (*Jetzt*) to form a constellation. In other words, image is dialectics at a standstill."[56] What Benjamin is calling image coincides with what for Agamben is its gestural dimension, revealed in a constellation when images are arrested. Benjamin describes a scene: "Picture to yourself a family row: the wife is just about to pick up a bronze statuette and hurl it at the daughter; the father is opening a window to call for help. At this moment a stranger enters. The process is interrupted; what becomes apparent in its place is the condition now exposed before the stranger's view: disturbed faces, open window, a devastated interior."[57] According to Benjamin, this interruption is an example of montage and reveals gestures that are both ordinary and yet otherwise obscured.[58] The repeatability of film turns the operation of stoppage described by Benjamin in the context of epic theater into a potential weapon against the colonization of our unconscious in the age of mass media and spectacle.

This practice corresponds to the Situationist strategy of détournement, namely, the strategy of removing a piece of culture from one sphere and exhibiting it in another, a strategy of hijacking and deliberate misuse of common language or imagery. Détournement referred not only to cinema but, as Debord, himself the maker of six films, argued (with collaborator Gil J. Wolman), "It is obviously in the realm of the cinema that détournement can attain its greatest effectiveness and, for those concerned with this aspect, its greatest beauty."[59] Of course, Agamben has Debord's conception of détournement in mind—which closely corresponds to his own investment in the idea of freeing up popular imagery for a new use—but notably he does not adopt the word in his essay on Debord's cinema. Perhaps this is a response to the fuzziness the term has acquired over time and how what was once an avant-garde strategy may be increasingly difficult to differentiate from what are now commonplace practices like the remix and all manner of found footage and appropriation films.

Any theory of détournement opens itself up to the query of what happens when détournement itself gets co-opted by bourgeois art or even advertising and spectacle. And more provocatively, is not the very logic of cooptation or appropriation—the taking of something with a critical or subversive or subcultural history and using it for mainstream practices—itself a form of détournement?[60] This question or problem is by no means lost on Agamben and was anticipated by Debord himself. The task then is not merely adopting détournement as a strategy, but adopting specific strategies of détournement—of repetition and stoppage—that interrupt the contemporary circulation of information and advertising that Badiou called the "ideological indicators of our epoch." The GIF, for example, frequently reifies gestures into symbolic content through stoppage and repetition, but even at its least inspired it also harbors an uncanny potential to deactivate some aspect of mainstream media and reactivate it for a new use.

THE HUMAN

One of Agamben's great insights is to think media less in terms of art, entertainment, or information than in terms of individuation both individual and collective. Media is a problem for, and symptom of, our changing conceptions of the human and how selves and communities can be imagined.

The importance of gesture for Agamben, while it extends far beyond the practice of filmmaking itself, concerns the sense in which man can be defined as "a moviegoing animal." Agamben is, of course, playing off of Aristotle's famous claim in *Politics* that man is a "political animal." For Agamben, man is not a moviegoing animal *as opposed* to being a political animal; rather, these are two different ways of saying the same thing. Politics, in other words, needs to be understood in terms of why human beings have an interest in the ritual of collectively watching images of ourselves.

For Aristotle, man's political nature is tied directly to the fact that man alone among the animals is capable of speech. Agamben cites the claim that unlike other animals, man remains fascinated by his image even when he knows it is only an image and not another person.[61] A primate, Lacan told us, will be excited by her mirror image as long as she mistakes it for another primate, quickly losing interest upon realizing it is only a reflection, whereas human beings, even after they realize the image is not another person and therefore a potential threat, remain fascinated. Human beings have a specific desire to observe images of themselves, despite (or because) the experience in some sense is useless or unproductive. It is the very uselessness of the experience of gazing on our own images and watching our gestures that puts us in contact with our potential. According to Agamben, "The fact that must constitute the point of departure for any discourse on ethics is that there is no essence, no historical or spiritual vocation, no biological destiny that humans must enact or realize."[62] This makes the act of gazing on our own likenesses— an act that has been dismissed by many moralists as a form of narcissism and a profound example of the distraction from meaningful politics embodied by the worst aspects of the media—central to what makes us human and therefore to understanding politics. We might say that gesture is the mark of the human as such for Agamben, but it is its indeterminability that makes it such. The essence of the human for Agamben is its lack of essence, which ties man's potentiality to a confrontation with his own uselessness or the imagelessness of his own image. Gesture is the mark of this confrontation.

Benjamin's emphasis on the actor or more broadly the presence of the human body on film is central to Agamben's conception of gesture in relation to cinema. Cinema's gestural dimension should ultimately be grasped in a more expansive sense than to refer exclusively to human bodily movements. At the very least, it refers also to technics, what Flusser calls the "tools" that are connected to body, which is to say McLuhan's "extensions of man."[63] But the corporeal dimension of the human is nonetheless very much Agamben's starting point. In "Notes on Gesture," he traces the sense of the bourgeoisie's loss of gestural legibility in the nineteenth century to Muybridge's proto-cinematic sequential photography often focusing on basic human actions and the frequent "bad acting" or excessive gesticulations as if to compensate for the lack of sound that are often found in the earliest films.

Meanwhile, the specific mode of human presence found in cinema, rather than the capacities of montage, is the central concern of the short 1992 essay, "For an Ethics of Cinema." Here, cinema is associated with an "essential mutation" in the "the principle of the individuation of the human species."[64] This concerns the development of the "type," which is when the productive potential of Brecht's social *Gestus* gets eliminated through what Balázs called "the leveling of gesturology." The type concerns the seemingly paradoxical way in which, according to Benjamin "the distinctive traits that at first appear to guarantee the uniqueness, the strict individuality of a person" become the traits that allow the individual to be subsumed within a series, to become typical.[65] As Agamben puts it, "The exclusive character becomes the principle of serial reproduction."[66] This is then another paradox of cinema, but one intimately connected to the temporal paradox already discussed because it is also an example of the singular merging with the generic.

Agamben draws out the logic implicit in Benjamin that authenticity is not so much vanishing in the age of cinema, as "The Work of Art" essay sometimes seems to suggest, but becomes a more powerful concept in a moment when it is being challenged. Cinema's repeatability (I'll use this term rather than reproducibility) does not mean the withering of "aura," Benjamin's famous term for what has traditionally marked the artwork, but a mutation of it. Aura may no longer be defined by the uniqueness of the object in time and space as it was for nature or the artwork before mass production, but the image as commodity or spectacle, as Adorno had objected to Benjamin, makes representations auratic in a new way.

The human "types" that saturate our mass media are a prime example of this mutation of aura. The type is given powerful form in the first decades of film, but finds an even more potent platform with the invention of television and, in particular, the TV advertisement. As Agamben suggests, the sense of the uniqueness or authenticity of an individual does not disappear with the model or unknown actor featured in an advertisement. Rather, with the "type," authenticity becomes generic. Agamben notes that this is a transformation so familiar to our culture that we can no longer perceive it. Advertising, pornography, and television

> have habituated us to those mutant beings who linger ceaselessly between individual and class and vanish utterly into a series precisely in their most characteristic idiosyncrasies. That young woman who smiles at us while drinking a beer, that other who rolls her hips so mischievously while running on the beach, they belong to a people whose members, like the angels of medieval theology (each of whom individually constitutes a species), elude the distinction between the original and the replica.[67]

This is one half of the mechanism of cinema—the capture of gesture, associated here, as is often the case for Agamben, with cinema insofar as it is not an art but a means of the culture industry. This is where cinema overlaps with media, which for Agamben is epitomized by advertising and pornography.

While cinema's capacity for potential is linked to the any-image-whatsoever, or what Godard called "just an image" as opposed to a "just image," as both singular and generic, this aspect of cinema can also be captured for the bad repetition associated with "the type." There is an additional mutation associated with the "star," a concept that, according to Agamben, is a new phenomenon specific to the cinema that makes the idea of the actor associated with theater no longer applicable. If the media provide cinema with this figure that, like the angel, is an individual that makes itself a species, with the star, "the type as such makes itself individual, becomes the type or the exemplar of itself." "The star's status," he explains, "is even more paradoxical from the perspective of the principle of individuation: 'Gary Cooper' or 'Marlene Dietrich' are not individuals but something that set theory would describe as classes containing only a single element (singletons) or belonging to themselves (a ∈ a)."[68] The type makes the singular generic, whereas the star makes the generic singular.

The novelty of the cinema star (as opposed to theater) is manifest in the way in which there is no firm distinction between the character and the actor. As Agamben argues, Oedipus and Hamlet exist independently of the actors who lend a body and voice to them on the stage, but Gregory Arkadin in *Confidential Report* cannot be separated from the body of Orson Welles.[69] This claim is not unfamiliar—Erwin Panofsky makes it in his influential and widely anthologized 1936 essay "Style and Medium in the Motion Pictures"—but for Agamben it is not merely a claim about the distinction between film and theater but concerns a transformation of the human in the twentieth century. "The type has realized in its flesh the abstractions and repeatability of the commodity; likewise, the *divo* constitutes a parodic realization of the Marxian 'generic being' in which individual practice coincides immediately with its genus."[70]

Marx read Feuerbach's conception of generic or species being (*Gattungswesen*) through the lens of historical materialism and argued that it was the outcome of the social organization of labor. Agamben rereads this concept for the age of spectacle. For him, generic being is found not in labor but in the failure to work: "Human beings are the animals capable of their own impotentiality."[71] The star, as Andy Warhol well understood, produces value without working—through what Benjamin called aura. That we still consider stars actors and give awards to them for acting is a way of legitimizing stardom by associating it with work and talent; but the essence of stardom is that stars produce aura by their mere presence. The star as spectacle, or today what we would call the celebrity, stands in relation to finance capitalism as the theater actor of old stands in relation to market capitalism.[72] But how do we wrest human impotentiality from its capture in spectacle? We need, according to Agamben, new forms of cinema that are also new forms of critique.

ART AS CRITIQUE

The functions of repetition and stoppage, cinema's transcendentals, are found not in creation but through how Benjamin defines critique. In a sentence from "Critique of Violence" that might be understood as the open sesame of all of Agamben's thought, critique is defined as based on a criterion "which would discriminate within the sphere of means themselves, without regard for the ends they serve."[73] Wresting something from the sphere of ends is, for Agamben, the function of not only critique but also art. Or rather, we might say that art and critique are bound together in a common project. Poetry deactivates language from the sphere of ends. Dance deactivates movement from the sphere of ends. Cinema deactivates time and spectacle.

This is a radically immanent form of critique that links art and philosophy. Critique is not here a form of symptomatic reading or pointing to the unasked question, but it is a way of deactivating the apparatus by exposing its gestural dimension, which is to say its immanent potentiality rather than its conditions of possibility. If all deactivations for Agamben are about wresting gesture from the sphere of ends, cinema has a specific connection to gesture through its capacity to stop and repeat time—the very time that has been subtracted from poetry or dance, the time of the ordinary. As Rancière remarks, cinephilia was characterized by the affirmation of the ordinary as spectacle: "The discovery of the splendor that even the most ordinary spectacle could display on the bright screen in a dark cinema: a hand lifting a curtain or playing with a door handle, a head leaning out of a window, a fire or headlights in the night, glasses clinking on the zinc bar of a café. . . ."[74] These are the types of familiar gestures that theorists from Bazin to Balázs, Kracauer, and Cavell all suggested that cinema somehow made visible—and, according to Bazin, lovable. Cinema's transcendentals for

Agamben are not time and movement as they are for Deleuze, but the ability to stop and repeat time and movement, yielding crystallizations of the ordinary and ephemeral, giving cinema a "weak messianic power." Agamben's conception of cinema brings it closer to the possibilities opened up by its remediation in the digital era, which remained latent but nonetheless evident in the classical and modernist moments covered in Deleuze's two *Cinema* books.

The significance of gesture for Agamben is not the exhibition or celebration of the ordinary, but, as it was for Bazin, Kracauer, and Benjamin—redemption of it. Redeeming gesture means wresting from the ordinary an unconscious sphere of action, which is ultimately the function of critique in his definition. In addition to critique, the terms that Benjamin uses in relation to Kafka that touch on this sphere of action are "play" and "study," which seek to reactivate gestures for use—not a use for an end or indeed an originary use value or purely aesthetic one, but, as Agamben insists, some new usage as yet undefined that might anticipate new forms of community.

FROM PRAXIS TO GESTURE

Agamben's conception of critique may seem rather unorthodox and at odds with the Marxist tradition. Therefore, it is worth looking at how Agamben nonetheless situates it within that tradition but in opposition to what he sees as the misappropriation of critique by certain Hegelian forms of Western Marxism. Indeed, Agamben's investment in a sphere of action outside the realm of means and ends is illuminated by seeing how it is intrinsic to his specific reading of Marx. In a revised version of *Infancy and History*, "Notes on Gesture" is preceded by a chapter in which Agamben quotes at great length an exchange of letters between Adorno and Benjamin from late 1938 in which Adorno expresses his disappointment with Benjamin's study of Baudelaire (later to be published as "The Paris of the Second Empire in Baudelaire") and what it implies for him about the future of the *Arcades* project. In a famous passage,

Adorno suggests that Benjamin's study is located at "the crossroads of magic and positivism." He continues, "That spot is bewitched. Only theory could break the spell."[75]

Theory, for Adorno, is then posed, as it will be in much film theory decades later, as the necessary means of destroying the pleasurable hold the object of our inquiry has over us. The magic spell of the object will be (and should be) snuffed out once it is properly theorized and brought into the fold of knowledge. Not just any theory is needed, of course, but a certain idea of theory in the Western Marxist tradition that demands that the realm of appearance taken in by the senses must be shown to be mediated in relation to the totality. This is again a version of Christian Metz's claim that we must win the imaginary on behalf of the symbolic.

According to Agamben, Adorno's insistence on mediation in his critique of Benjamin's Baudelaire is a way "to safeguard materialism from vulgarity," which he argues is made possible only by a misrecognition of the radicality of the Marxist problematic.[76] As Agamben claims, the relation between base and superstructure that has animated the Hegelian tradition of Western Marxism is a false problem. To insist on mediation and totality (as Adorno did), or the economic base as the final determining instance (as Engels did), is not to save Marxism but to exit it. Marxism does not demand a more complex theory of causality, as Althusser believed when he introduced "structural causality";[77] rather, true Marxism or historical materialism—in Agamben's reading of Marx by way of Benjamin—recognizes *all causality* as part of the Western metaphysical tradition.[78] As Agamben puts it,

> If man is human—if he is a *Gattungswesen*, a being whose essence is generic—his humanity and his species-being must be integrally present within the way in which he produces his material life—that is, within praxis. Marx abolishes the metaphysical distinction between *animal* and *ratio*, between nature and culture, between matter and form, in order to state that within praxis animality is humanity, nature is culture, matter is form.[79]

Agamben attributes to Marx precisely what Deleuze attributes to cinema—the undoing of the distinction between psychology and materiality. Cinema is indeed at the intersection of magic and facticity, and this is its strength, not what condemns it to ideology.

Marx's concept of praxis in Agamben's reading is a sphere of action outside what Aristotle called poiesis or production as well as, in Varro's terms, agere and facere. But Marx's praxis does not precisely correspond to what Aristotle called praxis in opposition to poiesis. For Aristotle, praxis is a mode of action that takes action as an end in itself as opposed to production, for which it is a means with an end; it is not pure means in the sense that Agamben wishes to define it. Perhaps this is why the concept that Agamben associates with praxis in Marx, defined as a sphere of means without ends, returns in "Notes on Gesture" not as praxis but as gesture. But something has shifted here—gesture, unlike Marx's praxis, is not man's production of his material life but the impersonal element that separates that production from man's sense of self-identity.

Why this shift? Why does gesture as an uncanny encounter with the potential of expression assume the role Agamben had wished to attribute to praxis? As he put it in 2012, "In the course of my research it emerged that the fundamental concepts of politics are no longer production and praxis, but *inoperativity* and *use*."[80] This shift in Agamben's thought is explicit when we compare *Infancy and History*, first published in 1977, with the final volume of the *Homo Sacer* series, *The Use of Bodies*, published in 2014. Politics for the late Agamben is what we have been calling deactivation or decreation, which make power inoperative and return gestures to common use. In 1977, when Agamben argued against the idea that Marx's analysis of political economy is dialectical and premised on contradiction, he attempted to define Marxist praxis outside the sphere of cause and effect, means and ends. But over time, he increasingly seems to recognize this mode of action that suspends causality as part of the problem it is meant to overcome.

Means without ends are frequently valorized in Agamben's work, but not always so. Pure means are not only lines of flight from an all-consuming capitalist logic, but also mobilized by capital itself in the age that Agamben, in his most quoted writings, has theorized in terms of the state of exception and biopolitics.[81] Deleuze's "Postscript on Control Societies" offered surfing as an illustration for this new mechanism of domination—a sport with no ends but keeping one's balance when confronted with forces beyond one's control. (The choice of "surfing" as emblematic of control was strikingly prescient given the word's later internet-era use).[82] Deleuze found another symptom of this new condition in the tendency for young people to describe themselves as "motivated," affirming, in effect, that energy as pure potential is good in itself regardless of where it is directed. In the society of control, motivation is healthy but motives are always suspicious.[83] Thus the aesthetic logic of pure means that Agamben associates with redemption sounds a lot like the very logic of neoliberal postmodern control that we wish to be redeemed from. We have already seen how the "star" parodically realized the logic of species being. It seems that Marx's conception of praxis may not be an overcoming of Western metaphysics so much as an example, like Nietzsche's concept of "eternal return" as analyzed by Agamben, of the impossible attempt to close a gap in subjectivity brought on by modern life.[84] As becomes clear in Agamben's later writings, the attempt by art and philosophy to overcome the split subjectivity of modern man gets mimicked by the spectacle's insidious logic of control in late capitalism. Therefore, praxis as the key to politics gets replaced by the more elusive concept of gesture.

Agamben's philosophy does not hide this sense in which catastrophe and redemption often seem to take the same form or to be positioned in relation to each other like two sides of a mobius strip, threatening to meet each other in a realm of indistinction. If, as Benjamin has claimed, "the state of emergency," which is to say the suspension of the force of law, has become the rule in today's society, then the task is not to return to the force of law but to bring about "the real state of emergency."[85]

This enigmatic proposition hinges on the sense that catastrophe and redemption are becoming blurred, that is, that resistance and power are under threat of becoming indiscernible. To distinguish this sphere of pure means from its appropriation in new forms of domination, Agamben needs another turn of the screw to give gesture, once described in terms of play and study, a messianic charge. De-Hegelizing Marx means accepting Guy Debord's logic of the society of the spectacle, namely the Feuerbachian idea of separation (or in the terms of Agamben's better known writings, "exception") as the rule.

The model for "separation," which is to say total alienation, is religion. As Agamben argues, "One can define religion as that which removes things, places, animals, or people from common use and transports them to a separate sphere. Not only is there no religion without separation, but every separation contains or conserves in itself a genuinely religious nucleus."[86] He is fond of repeating Benjamin's claim that capitalism is itself a religion, albeit the cruelest of all, because it offers no possibility for atonement. "Capitalism and other modern forms of power seem to generalize and push to the extreme the processes of separation that define religion."[87] In Agamben's Heideggerian reading, cinema, like all forms of modern technology, is an apparatus for separation and one of the most important ones in the twentieth century, but whether it will remain so for the twenty-first century remains unclear. For Agamben, the war against cinema as spectacle (epitomized by advertising and pornography) means neither using cinema "in the correct way" nor destroying it, but profaning it.[88] Profaning means taking something from the realm of the sacred or the logic of consumption and returning it to common use.

Let's look at how this takes place. As I have discussed, aura, which for Benjamin was the very thing that was decaying in cinema, is essential to spectacle. The gesture must then not be conceived auraticly. It cannot be a lure but the opposite, a void. For Agamben, cinema is not an art form in which aura is withering. Rather, it is an art form that can de-auraticize. If we follow Benjamin, we should attend to the sense in which "the withering of aura" is not the end of the story.

Indeed, there was always something questionable about Benjamin's thesis that the destruction of the unique existence of the work of art meant the withering of aura and cult value attached to the artwork. Adorno was quick to point out that the culture industry seemed to exacerbate the aura of mass art, noting, of course, that this was no longer the aura attached to the work's uniqueness and location within historical tradition but the phony spell of the commodity form. In Hollywood cinema, the aura formerly associated with beautiful semblance persisted in a new more dubious form. As he put it, "The culture industry is defined by the fact that it does not strictly counterpose another principle to that of aura, but rather by the fact that it conserves the decaying aura as a foggy mist."[89] But Benjamin was by no means unaware of this state of affairs. The strategy of the essay "The Work of Art in the Age of Its Technological Reproducibility" was to neutralize concepts associated with aura just when they were being appropriated by capitalism to deny the masses the egalitarian promise of the liquidation of bourgeois culture. Benjamin argued that capitalism using the weapon of *the star* sought to restore aura to a means of expression that was, in some sense, contrary to it. For Agamben, like Benjamin, cinema contains within it two conflicting tendencies—toward liquidating aura and toward re-creating it, toward exhibiting gestures and toward reifying them. If our experience is one of separation in which experiencing, dwelling, using, profaning are seemingly no longer possible, this is epitomized in spectacle—which is to say in cinema itself—at the same time as cinema bears the potential to render the spectacle inoperative. This potential then is not evident in all films but, on the contrary, is realized only in specific gestures or operations.

Agamben thus starts to sound closer to Adorno than he would like as the gesture becomes something like a flicker of nonidentity salvaged from universal catastrophe. And the strategy for resistance has a distinctly Hegelian ring as he argues we need a "separation of separation" or a "suspension of the suspension."[90] For Agamben, the anti-Hegelian, this redemptive potential is achieved not through *Aufhebung* but rather through exodus, that is, not through overcoming and arriving at a higher level but by subtracting the means from the ends they serve. Gesture is then a matter of critique. Critique in this sense is not a matter of deconstruction, which for Agamben is an infinite process of negotiation, nor a matter of Heideggerian destruction, but rather a matter of suspension or neutralization, which occurs only in fleeting gestures that are always already being folded back into spectacle.

SUSPENSE

The dialectical image in Benjamin, Agamben reminds us, involves, as Adorno put it critically, an "unpolarized latent ambivalence," or in Agamben's terms, "an unresolved oscillation between estrangement and a new event of meaning."[91] The ambivalence or lack of resolution is crucial for Agamben because potential is found in suspension rather than in its capture in a Hegelian dialectical overcoming. In the context of cinema, we could understand suspension as an interruption or stoppage of suspense—the effect and affect of suspense but wrested from narrative causality. Suspense, as Hitchcock once emphasized, derives not from withholding information but, on the contrary, from *offering* information to allow the viewer to grasp the withholding of the fulfillment of narrative causality.[92] But the information itself, Hitchcock famously pointed out, often serves only a formal function and, on closer inspection, is meaningless except as the means to the suspense.[93] Repetition and stoppage can suspend suspense and reveal the empty formal function of information and narrative fulfillment. Suspending suspense means wresting a gesture from the sphere of causality.

Hitchcock's genius might be seen to lie not in narrative economy, as is often believed, but rather in his use of repetition and stoppage to neutralize the cause and effect of narrative logic and render it, like the law in Kafka, as "in force without significance."[94] He is the master of suspending suspense. For Deleuze, Hitchcock began the break from the sensory-motor schema through his use of characters who could not act. This is exemplified literally by Jimmy Stewart's characters in *Rear Window* and *Vertigo* who, suffering from a broken leg and acrophobia, respectively, can only watch without acting. As Chris Marker has suggested, what *Vertigo* gives us is "a free replay," like a video game.[95] Marker harnesses this repetition, repeats it or remediates it through stoppage, in his CD-ROM *Immemory* (1998) (as he had already done in a different way in his 1983 film *Sans Soleil*) in which the "user"—the word is significant— navigates through *Vertigo* as a series of frozen moments to be repeated and placed in new associations.

Another remediation of Hitchcock much closer to Agamben is found in Godard's *Histoire(s) du cinéma* (1988–1998), which was the subject of a short essay by the philosopher in 1995. Here we can see the use of repetition and stoppage as the power to interrupt or to hesitate. Godard, according to Agamben, wrests images from the narrative logic to allow them to "exhibit themselves as such."[96]

Godard speaks these lines over a montage of corresponding images from Hitchcock's films:

> We've forgotten why Joan Fontaine leans over the edge of a cliff and what it was Joel McCrea was going to do in Holland. We don't remember why Montgomery Clift was maintaining eternal silence or why Janet Leigh stops at the Bates Motel or why Teresa Wright is still in love with Uncle Charlie. We've forgotten why Henry Fonda is not entirely guilty and exactly why the American government employed Ingrid Bergman. But we remember a handbag. But we remember a bus in the desert. But we remember a glass of milk, the sails of a windmill, a hairbrush. But we remember bottles in a line, a pair of glasses, a passage of music, a bunch of keys, because it's thanks to them that Alfred Hitchcock succeeded where Alexander, Julius Caesar, and Napoleon failed: to become master of the universe.[97]

According to Godard, Hitchcock gives us, on the one hand, stories of narrative suspense that require a plausible enough explanation and set up a situation in which we wonder what will happen next. On the other hand, we have images of objects, which Godard shows us—bottles in a wine cellar from *Notorious* (1946) that do not look quite right, the hair brush picked up by Rose (Vera Miles) after she's gone mad in response to the suspicion cast on her husband (Henry Fonda) in *The Wrong Man* (1956), and so on. The two are put in opposition. The narrative details are dismissed as relatively unimportant, whereas it is these images of objects that are seared in our collective memory after the narrative logic has been forgotten—like dream objects or those found in Magritte's paintings, ordinary objects pregnant with unconscious meaning that can never be adequately explained by any interpretive key. Agamben's conception of cinema suggests that we should take Godard's claim seriously. Hitchcock offers us part objects exhibited as gestures, objects we cannot buy or own that become pure means extracted from the ends they serve in the narrative causality. As such, they become available for a new common use.

This is why Hitchcock "succeeded where Alexander, Caesar, and Napoleon failed": because he was concerned not with the ends of victory but with the pure means of the collective optical unconscious. As Jean Epstein put it in 1921, "No film ends badly" because "Cinema is true. A story is a lie."[98] With Hitchcock, we might invert Epstein's claim while retaining the same general argument and say, "No film ends happily." The formulaic resolutions that supply the "happy endings" of *The Wrong Man* and *Suspicion* (1941) do not undo the haunting images of madness and paranoia that preceded them. Hitchcock succeeded where the figures of political power failed by harnessing what Benjamin called "exhibition value," a sphere of action connected to play. Gesture is suspended meaning, the exhibition of the capacity for meaning or, in the case of cinema, of the cinematic as such. The list of what to a Lacanian would be Hitchcockian fetish objects, signifiers of cinephilia, are truly gestures more than they are objects—a glowing glass of milk, carried on a tray by Cary Grant as he ascends a staircase, that begins to consume the field of vision, a ring of keys pushed behind a table by Ingrid Bergman's foot in the moment of an embrace. The object's unspecifiable power is crystallized in a movement, a gesture, that is encompassed by the image as such as much as it is the movements of the figures within the image.

But as Rancière has pointed out in an analysis of this scene of Godard's remediation of Hitchcock, whatever intuitive sense we might have that Godard is right that these images lodge themselves in our memories quite apart from the logic of the plot, they nevertheless rely on that very structure to acquire an affective charge.[99] Narrative causality and the desires it animates must be in force to be suspended or deactivated. The glowing glass of milk in *Suspicion* takes on its visual power because Joan Fontaine's character (and we, the viewers) fears that Cary Grant's character, her pathologically irresponsible husband, may be trying to poison her. And while Godard's claim is that it is Hitchcock who has liberated these gestures from their representative function and freed them for a new use, it is also Godard who is literally doing exactly that, suspending suspense, dissociating these images from the narrative within which they originally figured. Through stoppage and repetition he exhibits the potentiality of these gestures having subtracted them from their use in the apparatus of the plot—making them what Deleuze called affect-images—but only paradoxically by inserting them into a new narrative about Hitchcock's ability to realize, if fleetingly, the very possibility of a mass art, which is to say the intersection of aesthetics and politics. Godard also inserts them in a new medium: this narrative about cinema as a mass art is notably constructed not through the mass art of the projected feature film but through an artisanal form of degraded video in a work made for television.

The gesture as pure means must be rescued from the narrative schema of cause and effect, and at the same this rescue operation is legible only through another logic of cause and effect in which these images that speak for themselves require a narration *that tells us that they do so*, the name of the auteur and even image of the auteur is used to forge a new link between these objects. In this video remediation of film, the images of a handbag, keys, hairbrush, lighter, and so on form a constellation that signifies "Hitchcock," the auteur as puppet master, the master of forms exponentially more powerful than Cézanne because the forms and technique are invisible (as we hear Hitchcock explain in voice-over), the elusive result of the hold and lure of a narrative logic put in suspension and rendered inoperative by memory. Despite Agamben's claims to contrary, gesture is never pure means, but derives its messianic charge from an operation that relies on the narrative logic of cause and effect that it suspends, and must constantly return to, to verify its power.

DELEUZE AND BENJAMIN

Rather than seeing this valorization of gesture on Godard or Agamben's part as always mired in performative contradiction, we can look at the work of both as revealing something about the persistence of dialectical thought necessary to thinking new image relations today. To conclude this chapter, I summarize what Agamben allows us to do with Deleuze and Benjamin and show how Agamben allows us to think about new image operations in the post-film, post-spectacle age of digital media.

He allows us to move us away from the image of Deleuze as a kind of neo-phenomenologist who valorizes cinema for its affective dimensions rather than as a means of signification, and toward Deleuze as someone who offers a different way of thinking about the relation between cinema and philosophy, concept and image, brain and body, that does not give priority to one over the other. At the same time, the concepts of repetition and stoppage offer a way of thinking cinema that is not possible in Deleuze's schema without significant modification. The great thinker of difference and repetition defines cinema in such a way as to restrict its operations to the production of new images and not to think about the ways that repetition and stoppage can perform a different kind of work on the image that radically opens up its capacity for use. One need only think of the symptomatic absence from Deleuze's cinema books of not only Debord, but also Chris Marker or indeed Esfir Shub, Joseph Cornell, Santiago Alvarez, Alexander Kluge, or any filmmaker whose images are appropriated from other sources and therefore have a prior history.[100] Repetition and stoppage give us a way of thinking about montage in a more expansive sense, one that illuminates the history of moving images as forms of objectified memory and connects us to new fields of cinematic experience increasingly informed by a logic of networks and databases rather than teleological plots.[101] It is in reactivating the potential of the past for a new use outside a fated history that cinema remains a vital field for thought.

An understanding of cinema's transformations away from the hegemony of the projected feature film has all too often been lodged in discourses that fetishize technique and technology and treat the digital, the array of platforms, software codes, and internet protocols, as causal agents. Yet the possibilities that are currently being opened up for new forms of reception, production, and distribution as well as accompanying new forms of montage (a word that we know is no longer adequate) and gesture remain scarcely understood. Agamben allows us to grasp Benjamin as a thinker of these new possibilities, not one who, as is so often thought, ties the ontology of media to its technology, but rather someone whose thought is always oriented toward disrupting this very teleological logic.

The chapter that ends Agamben's *Profanations*, "The Six Most Beautiful Minutes in the History of Cinema," describes a sequence from Orson Welles's unfinished film of *Don Quixote*. It offers a succinct and charming example of Agamben's idea of cinema as decreation. It also leads us to the limits of Agamben's thought. The chapter is brief enough that it is worth quoting in full:

> Sancho Panza enters a cinema in a provincial city. He is looking for Don Quixote and finds him sitting off to the side, staring at the screen. The theater is almost full; the balcony—which is a sort of giant terrace—is packed with raucous children. After several unsuccessful attempts to reach Don Quixote, Sancho reluctantly sits down in one of the lower seats, next to a little girl (Dulcinea?), who offers him a lollipop. The screening has begun; it is a costume film: on the screen, knights in armor are riding along. Suddenly, a woman appears; she is in danger. Don Quixote abruptly rises, unsheathes his sword, rushes toward the screen, and, with several lunges, begins to shred the cloth. The woman and the knights are still visible on the screen, but the black slash opened by Don Quixote's sword grows ever larger, implacably devouring the images. In the end, nothing is left of the screen, and only the wooden structure supporting it remains visible. The outraged audience leaves the theater, but the children on the balcony continue their fanatical cheers for Don Quixote. Only the little girl down on the floor stares at him in disapproval.
>
> What are we to do with our imaginations? Love them and believe in them to the point of having to destroy and falsify them (this is perhaps the meaning of Orson Welles's films). But when, in the end, they reveal themselves to be empty and unfulfilled, when they show the nullity of which they are made, only then can we pay the price for their truth and understand that Dulcinea—whom we have saved—cannot love us.[102]

It is fitting that Agamben focuses on a fragment of an unfinished film by a filmmaker who worked within a Hollywood system that continuously undermined him to show cinema's beauty as its potential, which is also to say, its failure. Welles, as the legend goes, was part of the spectacle, but also always at war with it and destroyed by it in the end. His *Don Quixote* was one of his many unfinished or compromised projects, and like so many of them, its plot seemed to allegorize Welles's own plight—the heroic yet ultimately failed attempt to evade an apparatus of capture. It is fitting that the narrative is centered around Don Quixote, who refused to treat the world of the imagination as a separate sphere, who sought to deactivate the distinction between fiction and nonfiction, imagination and reality. What Agamben's fable tells us, by way of Welles (and this is clear enough in Debord's films as well), is that the gesture of exhibiting the means as such is at the cost of their destruction. Though profanation, Agamben has told us, does not mean destruction, he cannot envision our salvation without exposing the emptiness of the apparatus. If we are not seduced by nostalgia for the film that never came to be—in which case we cannot profane it—then we are left with the screen in tatters and the disapproval of the one whose love we wish to have returned. If we are always already in a separate sphere, our gestures captured by the apparatus of spectacle, then the truth cannot be anything other than the impossibility of the capacity to imagine another world.

If Agamben can help us reread Deleuze and Benjamin for new uses of their thought, we also must seek ways of unhinging the potential of Agamben's own work from the powerful logic of separation that condemns us to always be seeking our disenchantment in an undecidable operation in which the veil is removed and we discover only the void.

CONCLUSION: EXHIBITION VALUE IN
THE AGE OF SOCIAL MEDIA

Both Godard's *Histoire(s)* and Welles's *Quixote* suggest that, paradoxically, if the gesture is to be pure or "unsullied" (to evoke Bazin) it must always be subtracted from another body. It cannot be exhibited for our gaze consciously or deliberately. That the deliberate exhibition of gestures either is grotesque or points to a kind of exhaustion of the means of expression is found in the exaggerated gesticulations that Agamben highlights in the first decades of cinema. It has also been a central theme of video art since the seventies, which Rosalind Krauss called "an aesthetics of narcissism," a theme that has taken on a new incarnation in the first decade of the twenty-first century, both more promising and more ambiguous in video blogs (or vlogs), featured on YouTube (founded in 2005) and other video sharing sites, composed mostly by teenagers and preteens who in exhibiting themselves oscillate between the will to pure praxis performed as sincerity and a deliberately strained mimicry of their own gestures.

It is easy to have a cynical approach to vernacular videos of the types sent to friends, posted on Snapchat or YouTube, as it is to the information and images that make up Facebook, Tumblr, Twitter, and Instagram accounts. That they are called "accounts" is telling enough. From a very young age children on the right side of the digital divide are quickly made to see themselves as what Foucault called entrepreneurs of the self.[103] They submit their libidinal economy to apparatuses that extract value from their social investments and leisure time, but these same apparatuses make possible what Benjamin called a vast new field of play (*Spielraum*) or, we might say, new possibilities for use. The submitting of one's self to an economy of ratings, a logic of accumulation (whether of likes or view counts or followers/subscribers), the way we are all increasingly unembarrassed to speak of ourselves as a brand and participate willingly in nonstop algorithmic surveillance, suggests a new kind of apparatus of control that fuses advertising and pornography and captures every aspect of our forms of life, making work and play virtually indiscernible.

According to Agamben "capitalism is nothing but a gigantic apparatus for capturing pure means, that is, profanatory behaviors."[104] More ominously, he adds, "The capitalist religion in its extreme phase aims at creating something absolutely unprofanable."[105] Nonetheless, there remains hope but it is given in an elliptical formula: "The profanation of the unprofanable is the political task of the coming generation."[106]

How do we profane the unprofanable today? Agamben more explicitly than Rancière and Badiou has suggested that cinema is no longer emblematic of our situation. As he wrote in 1992, "The end of the cinema truly sounds the death knell of the ultimate metaphysical adventure of *Dasein*. In the twilight of post-cinema, of which we are seeing the beginning, human quasi-existence, now stripped of any metaphysical hypostasis and deprived of any theological model, will have to seek its proper generic consistency elsewhere."[107] We are no longer moviegoing animals seeking images of ourselves among a collective in the dark, but users interfacing with a network within which moving images are reduced to one form of information among many.[108]

Though he has barely discussed it himself, Agamben points us to the importance of examining social media as an apparatus where gesture gets exhibited and captured. One of the shifts Benjamin identified was happening to the work of art in the age of its technological reproducibility was a shift from its cult value (associated with the unique work) to its exhibition value (associated with social act of viewing as part of a mass). These have not been the most enduring of the terms offered by Benjamin. For one thing, cult value, like aura, far from seeming to have disappeared, remains a central condition of contemporary commercial culture, which Benjamin well understood would happen if film remained under the control of private property. For another, exhibition value (*Ausstellungswert*) was barely defined. But according to Agamben, "nothing better characterizes the new condition of objects and even of the human body in the era of fulfilled capitalism."[109] Indeed, as Krauss cannily anticipated in her analysis of artists' videos in the 1970s, the essence of so-called social media and video blogging is not the ostensible content but exhibiting oneself as such.

This is beautifully rendered in *need ideas!?!PLZ!!*, a 2011 video by Elisa Giardina Papa.[110] The video is a repurposing of videos posted on YouTube by preteens or young teens asking for ideas for their videos. It takes the form of what has been called a supercut, a genre of vernacular video that compiles a series of examples of the same type of action—through stoppage and repetition it thus either fetishizes or parodies a particular gesture. Whether by showing a series of people on many different reality shows all saying "I'm not here to make friends" or a tic, a certain jaw movement, by George W. Bush repeated in various circumstances over a period of time, supercuts expose a kind of optical unconscious, a psychopathology of everyday mediated life, to different purposes. In *need ideas!?!PLZ!!*, Giardina Papa edits together variations of requests for content by these young individuals, mostly (but not exclusively) girls, who want views, who want comments, who want subscribers, but have nothing to offer for them except the solicitation for ideas for what they should do in their videos. I have no ideas, each one tells their unknown anonymous audience, please tell me what to do. Each young girl (or boy) keeps insisting that she wants to please us and work on our behalf. These individuals are, in effect, pure exhibition value, literally watching their own images as they record them (a function built into the technology of the webcam), as they request a response from an unseen collective who is seeing what they see, themselves. Agamben quotes Ingmar Bergman describing the famous scene in *Summer with Monika* (1952) when Harriet Andersson looks back directly at the apparatus: "Here for the first time in the history of cinema there is established a shameless and direct contact with the spectator." Agamben notes that pornography has rendered this banal.[111] The webcam and the existence of video sharing sites open up this banality to a new level. Today direct address establishes the gestural as a form of currency that calls for profanation.

Agamben's emphasis on repetition and stoppage, and the examples of Godard and Debord, may suggest that when he refers to cinema, he means avant-garde cinema, but it is the strength of his conception of cinema that he moves us away from cinema as art and toward cinema as strategy. Repetition and stoppage are not esoteric or elitist gestures but the forms of vernacular engagement with moving images and spectacle that every young person, now movie*making* animals, in the advanced postindustrial world is familiar with today. They are the basis for videos exposing police injustice as well as any fan culture that revolves around popular characters or media celebrities. The familiarity or banality of these operations today might seem to mute their radicality, but on the contrary, it opens up gestures today to a much wider field of common use no longer restricted by the limited realm of the art world.

I therefore regret that, although it is available for free viewing on the internet, *need ideas!?!PLZ!!* is a video that has exhibited in galleries. The museum, as Agamben has noted, is the epitome of an apparatus that makes things and ideas no longer available for common use. But despite the limitations of the original exhibition context, what Giardina Papa makes visible is the social *Gestus* of the preadolescent girl or boy searching for recognition, a new use for themselves within a community. The declared total absence of ideas, an absolute exhaustion of content, exposes and neutralizes the libidinal economy of the apparatus. The profaning of the image of the self is necessary to release it from the inescapable expectations of a neoliberal attention economy.

Cinema touches on the mute private singular aspects of our forms of life and brings them into common use. This is its political dimension. At the same time, it captures gestures and converts them into information that can be quantified. The struggle between these two sides of a moving image that is now increasingly available to anyone can be seen in this serial depiction of young people who self-exhibit, who stare back into the mirror with a memory asking for a response that comes from elsewhere; though explicitly asking for quantifiable fame, the acknowledged absence of ideas that would earn that fame suggests at some level that they desire something else, some other way of being. We witness vernacular gestures calling out for a new use outside the realm of instrumentality. A new politics of media may not be exhibited here, but a demand for it is if only through the minor differences of gesture that come through repetition. These mediated images of young girls and boys are asking what to do with the burden of their own bodies as images. Individually they demand a big Other that tells them what to do, but what we encounter collectively is a social *Gestus* that evades ownership and control. As Badiou would agree, we need a cinema that makes a demand for new ideas. Here we see the anonymous capacity of anyone whatsoever to make this demand not for the sake of art, but for new forms of life.

4

RETHINKING THE POLITICS OF
THE PHILOSOPHY OF CINEMA

CINEMA AS THOUGHT

By the turn of the twenty-first century, as the influence of seventies film theory was waning, one of the most high-profile defenses of theory came from Slavoj Žižek in his *The Fright of Real Tears: Krzysztof Kieślowski Between Theory and Post-Theory*, published in 2001.[1] The differences between Žižek and the legacy he wishes to defend are telling. While Žižek insists on preserving the political project of film theory against the post-theory turn, there is little trace of the "political modernism" of his predecessors. Like Metz, Wollen, Comolli, and Mulvey, he privileges the symbolic over the imaginary, but the process of passing from perception/recognition to knowledge is now on the side primarily of theory rather than art. For this reason he tends to focus on popular cinema and art films, not the formally radical cinema valorized by seventies film theorists. In regard to his use of Krzysztof Kieślowski, Žižek says that his aim is "not to talk *about* his work, but to refer to his work in order to accomplish the *work* of Theory. In its very ruthless 'use' of its artistic pretext, such a procedure is much more faithful to the interpreted work than any superficial respect for the work's unfathomable autonomy."[2] For Žižek, the relation between film and theory is viewed as just that, a relation, and not a "non-relation" in the Lacanian sense. The tendency is for film to have an instrumental function in the illustration of Lacanian concepts. It is part of his charm to have made this so explicit, and few people have made, and embodied, as compelling a case for the *jouissance* of theory itself as Žižek.

But we need to recognize that the relationship between theory/philosophy and cinema for Žižek denies films the possibility of producing new ideas for thought. It would be wrong to accuse Žižek of merely applying Lacanian concepts to films. Theory is not applied to films so much as films become an arena for the staging of theory: "Hollywood is conceived as a 'phenomenology' of the Lacanian Spirit, its appearing for the common consciousness."[3] The concepts that Žižek finds in films are not the concepts cinema gives rise to, as they are for Deleuze, but mere repetitions of the same Lacanian apparatus. For Žižek, film, like all art, is indistinguishable from the cultural product in that it illustrates an ideological impasse. This idea is also the premise of two films starring Žižek directed by Sophie Fiennes, *The Pervert's Guide to Cinema* (2006) and its sequel, *The Pervert's Guide to Ideology* (2012), in which films are taken as an illustrated guide for the logic of psychoanalysis and contemporary ideology with Žižek as the mediator.

Žižek is right that theory should not lie prostrate before the work of art as autonomous entity, but this should not mean relegating it to the status of a pretext for theory. Indeed, for Žižek, the effect of the work of art is finally imaginary in Lacan's sense, or rather, ideological in Althusser's sense. The ultimate goal of theory for Žižek is not oriented toward wresting the symbolic from the imaginary so much as reaching the point at which the symbolic fails—the way that films, and generally filmic narratives, reach an impasse in the traumatic void of what Lacan called the Real. By focusing on narrative, however, the Real in his uses of cinema is an imaginary Real, a figuration of the traumatic void occluded by what passes for common sense about our shared culture.

As Žižek points out, Lacan multiplies the permutations of the Real, Imaginary, Symbolic triad by proposing that there is an Imaginary Real, a Symbolic Real, a Real Real, a Real Imaginary, a Symbolic Imaginary, and so on.[4] However, Žižek rarely makes explicit use of this in his analyses. When he offers a filmic example of the Real such as the alien bursting through a man's stomach in *Alien* (1979), this image may provide an example of the Real as traumatic void that cannot be properly symbolized, but if we are talking about the scene in the film, it remains in some sense imaginary.[5] It is in that sense an "imaginary Real." We might add that insofar as it serves as an example for Žižek himself, it is also a "symbolic Real." But the cinematic as such for Žižek remains imaginary. In Žižek's analyses of film, art is capable not of truth, but only of illustrating it or narrativizing it. Though Žižek puts himself in opposition to both analytic philosophy and cognitive forms of theory, because he privileges theory over art, he shares with these other approaches the assumption that theory explicates an object that it does not transform, and theory, in turn, is not transformed in the process. Bordwell, Žižek's adversary, wants to show how films work to create specifiable effects, Žižek wants to show how films illustrate ideological content, but they both relegate films to the side of the imaginary and put knowledge on the side of theory or philosophy.

This is where Deleuze, Badiou, Rancière, and Agamben offer a different way of conceiving of the relationship between theory/philosophy and cinema. Cinema, according to Badiou, is a truth procedure. Like Deleuze, he argues that films create new ideas through new images and signs. For Rancière, cinema can disrupt the distribution of the sensible. He has written about the potential for images to be "pensive," which is to say producing thought by being suspended between different regimes of representation or expression.[6] For Agamben, cinema can create new kinds of signs, called gestures, that deactivate our relation to time, or rather, history and memory. This gets us beyond the dead end binary of seeing cinema/art as either autonomous from theory or as merely a pretext for theory.

Moving images are forms of thought and produce effects for conceptual thought. As a mode of thought, cinema is one of philosophy's conditions, one of the realms of expression or creativity that philosophy must think. This means we should not privilege the symbolic over the imaginary or the bodily/material over the ideational. The thought of cinema constructs a relation between the symbolic and imaginary and neutralizes the frequently hierarchical opposition between them. Philosophy or theory thinks cinema's thought in its own way and for its own purposes—not to explicate it but to learn from it and create its own ideas from what it learns.

CINEMA AS ART

To construct a different relationship between cinema and philosophy, Rancière, Badiou, Deleuze, and Agamben all ask us to consider what cinema is—if it is a form of thought different from conceptual thought, then how do we characterize it? Each asks us to consider cinema within the broader category of art, but this in turn leads us to reconsider the concept of art itself. As André Bazin well understood, to think the ontology of cinema means to acknowledge the porousness of its boundaries—its paradoxical relationship to the real and to the other arts. Recognizing this fundamental impurity of cinema does not negate the value of the question of what makes cinema an art, but, on the contrary, it is what makes it a question of philosophy.

In the 1930s, Walter Benjamin famously proposed that the question should not be whether film and photography are arts, but whether they have changed the very nature of art.[7] While today few would dispute film's claim to being "an art," what is meant by this tends to remain remarkably vague. To confuse matters, "Art" has, in many arenas (not least the academic discipline of art history), continued to be associated with what appears on museum walls or, in other words, the idea of art that Benjamin thought was disappearing and not film or even (with some exceptions) music, drama, literature, or poetry. Given this semantic confusion, the question should be not only whether the category of art is applicable to film, but also what is meant by art and how film is understood when it is not understood as an art.

In regard to what we can *think cinema as* if not art, two possibilities present themselves. To be clear, these two possibilities do not necessarily preclude also seeing some films as art, as I will explain below, and they are not always necessarily mutually exclusive, but nonetheless they are common relatively distinct ways of identifying film as something other than art:

1)   The first category I will propose is seeing film *as ideology*. I use the word "ideology" as shorthand, but in this category I wish to include seeing film as "commodity" as well as seeing film as "myth" in the Roland Barthes sense, while acknowledging that neither commodity nor myth is strictly equivalent to ideology. Nonetheless, what unites this category is the logic of demystification or the "hermeneutics of suspicion" as an approach to film in a way that Rancière has criticized for reproducing the position of the master in the know and the logic of inequality.[8]

One needs to be careful here because Barthes did not wish to conceive of myth as something that could be unveiled. And this also is true the more sophisticated forms of ideology critique, especially those derived from Althusser's concept of ideology, which takes ideology as an a priori condition of daily life not to be confused with false consciousness.[9] The "hermeneutics of suspicion" as defined by Paul Ricoeur, which starts with Marx, Nietzsche, and Freud, has from the very beginning been suspicious of the hermeneutics of suspicion itself.[10] Nonetheless, the tradition of ideology critique must retain the notion that theory can say something that the film itself cannot—that, as Laura Mulvey put it, theory can be "a political weapon" against the unreflective pleasures offered by film.[11] Or as Metz put it, theory can wrest film from the imaginary and win it for the symbolic.[12] Seeing film as ideology presumes that film is first an imaginary or idealist phenomenon and that one can extract meaning from the text of the film that it simultaneously contains and seeks to obscure.

2)   The second way of seeing film as something that is not art I will call seeing film *as culture*. By *as culture* I mean asking how film or films function culturally without necessarily treating them as ideology that needs to be demystified or art that needs to be appreciated. I do not intend this category to be strictly correlative to the work done on film by writers and academics that identify with the tradition of cultural studies, but obviously there is overlap. By seeing film as culture I mean a way of seeing film that is committed to retaining as its object the ordinary

ways that films are received and experienced without (necessarily) denouncing or unveiling them, on the one hand, or championing them, on the other. It means a way of approaching films less in terms of how meaning inheres within the film text than in how films take on or acquire meanings.

With these two ways of conceiving of film as something other than art in mind, I will turn to five different approaches to seeing film as art:

1) The first way I will call the *Romantic Approach*, though it has certain variants that may sound more modernist than romantic.[13] The paradoxical logic is the following: Film is an art like any other, that is, the seventh art, because film is an art like no other. In other words, the logic behind the titles of both Rudolf Arnheim's *Film as Art* and V. F. Perkins's *Film as Film* would fall into this category.[14] In this category not all films are art and seeing films as art means focusing on representative masterpieces to show how they use the specificity of the medium to transcend the medium.

2) The second model I will call the *Utilitarian Approach*. We could also call it the poetic model, not in the sense of romantic poetics, but because it sees art as *poiesis* or in terms of ways of doing or making. Here I am thinking of the popular American textbook *Film Art* by David Bordwell and Kristin Thompson. Bordwell and Thompson insist that when they refer to film art, pedigree is not an issue. They are using a concept of art that does not require transcendence, but rather acknowledges the wide variety of types of films and audiences. Cinema is an art, they tell us, because it offers filmmakers ways to "design" experiences that viewers find "worthwhile" or "valuable." They tell us that we can analyze cinema as an art because it is an intentional formal construct.[15] The criteria for art are then three things: (a) analyzable form (patterns are discernable, as are innovations within available patterns); (b) authorship (the effects of these formal constructs they tell us are not accidental; we analyze cinema as art because we attribute design or intention to it); and (c) identifiable positive effects, effects that Bordwell and Thomson call "worthwhile" or "valuable," though these adjectives are left vague because

they are meant to encompass an enormous range of effects. What is key in this model is that art cannot produce immanent singularities in Badiou's terms or be pure means in Agamben's sense, but that it has identifiable ends.

3) The third category I propose is what I will call the *Didactic Approach*. This category supplements the category that sees film as primarily ideology. In that approach, film can become political when it becomes art or vice versa. Art is understood here in an avant-garde or political modernist sense as that which breaks from film as ideology.[16] Those who conceive of film as ideology often reserve film's power as art to its critical capacity, its politics. Political film is not film about politics but film that uses film form to disturb our normal relation to film through what Althusser called a knowledge effect. This argument is perhaps most explicit in Comolli and Narboni's "Cinema/Ideology/Criticism,"[17] and it can also be found in many of the most influential essays published in the British journal *Screen* in the 1970s. It corresponds to the discourse of political modernism as described by David Rodowick.

4) The fourth category I will call the *Sociological Approach*. It corresponds to the category that sees film as culture. As I suggested, seeing film as culture goes against seeing film in general as art, but what it recognizes is the *art effect* of a certain category of film. It is from this category that we get not the syntagma "film art," but that of "art film," which is to say that "art" when applied to film refers not to its practice in general or its exceptional instances but is more like a genre or mode of film practice with a specific institutional history and specifiable codes and conventions that appeal to an elite cultural milieu. According to this approach, we can read film as art only to the extent that it circulates as art. This category need not be evaluative but is available for the Bourdieusian critique of art cinema or the "festival film" in which the art effect of certain films is read in a class context.

"Art film," in this approach, is often in opposition to subversive or resistant cinema, the examples of which are found more often than not in popular cinema or television. This is because the real-world effects are privileged over what in the seventies was called the work at the level of the signifier. In the progressive versions of this model, the politics of cinema is therefore rarely located in new kinds of images, but rather in challenging hegemonic cultural stereotypes or affirming nonhegemonic ones.

5) The fifth category of seeing cinema as art, shared by the thinkers discussed in this book, I will call the *Philosophical Approach*. This approach asks in what ways cinema can produce new possibilities for thought. Or as Badiou put it, "What does cinema think that only it can think?" Art signifies a transformation of sensible forms to create a new idea possible only through its own means. What the other approaches all share is a logic that assumes that the operations of art have specifiable effects. Like the ignorant master, the emancipated idea of art dissociates cause and effect. What aesthetics means in Rancière's analysis is the suspension of the rules of appearance that define the difference between art and non-art. This means seeing art as means without ends, as Agamben argues, or as capable of new kinds of immanent relations between incommensurables, in Badiou's terms. This does not mean being indifferent to cinema's function as either ideology or culture—on the contrary—but it does mean the refusal to reduce it to that function. The philosophical approach, understood through the writings of Agamben, Badiou, and Rancière, means that art performs work on its ideological and cultural dimensions but gains its importance for philosophy in how it transforms and reveals those functions, or rather in how it intervenes in the distribution of the sensible.

Whether art remains the right term is an open question. We should, nevertheless, insist that this is not an elitist conception of art but that art is a term for any arrangement of sensible material that is not merely symptomatic but rather produces effects for thought by positing that something else is possible. Cinema as an impure mass art, as Badiou would put it (though with Rancière, we must go further than Badiou and say that all arts are impure arts), can be made by anyone and is addressed to anyone. Agamben pushes the farthest in respect to questioning the category of art and implies that we should go beyond art to the question of human expression as such. And this indeed is where cinema today is leading—to new vernacular forms that can proliferate outside of the institutional apparatuses that make art legible as art. The danger of abandoning the category of art is sacrificing the legibility of cinema's operations. As Deleuze or Badiou would argue, in an age in which everything tends to get reduced to communication or information, we must be able to isolate and name the assemblages that disrupt this tendency and in doing so challenge our habits of engaging with the world. So even if "art" is no longer applicable to these modes of expression, the philosophical approach involves making a distinction between information and communication embedded within contemporary capitalism's logic of control and any cinematic expression whatsoever that has a claim on philosophy, that produces new resources for thought.

CINEMA AS POLITICS

Cinema as art in the philosophical approach produces new resources for thought when it says: Something else is possible. The people are missing. When it perturbs the ordinary relationship between sense and sense. When it interrupts our habitual modes of being and exposes an unconscious gesture, a new use for the data of common experience resistant to instrumental rationality. These are all ways of understanding how cinema is political as simultaneously a mode of critique and a form of affirmation of another possibility or potentiality.

This very much places our thinkers in the lineage of seventies film theory since they all affirm an axiomatic politics of cinema. But for these thinkers, this does not mean that all films are inherently political simply because they are ideological, but that philosophy extracts a political dimension from cinematic operations that are, at least in part, predicated on art's relative autonomy from political action. They all acknowledge a different relationship between philosophy and art, one that makes the old formulas for critical art problematic.

The shift in the politics of cinema from the seventies to the philosophers discussed in this book can be exemplified by looking more closely at the discourses about cinema related to the binary activity/passivity.

One central tenet of seventies film theory and the discourse of political modernism or didactic approach was that the ordinary cinema spectator, as Rancière put it, was "separated from both the capacity to know and the power to act."[18] Rancière was writing about discourses about theater, but film in the twentieth century, associated with the mindless rapt fascination of the images of mass media and aura of Hollywood stars, became the primary target for the accusation that its viewers were in some fundamental sense *passive*. This assumed position of passivity was the basis, for example, of Baudry's analogy between cinema spectatorship and the unenlightened shackled in Plato's cave mistaking shadows for reality. For seventies film theory, cinema was an inherently idealist medium and, correspondingly, a powerful vehicle for the smooth transfer of ideology. The politics of cinema, needless to say, were about countering this tendency, making active spectators aware of the mechanisms that transformed reality into wish fulfillment.

Meanwhile the critique of this era of film theory has often taken the form of a heroic defense of the presumably maligned average cinema viewer who we are told is indeed active, both bodily and cognitively. (We find different versions of this in the utilitarian and sociological approaches discussed above.) There is no doubt some truth to this counter-charge on two accounts. First, it is true that many instances of seventies film theory by focusing of how the apparatus and the text of the Hollywood film interpellated spectators in such a way as to reproduce, naturalize, and universalize ideological content seemed to leave little room for the kinds of negotiated or oppositional readings Stuart Hall would theorize in his important 1973 essay "Encoding/decoding."[19] Second, it is a banal truth that all spectators are always, at least in some sense, *active*; all spectators have physical and affective responses, and use cognitive skills and different forms of prior knowledge to create inferences to follow and anticipate the plot, and so forth, and these are all literally activities of a sort.

But what is frequently ignored by revisionist critiques of seventies film theory that lay special emphasis on the spectator's activity is the extent to which a certain desire for passivity, if we can call it that, a desire to forget one's body, one's identity, and daily responsibilities, permeates cinephilia even in its most presumably sophisticated forms. And this desire is by no means something we should reject out of hand or place in strict opposition to politics. Not only did Pauline Kael title one of her collections of criticism *I Lost It at the Movies*, but Andrew Sarris, her famous rival in American film criticism in the sixties and seventies whom she accused of elitism for championing auteurist rankings, had identified himself as a "professional voyeur" and explicitly celebrated "the voluptuous passivity of moviegoing."[20] Susan Sontag, for her part, wrote, "The strongest experience was simply to surrender to, to be transported by, what was on the screen. You wanted to be kidnapped by the movie."[21] But perhaps it was Stanley Cavell who understood best the profound effect that came from relinquishing power in front of the film screen:

> How do movies reproduce the world magically? Not by literally presenting us with the world, but by permitting us to view it unseen. This is not a wish for power over creation (as Pygmalion's was), but a wish not to need power, not to have to bear its burdens. It is, in this sense, the reverse of the myth of Faust. And the wish for invisibility is old enough. Gods have profited from it, and Plato tells it in Book II of the *Republic* as the Myth of the Ring of Gyges. In viewing films, the sense of invisibility is an expression of modern privacy or anonymity. It is as though the world's projection explains our forms of unknownness and of our inability to know.[22]

For Cavell, the desire not to be present and the desire not to know and be known were directly related to cinema's unique ethical function in modern life.

Seventies film theory rejected this celebration of a kind of passivity on the assumption that it was in direct opposition to political action. Correspondingly, it shares the same premise with the contemporary film studies that has rejected it—whether cognitivist, phenomenological, or Deleuzian—that passivity is a bad thing. Where they differed was in whether it described a dominant condition of cinematic spectatorship. If the rejection of seventies film theory has been in large part grounded in the claim that cinema viewers are all always active, we need to recognize that it is not a coincidence that this new consensus coincides with the age of social media, the attention economy, and participatory culture.[23] If the age of spectacle and the culture industry did make a certain passivity compulsory (a passivity that had its own intellectual pleasures), the age of control makes activity compulsory, turning us all into "users." Hence the appeal of the figure of Melville's Bartleby the scrivener for a number of contemporary philosophers including Deleuze, Žižek, and Agamben—the passive refusal to participate begins to seem like a radical act.

But the politics of cinema is no more about affirming passivity than it is about affirming activity. It is rather about challenging received ideas of what constitutes activity and what constitutes passivity—it recognizes that a certain suspension of activity characteristic of twentieth-century cinema made cinema a pleasurable vehicle for naturalizing capitalism, patriarchy, and racial and cultural hierarchies at the same time as it made possible ways of suspending and thwarting those relations. Seventies film theory understood this but assumed that those relations needed to be thwarted by producing knowledge of the conditions of possibility of the spectacle either through theory or through reflexivity and self-consciousness within films themselves. But being made aware that we are trapped by a system we cannot control can be as disabling as enabling—and neither the complex multiplicity that makes up a given film nor the specific work of certain aesthetic operations should have to be converted into knowledge. According to Rancière, "emancipation begins when we challenge the opposition between viewing and acting."[24] Politics does not mean a determinate idea by an auteur that will be directly transmitted to the spectator through a reproducible formula. Nor should it mean an injunction to become active. It means a work "whose meaning is owned by no one."[25] Similarly, Agamben finds the politics of cinema in gesture because gestures do precisely that—interrupt the opposition between passivity and activity and the logic of cause and effect, and as such they are figures for new forms of collective being to come. To affirm that something else is possible (that there is something other than just bodies and languages) or that the people are missing (that there is no community whose response we can predict in advance) is to initiate a fold in the distribution of the sensible. It is the affirmation of a suspended meaning that is available to anyone because it is owned by no one.

How unsatisfying it may be to think of the politics of cinema outside the realm of explicit political content and to critique the legacy of committed art that sought to produce knowledge of oppression as a call to action. But it is not a matter of rejecting this history. Among the most powerful theories, and examples, of political cinema in the sixties and seventies came from Latin America, where a number of great filmmakers and thinkers sought to challenge the idea that cinema should be a space for either "voluptuous passivity" or intellectual puzzles, and proposed instead that it must become a revolutionary space in which the realities of colonial violence, imperialism, and neocolonialism should be exposed. Films could be like weapons that armed their viewers. Brazilian filmmaker Glauber Rocha demanded an aesthetics of hunger and of violence.[26] Argentinian filmmakers Fernando Solanas and Octavio Getino coined the term "third cinema," defined as a lucid anticapitalist cinema that did not seek refuge in the ambiguity of the bourgeois art film (second cinema) any more than in immediate pleasures of mass spectacle (first cinema). But what third cinema did in Solanas and Getino's conception (and in the underground screenings of their *Hour of the Furnaces*) was to reorient the space of the cinema as one of discussion. "The film," they claimed, "is the pretext for dialogue, for the seeking and finding of wills. It is a report that we place before you for your consideration, to be debated after the showing."[27] This is then not merely the reconfiguration of the space of viewing as one for action, but rather an attempt to initiate a new kind of relationship between cinema and action by making the space of the film into one for debate and dialogue beginning from a challenge to consensus. The suspended meaning that forms the political dimension of a given film does not mean art house ambiguity and ennui, nor does it mean that there is no place in cinema for exposing injustices or offering knowledge about how governments or economic systems perpetuate violence and inhibit the forms of life of individuals and communities, but it does mean sacrificing the idea that the politics of a given film are equivalent to its explicit message or that the effects of the film, or the affective response to the film, can be predicted.

It means that philosophy or theory creates its own political idea from the ways in which cinematic forms create a new sensible relation to the world. The philosophical approach means responding to the concrete specificity of individual films, their singularity, but at the same time, it is freed from having to account for explanations of the effects of those films. It seeks not knowledge of the films but their effects for thought, which always means a challenge to the logic of consensus. With the demise of the authority of so-called high theory and cultural studies, certain quarters of film studies seek refuge in the kinds of uncontroversial knowledge that shore up the discipline and the expertise of the professors who teach and publish in it. But scholarship always means making a decision about what aspects of cinema and media history are worth thinking about. Scholarship needs to be supplemented not only by explanatory theories, but by ideas that initiate conflict over the sensible.

As Rancière argues, philosophers and theorists writing on cinema are like filmmakers adapting a script or audiences remembering a film in the sense that they all extract one fable from another. To move beyond political modernism, to look for the specific ways that contemporary cinematic forms produce new resources to imagine a reconfiguration of places and identities against the police logic of control, means preserving the aesthetic dimension of theory and philosophy as a place where conflict over shared experience can be initiated. Militant cinema is only one form of political cinema, but by being subjected to political imperatives, it risks sacrificing the truths of its own immanent material, which are the sounds and images of history and the contemporary world. Similarly, the aesthetic formulas of counter-cinema, or the familiar ideas of subversive or resistant aesthetics that seek to expose the apparatus or cross a threshold in which the spectator becomes an actor, work only within certain situations that are attuned to the nuances of the dominant forms that they are undermining and not if they are reproducing now familiar gestures that merely reinforce dominant or dated conceptions of what makes cinema political. The works that make a claim on philosophy are the ones that challenge our ideas of what cinema can do, how cinema is related to thought, and what makes cinema political. Philosophy, in turn, shows how cinema allows us to rethink what can be seen, said, and done, and who is capable of seeing, saying, and doing.

ACKNOWLEDGMENTS

When I received my PhD from the Program in Literature at Duke University in 2009, I did not yet have the idea for this book. Nonetheless, looking back on my graduate work today, it strikes me how much of the book still feels inextricable from the thinking I did in Durham, North Carolina, from 2002 to 2008. My first debt is to the many mentors and friends from that period of my life. I want to thank Negar Mottahedeh and Michael Hardt for their comments and encouragement. Cohort and friends, including Russ Leo, Shilyh Warren, and Alvaro Reyes, among many others, left their marks on my thought. In particular, I want to acknowledge Luka Arsenjuk and Abe Geil. Together we brought our shared theoretical commitments to the Society of Cinema and Media Studies, where I first rehearsed some of the arguments in this book. In addition I want to thank Abe for his comments on chapter 3.

It is hard to find the right words to express my debt to Fredric Jameson. He was my advisor at Duke and he will always be an intellectual model for me. It is strange to realize his name is absent from these pages, as if to cite him was somehow to give the game away—too deep and direct has his influence been on my thinking and writing that I unconsciously repressed the traces.

Jane Gaines, another advisor on my graduate work, also requires a paragraph all her own. She has remained a mentor and inspiration and also has become a colleague. Nobody else has done so much to help create the conditions for me to finish this book. I am enormously grateful for her belief in me and for her gentle pressure to always make this book my first priority.

I still feel indebted to my undergraduate professors and advisors at Brown University, Mary Ann Doane and Philip Rosen. It was in their classes that I first read so many of the essays that I discuss in this book, it was their responses to my undergraduate papers and thesis that helped convince me to go on to graduate school, and somewhere in the back of my head it is still their approval I am seeking when I write.

At Columbia, I am grateful to be a member of the Film Program and to have such terrific colleagues including Richard Peña, Annette Insdorf, Ron Gregg, and Thomas Elsaesser. I want to give special thanks to Rob King and James Schamus for support, inspiration, and conversations over the years. I would also like to thank all of the members the Comparative Media group, especially Brian Larkin for mentorship and Noam Elcott for friendship, advice, and occasional arguments over chartreuse cocktails.

This book has benefited immeasurably from conversations with many other friends, colleagues, and students too numerous to name. I would like to single out Genevieve Yue for comments on an early draft of chapter 3. For in-depth comments on the book in its entirety, I am especially grateful to Rachel Price and Damon Young. This book has improved enormously due to their careful reads and probing questions. Anonymous readers at both University of Minnesota Press and Columbia University Press also provoked me with their thoughtful feedback and suggestions. I feel fortunate to have been in such good hands with my editor, Philip Leventhal.

Thanks to my parents, Jonathan Baumbach and Georgia Brown, to my siblings, Noah, David, and Nina Baumbach, to many friends who I have felt supported by over the years, including Seth Price, Bettina Funcke, Taryn Simon, Carolyn Funk, and Jake Perlin.

Parts of this book include modified versions of ideas that I developed in a number of conference papers and publications. Chapter 1 builds on my essay "Jacques Rancière and the Persistence of Film Theory," published in *Critical Cinema: Beyond the Theory of Practice* (Wallflower Press, 2012). This essay was first given as a conference paper at the Jacques Rancière Day Conference at Roehampton University in 2008. I would like to thank Paul Bowman for organizing this conference and Clive Myer for including the essay in his collection. Traces of a second essay on Rancière, "The Politics of the Aesthetics of Theory," also found their way into chapter 1. This essay is forthcoming in *Jacques Rancière: Politics and Aesthetics*, edited by Scott Durham and Dilip Gaonkar (Northwestern University Press, 2018), and was first given as a paper at the conference "Rancière: Politics and Aesthetics" at Northwestern University in 2011. I would like to thank Scott and Dilip and André Munro. Sections of chapter 2 derive from "Something Else Is Possible: Thinking Badiou on Philosophy and Art," published in *Polygraph* #17, *The Philosophy of Alain Badiou* (2005). I would like to thank Matthew Wilkens for publishing this paper and for being an interlocutor on Badiou's philosophy in reading groups and on the tennis court. Ideas throughout this book found their way into "Metz with Deleuze," first written as a paper for the conference "The Semiological Paradigm and Christian Metz's Cinematographic Thought" at the University of Zurich in 2013 and later published in *Christian Metz and the Codes of Cinema: Film Semiology and Beyond* (Amsterdam University Press, 2018). I want to thank Margrit Tröhler, Guido Kirsten, and especially Julia Zutavern for inviting me to the conference. I would like to thank Arne de Boever for enlisting me to review Badiou's *Cinema* for the *Los Angeles Review of Books*, which helped me rethink the framing of chapter 2. Certain ideas in chapter 4 were first developed in "What Does It Mean to Call Film an Art?" in *Rancière and Film*, ed. Paul Bowman (Edinburgh University Press, 2013). This essay grew out of a response to a paper by Philip Watts at the Columbia University Seminar on Cinema and Interdisciplinary Interpretation. I would like to thank Phil for that paper, for conversations on Rancière, and for his warmth and generosity. I miss him.

Annie Baker has also given me invaluable comments on the manuscript, but more than that, she has shown me how and why it is done. The "it" here is writing, perhaps, but it is much more than that too. When I try to start to say something about what I have learned from her that is so important to my work, to my understanding of what it means to work and how it connects to everything else, I keep returning to the line from Malebranche cited by both Benjamin and Celan: "Attentiveness is the natural prayer of the soul."

NOTES

INTRODUCTION

1. Walter Benjamin, "The Work of Art in the Age of Its Technological Reproducibility," in *Selected Writings Volume 3: 1935–1938*, trans. Edmond Jephcott and Harry Zohn (Cambridge, Mass.: Harvard University Press, 2002), 106. There are three versions of the essay, the first published in German in 1935. I am quoting from the second version, first published in French in 1936. "But as soon as the criterion of authenticity ceases to be applied to artistic production, the whole social function of art is revolutionized. Instead of being founded on ritual, it is based on a different practice: politics." Film "emancipates" art from authenticity and ritual because "film is the first art form whose artistic character is entirely determined by its reproducibility" (109).

2. Giorgio Agamben, *Infancy and History: On the Destruction of Experience*, trans. Liz Heron (London: Verso, 2007), 154, 156.

3. The title of this book plays on the title of Comolli and Narboni's essay. The goal of this book is, in some sense, to continue their legacy. But rather than focusing on the critique of ideology, the approach emphasized in this book affirms the politics of cinema through philosophy. Philosophy and politics are not in opposition to criticism and ideology. Philosophy here means, rather, a step that goes beyond the criticism or the critique of ideology. This additional step is an affirmation or a new possibility that emerges out of a critique of ideology but is never reducible to it. This book therefore advocates for the persistence of ideology critique, analyzing the way configurations of race and gender, class and property relations are transformed into common images and common sense. But philosophy does not stop there but affirms the existence of something that does not correspond to this world. And philosophy therefore views cinema as not only ideological (though it is that too) but also political—politics understood (pace Comolli and Narboni) as not a synonym for ideology but its opposite, as, to borrow a phrase from Badiou, that which "punctures a hole" in ideology.

4. Jean-Louis Comolli and Jean Narboni, "Cinema/Ideology/Criticism," trans. Daniel Fairfax, in Jean-Louis Comolli, *Cinema Against Spectacle: Technique and Ideology Revisited* (Amsterdam: Amsterdam University Press, 2015), 253.

5. Laura Mulvey, "Visual Pleasure and Narrative Cinema," in *Narrative, Apparatus, Ideology*, ed. Philip Rosen (New York: Columbia University Press, 1986), 198.

6. Christian Metz, *The Imaginary Signifier: Psychoanalysis and the Cinema*, trans. Celia Britton, Annwyl Williams, Ben Brewster, and Alfred Guzzetti (Bloomington: Indianan University Press, 1982), 3.

7. It is important to note that Metz attempted to develop a descriptive (as opposed to normative) theory and his work was not explicitly political. Nonetheless, his formula that the symbolic should be wrested from the imaginary aptly summarizes the goals of much Marxist film theory despite Metz's reticence about bringing his own work in this direction.

8. As Lacan himself put it, "The structures of society are symbolic." See *Écrits*, trans. Bruce Fink (New York: Norton, 2006), 108. It was by way of Althusser, however, that Lacan's concept of the symbolic was used for ideology critique.

9. Pier Paolo Pasolini, *Heretical Empiricism*, trans. Ben Lawton and Louise K. Barnett (Bloomington: Indiana University Press, 1988), 197.

10. For Althusser's conception of the "knowledge effect," see Louis Althusser and Étienne Balibar, *Reading Capital* (New York: Verso, 1997), 62.

11. For the way that the auteur cinema celebrated by an earlier generation of cinephiles manages to, in effect, say what it does not want to say, see in particular Editors of *Cahiers du Cinéma*, "John Ford's *Young Mr. Lincoln*," trans. Helen Lackner and Diana Matias, in Rosen, *Narrative, Apparatus, Ideology*, 444–482. For an influential example of an analysis of oppositional or "counter-cinema" in this mode, see Peter Wollen, "Godard and Counter-Cinema: *Vent D'est*," reprinted in the same volume, 120–129.

12. The often-cited statement is from a line of dialogue in *La Chinoise* (Godard, 1967) that has its origins in what was then a recent essay by a young Maoist student of Althusser, Alain Badiou, called "The Autonomy of the Aesthetic Process." See "The Autonomy of the Aesthetic Process," in *The Age of the Poets, and Other Writings on Twentieth-Century Poetry and Prose*, trans. Emily Apter and Bruno Bosteels (London: Verso, 2014), 111–131.

13. A thorough accounting of the relationship between "cultural studies" and seventies film theory is beyond the scope of this book. Nonetheless, it is worth noting that while certain tendencies in cultural studies can be seen as a continuation of seventies film theory, as Mary Ann Doane has analyzed, the way that cultural studies sometimes rejected theory bore affinities to "post-theory," despite their mutual antagonism. Here is Doane: "In its commitment to the local and the context driven, if not in its constant appeal to political immediacy, cultural studies shares with Post-Theory an aversion to the abstraction and perceived totalization or systematization of theoretical constructs. The strategy of localization also entails a certain proliferation of objects that are presumed to be 'out there,' just waiting to be studied (many of which, for cul-

tural studies, are located in the domain of popular culture). Both tendencies embrace a certain Taylorization of knowledge production in their appeal to the soluble problem, the answerable question, the usable thesis. All of this is at the expense of speculation." "The Object of Theory," in *Rites of Realism: Essays on Corporeal Cinema*, ed. Ivone Margulies (Durham, N.C.: Duke University Press, 2002), 82.

14. The most well known is probably *Post-Theory*, discussed below. See also Noël Carroll, *Mystifying Movies* (New York: Columbia University Press, 1988). These books should probably be understood within the broader context of debates about theory across the humanities as well as the even broader context of the so-called culture wars. In a less combative tone, see, for example, D. N. Rodowick's *The Crisis of Political Modernism* (Berkeley: University of California Press, 1994) or Christine Gledhill and Linda Williams's *Reinventing Film Studies* (London: Arnold, 2000). These latter books are in critical dialogue with the period of seventies film theory and situate it, not dismiss it. My work could be seen as part of this project. If I choose these two titles as examples, it is because I think that the words "crisis" and "reinventing" are symptomatic of not only trends in publishing but the perceived state of film studies after the demise of the cachet of high theory.

15. For a discussion of the historical turn in film studies, see, for example, Sumiko Higashi, "In-Focus: Film History, or a Baedeker Guide to the Historical Turn," *Cinema Journal* 44, no. 1 (2004): 94–100; or, in a more critical mode, Jane Gaines, "What Happened to the Philosophy of Film History?," *Film History* 25, nos. 1–2 (2013): 70–80.

16. See David Bordwell and Noël Carroll, eds., *Post-Theory: Reconstructing Film Studies* (Madison: University of Wisconsin Press, 1996). Bordwell and Carroll refer to "the Theory" as "top-down," "homogeneous," "univocal," etc. If I use Metz's statement to unite "seventies film theory," it is not to support these characterizations. Rather, I wish to isolate a tendency that I believe connects a complex range of material within which there were internal divisions and debates.

17. David Bordwell, "Never the Twain Shall Meet," *Film Comment*, May/June 2011: http://www.filmcomment.com/article/never-the-twain-shall-meet/.

18. An influential book in the return to phenomenology in American film studies is Vivian Sobchack, *Address of the Eye: A Phenomenology of Film Experience* (Princeton, N.J.: Princeton University Press, 1992). Deleuze's *Cinema 1* is likely the main source for a renewed interest in Bergson, though not all current Bergsonian theories of the image are strictly Deleuzian. For Deleuze and questions of the body, see chapter 2. These trends, along with more classical approaches to aesthetics and ethics, get folded into the new market for readers on film and philosophy. See the readers *Thinking Through Cinema: Film as Philosophy,* ed. Murray Smith and Thomas E. Wartenberg (Oxford: Blackwell, 2006), *Philosophy of Film Motion Pictures*, ed. Noël Carroll and Jinhee Choi (Malden, Mass.: Blackwell, 2005), and *Film Theory and Philosophy*, ed. Richard Allen and Murray Smith (Oxford: Oxford University Press, 1999). For overviews on the "philosophical turn," see *New Philosophies of Film: Thinking Images*, by Robert Sinnerbrink (New York: Continuum, 2011) and *Refractions of Reality: Philosophy and the Moving Image*, by John Mullarkey (New York: Palgrave, 2008). For the

return to Jean Epstein, see the fine collection *Jean Epstein: Critical Essays and New Translations*, ed. Sarah Keller and Jason N. Paul (Amsterdam: Amsterdam University Press, 2012). As for Bazin, a rich and provocative reappraisal of his work can be found in Philip Rosen, *Change Mummified* (Minneapolis: University of Minnesota Press, 2000). See also *Opening Bazin: Postwar Film Theory and Its Afterlife*, ed. Dudley Andrew with Herve Joubert-Laurencin (Oxford: Oxford University Press, 2011).

19.   Dudley Andrew, Anton Kaes, Sarah Keller, Stuart Liebman, Annette Michelson, and Malcolm Turvey, "Roundtable on the Return to Classical Film Theory," *October* 148 (Spring 2014): 22.

20.   For a brilliant example of this more expansive theory of mediation, see John Durham Peters, *The Marvelous Clouds: Toward a Philosophy of Elemental Media* (Chicago: University of Chicago Press, 2015).

21.   See, for example, much of the field of new media studies that concentrates on moving images, including Lev Manovich, *The Language of New Media* (Cambridge, Mass.: MIT Press, 1998), and Mark Hansen, *New Philosophy for New Media* (Cambridge, Mass.: MIT Press, 2006). See also the influential work of Bernard Stiegler and Friedrich Kittler. Gertrud Koch argues that the approach which takes technology to play much the same role that structuralists accorded to language can be traced to Heidegger. Here is her gloss on this premise of much New Media theory: "Technology encompasses the idea of technē in the sense that at its base it is not only a tool for constructing objects *in* the world but also a construction *of* a world in the radical sense that Martin Heidegger read the Aristotelian conception of technē." Gertrud Koch, "Carnivore or Chameleon: The Fate of Cinema Studies," *Critical Inquiry*, Summer 2009, 921.

22.   One notable exception is Eugenie Brinkema's *The Forms of the Affects* (Durham, N.C.: Duke University Press, 2014). Her emphasis on textual form is in conjunction with a critique of the abandonment of form in the vast majority of what counts as "affect theory."

23.   In a sense, we might identify this as a kind of turn to the spectator with a new emphasis on the body, perception, and affection from Deleuzians and neo-phenomenologists, or perception and cognitive processing from cognitivists. The "subject" in seventies film theory referred not to an empirical spectator but rather to how the subject was positioned or interpellated by the apparatus or dispositif of cinema. It was an effect of the film text or film work and its cultural and economic conditions. It should be added that Deleuze himself makes no mention of spectators. In his writings, affects and percepts are not presented in reference to either empirical or transcendental spectators. For the difference between Deleuze's cinema books and certain tendencies in Deleuzian film theory, see chapter 2.

24.   See Carroll, *Mystifying Movies*.

25.   Jacques Rancière, *The Politics of Aesthetics: The Distribution of the Sensible*, trans. Gabriel Rockhill (New York: Continuum, 2004), 34.

26.   In the famous passage from chapter 1 of *Capital Volume One*, Marx states, "A commodity appears as first sight an extremely obvious, trivial thing. But its analysis brings out that it is a very strange thing, abounding in metaphysical subtleties and theologi-

cal niceties." Karl Marx, *Capital Volume One: A Critique of Political Economy*, trans. Ben Fowkes (New York: Vintage, 1977), 163.

27. While Žižek is the most well-known figure, here it is worth mentioning writings by Joan Copjec, Todd McGowan, Mladen Dolar, and Alenka Zupančič, among others, who, in recent decades, have used Lacan to theorize film in a way that goes well beyond the almost exclusive focus on "The Mirror Stage as Formative of the I Function" that tended to mark the engagement with Lacan in seventies film theory.

28. Žižek, *The Fright of Real Tears: Krzysztof Kieślowski Between Theory and Post-Theory* (London: BFI, 2001), 1.

29. In addition to Žižek's *Fright of Real Tears*, other important critical assessments of post-theory include D. N. Rodowick's *Philosophy's Artful Conversation* (Cambridge, Mass.: Harvard University Press, 2015) and Francesco Casetti's "Theory, Post-theory, Neo-theories: Changes in Discourses, Changes in Objects," *Cinémas: Revue d'études cinématographiques/Cinémas: Journal of Film Studies* 17, nos. 2–3 (2007): 33–45.

30. Rodowick, *Crisis of Political Modernism*, 274.

31. Rodowick, xiv.

32. See David Bordwell, "Slavoj Zizek: Say Anything," April 2005, http://www.davidbordwell.net/essays/zizek.php. See also Malcolm Turvey, "Theory, Philosophy, and Film Studies: A Response to D. N. Rodowick's 'An Elegy for Theory,'" *October* 122 (Fall 2007): 114; and Carroll in *Post-Theory*, 46–47.

33. Rodowick, *Elegy for Theory* (Cambridge, Mass.: Harvard University Press, 2014), 100.

34. See Stephen Best and Sharon Marcus, "Surface Reading: An Introduction," *Representations* 108 (2009): 1–23.

35. For an interesting argument about why object-oriented philosophy has so far had less success in film studies than in other fields in the humanities, see Luka Arsenjuk, "On the Impossibility of Object-Oriented Film Theory," *Discourse* 38, no. 2 (Spring 2016): 197–214.

36. Bruno Latour, "Why Has Critique Run Out of Steam? From Matters of Fact to Matters of Concern," *Critical Inquiry* 30, no. 2 (Winter 2004): 225–248.

37. Rancière, "The Gaps of Cinema," trans. Walter van der Star, http://www.necsus-ejms.org/the-gaps-of-cinema-by-jacques-ranciere/. See also Rancière, *The Intervals of Cinema*, trans. John Howe (London: Verso, 2014), 5. Here I have used van der Star's translation, which, in this instance at least, provides, in my view, a more accurate rendering of the original than John Howe's translation.

38. The statement that "tracking shots are a question of morality" is often attributed to Godard. He made the comment in a 1959 roundtable discussion of *Hiroshima Mon Amour* in *Cahiers du Cinéma*. See *Cahiers du Cinéma, the 1950s: Neo-realism, Hollywood, New Wave*, ed. Jim Hiller (Cambridge, Mass.: Harvard University Press, 1985), 62. Godard was reformulating a statement made by Luc Moullet. For more detail, see Antoine de Baecque, *La Cinephilie: Invention d'un regard, histoire d'une culture (1944–1968)* (Paris: Fayard, 2003), 206–209.

39. Theorists influenced by the analytic tradition sometimes use Gilbert Ryle's notion of "category mistake" as a charge against claims that blur different spheres of thought.

40. Rancière, "Gaps of Cinema."

1. CINEMATIC EQUALITY

1. Warren Montag's *Althusser and His Contemporaries: Philosophy's Perpetual War* (Durham, N.C.: Duke University Press, 2013) makes a compelling case that the influence of both structuralism and Lacanian psychoanalysis has tended to be exaggerated in readings of Althusser. Instead, Montag emphasizes, for example, the influence of Spinoza rather than Lacan on Althusser's use of the term "imaginary." I find Montag's analysis largely convincing, though I believe he may underestimate the role Lacan plays for Althusser for the purpose of demonstrating the neglected importance of Spinoza in Althusser's work. Either way, Lacan and structuralism were undeniably central to the reading of Althusser that became orthodoxy in film theory. My central concern is less Althusser's body of work as a whole than Althusserianism in film studies—how a few key texts by Althusser were used by film critics (who were frequently not academics) to bring together Marxist critique, Lacanian psychoanalysis, and structuralism.

2. The other three were Étienne Balibar, Roger Establet, and Pierre Macherey.

3. See in particular *The Philosopher and His Poor,* trans. John Drury, Corinne Oster, and Andrew Parker (Durham, N.C.: Duke University Press, 2004) and *Hatred of Democracy,* trans. Steven Corcoran (London: Verso, 2006).

4. See Rancière, *Disagreement: Politics and Philosophy,* trans. Julie Rose (Minneapolis: Minnesota University Press, 1998), 32. "What makes an action political is . . . the form in which confirmation of equality is inscribed in the setting up of a dispute."

5. Rancière, *Disagreement,* 77.

6. Peter Hallward, in his essay "Staging Equality: On Rancière's Theatocracy" (*New Left Review* 37 [January/February 2006]: 109–129), notes and critiques the importance of the theatrical metaphor in Rancière's political thought. Leaving aside Hallward's broader concerns, I just want to note here that I think it is a mistake to think that Rancière accords a privileged place to theater in particular and that the metaphor of "staging" is only one of the metaphors from various artistic realms that Rancière uses to think the aesthetics of politics.

7. Rancière no longer uses the term "ideology" and would reject the notion that "le partage du sensible" (the distribution of the sensible) is a synonym for "ideology." As I will show over the course of this chapter, while I do not consider the words synonyms exactly, I do think we can think of "the distribution of the sensible" as a kind of reconceptualization of what Althusser meant by "ideology."

8. Rancière, "The Aesthetic Revolution and Its Outcomes," *New Left Review* 14 (March/April 2002): 151.

9. Hal Foster, "Post-Critical," *October* 139 (Winter 2012): 6.

10. Louis Althusser, "On Brecht and Marx," trans. Max Statkiewicz, appendix to *Louis Althusser (Transitions),* by Warren Montag (New York: Palgrave, 2003), 141.

11. Althusser, "On Brecht and Marx," 141.

12. Althusser, 142.

13. Althusser, 145.

14. Althusser, "A Letter on Art," in *Lenin and Philosophy and Other Essays*, trans. Ben Brewster (New York: Monthly Review Press, 1971), 223.

15. Althusser, "A Letter on Art," 224.

16. Althusser, "The Humanist Controversy," in *The Humanist Controversy and Other Writings (1966–67)*, ed. François Matheron, trans. G. M. Goshgarian (London: Verso, 2003), 232.

17. Althusser, "Marxism and Humanism," in *For Marx*, trans. Ben Brewster (London: Verso, 2005), 223.

18. Althusser, "Ideology and Ideological State Apparatuses: Notes Towards an Investigation," in *Lenin and Philosophy*, 162.

19. Metz, *The Imaginary Signifier*, 3.

20. Peter Wollen, "'Ontology' and 'Materialism' in Film," *Screen* 17, no. 1 (1976): 18–19.

21. Wollen, "'Ontology' and 'Materialism,'" 17.

22. Jean-Louis Baudry, "Ideological Effects of the Basic Cinematographic Apparatus," in *Narrative, Apparatus, Ideology*, ed. Philip Rosen (New York: Columbia University Press, 1986), 295–296. The concept of the "film work" was often used in analogy to Freud's concept of the dream work to refer to the formal methods of encoding the repressed content. See, for example, Thierry Kuntzel, "The Film-Work," *Enclitic* 2, no. 1 (Spring 1978): 38–61.

23. Baudry, "Ideological Effects," 296.

24. Jean-Louis Comolli and Jean Narboni, "Cinema/Ideology/Criticism," trans. Daniel Fairfax, in *Cinema Against Spectacle: Technique and Ideology Revisited* (Amsterdam: Amsterdam University Press, 2015), 254.

25. Philip Rosen, "Screen and 70s Film Theory," in *Inventing Film Studies*, ed. Lee Grieveson and Haidee Wasson (Durham, N.C.: Duke University Press 2008), 272.

26. C. Wright Mills, *The Sociological Imagination* (Oxford: Oxford University Press, 1959), 25–49.

27. Bordwell, "Film Studies and Grand Theory," in Bordwell and Carroll, *Post-Theory*, 18–26.

28. Jean-François Lyotard, *The Postmodern Condition: A Report on Knowledge*, trans. Geoff Bennington and Brian Massumi (Minneapolis: University of Minnesota Press, 1984), xxiv.

29. Rosen, "Screen and 70s Film Theory," 264–265.

30. Comolli and Narboni, "Cinema/Ideology/Criticism," 253.

31. Comolli and Narboni, 256.

32. As Daniel Fairfax points out in the introduction to his revised translation to "Cinema/Ideology/Criticism," Comolli and Narboni never actually used the phrase "scientific criticism," despite it appearing in the widely anthologized and cited English translation of the essay by Susan Bennett. They distinguished themselves from *Cinéthique*, which did use that phrase. Nonetheless, whether or not we call it "scientific" (as many who read Bennett's translation did), the Marxist criticism they advocated did become the basis for a new kind of theoretically rigorous criticism that challenged ideology.

33. Mulvey, "Visual Pleasure and Narrative Cinema," in Rosen, *Narrative, Apparatus, Ideology*, 199.

34. Mulvey, 203.

35. Mulvey, 200.

36. Mulvey, 209.

37. Mulvey, 200.

38. Mulvey, 199.

39. Mulvey, 208.

40. Mulvey, 200.

41. Mulvey, 200.

42. Laura Mulvey and Peter Wollen with Lee Grieveson, "From Cinephilia to Film Studies," in Grieveson and Wasson, *Inventing Film Studies*, 228.

43. Mulvey, "Visual Pleasure," 207.

44. Friedrich Kittler, *Optical Media: Berlin Lectures 1999*, trans. Anthony Enns (Cambridge: Polity, 2010), 148.

45. Brinkema, *Forms of the Affects*, 26.

46. Brinkema, 29, 27.

47. Bordwell, "Slavoj Zizek."

48. Bordwell's most in-depth analysis of the relationship between theory and interpretation in film criticism can be found in *Making Meaning: Inference and Rhetoric in the Interpretation of Cinema* (Cambridge, Mass: Harvard University Press, 1991).

49. David Bordwell, *Figures Traced in Light* (Berkeley: University of California Press, 2005), 265.

50. Wollen, "Godard and Counter-Cinema," 122.

51. See Bordwell, "Slavoj Zizek."

52. Jacques Rancière, *Dissensus: On Politics and Aesthetics*, trans. Steven Corcoran. (London: Continuum, 2010), 147.

53. Jacques Rancière, *Aesthetics and Its Discontents*, trans. Steven Corcoran (Malden, Mass.: Polity, 2009), 6.

54. Jacques Rancière, "The Politics of Literature," *SubStance* 33, no. 1 (2004): 10.

55. Rancière, 10.

56. Jacques Rancière, "Identifications of the People," in *Dissenting Words: Interviews with Jacques Rancière*, ed. and trans. Emiliano Battista (London: Bloomsbury, 2017), 167.

57. For the most thoroughgoing articulation of this critique of modernism, see Jacques Rancière, *Aisthesis: Scenes from the Aesthetic Regime of Art*, trans. Zakir Paul (London: Verso, 2013).

58. Jacques Rancière, *The Future of the Image*, trans. Gregory Elliott (London: Verso, 2007), 123.

59. Georg Wilhelm Friedrich Hegel, *Aesthetics: Lectures on Fine Art, Volume 1*, trans. T. M. Knox (Oxford: Oxford University Press, 1975), 605.

60. I briefly discussed Hal Foster's essay "Post-Critical" earlier in this chapter.

61. Althusser, "Ideology and Ideological State Apparatuses," 174.

62. Althusser, 127–186, esp. 174–175.

63. Rancière, *Disagreement*, 28.

64. Jacques Rancière, "Politics, Identification, and Subjectivization," *October* 61 (1992): 58–64.

65. Jacques Rancière, "Ten Theses on Politics," *Theory & Event* 5, no. 3 (2001), https://muse .jhu.edu/article/32639 (accessed May 6, 2018).

66. Jacques Rancière, "The Aesthetic Dimension: Aesthetics, Politics, Knowledge," *Critical Inquiry* 36 (Autumn 2009): 11.

67. Rancière, "Politics, Identification, and Subjectivization," 60.

68. Rancière, *Disagreement*, x.

69. To seriously address Spivak's concept of the subaltern is beyond the scope of this book. For now I wish to note that she later modified her original claim that the subaltern *cannot* speak. See Gayatri Chakravorty Spivak, *A Critique of Postcolonial Reason: Toward a History of the Vanishing Present* (Cambridge: Harvard University Press, 1999), 308.

70. Jacques Rancière, *The Ignorant Schoolmaster: Five Lessons in Intellectual Emancipation*, trans. Kristin Ross (Stanford: Stanford University Press, 1991), 138.

71. It is worth mentioning that there is a sometimes a misunderstanding of Lacan's devaluation of the imaginary that pervades the accusation that Lacan's work enforces a tyranny of the signifier. The imaginary is a negative term only to the extent that it is conceived without supplement or lack, as long the imaginary's fragmentation and heterogeneity are ignored. For Lacan, the imaginary tends toward a fictional unity, but is always marked by its own failure. The imaginary's difference from itself is precisely what it attested to by the symbolic and the real.

72. Rancière, *Disagreement*, 114.

73. Noël Burch, "The Sadeian Aesthetic," in *The Philistine Controversy*, ed. Dave Beech and John Roberts (London: Verso, 2002), 193.

74. Rancière, *Politics of Aesthetics*, 57.

75. Rancière, 40.

76. Rancière, *Disagreement*, 104.

77. Jacques Rancière, *La Parole Ouvrière* (Paris: La Fabrique, 1976), 19.

78. Jacques Rancière, "The Misadventures of Critical Thought," in *Emancipated Spectator*, trans. Gregory Elliott (London: Verso, 2009), 48.

79. Rancière, "Misadventures of Critical Thought," 49.

80. Althusser, *Lenin and Philosophy*, 184.

81. See Carroll, "Prospects for Film Theory," in Bordwell and Carroll, *Post-Theory*, 61.

82. Althusser, *Reading Capital*, 142–143.

83. Althusser, 22.

84. Jacques Rancière, *The Flesh of Words: The Politics of Writing*, trans. Charlotte Mandell (Stanford, Calif.: Stanford University Press, 2004), 132.

85. Rancière, *Flesh of Words*, 133.

86. Rancière, 135.

87. Rancière, 136.

88. Rancière, *Politics of Aesthetics*, 34.

89. See, for example, Slavoj Žižek, "You May!," *London Review of Books* 21, no. 6 (March 18, 1999): 3–6.

90. Metz, *Imaginary Signifier*, 48.

91. Walter Benjamin, "Little History of Photography," in *The Work of Art in the Age of Its Technological Reproducibility*, ed. Michael W. Jennings, Brigid Doherty, and Thomas Y. Levin (Cambridge, Mass.: Harvard University Press, 2008), 276.

92. Jean Epstein quoted in Jacques Rancière, *Film Fables*, trans. Emiliano Battista (New York: Berg, 2006), 1.

93. Rancière, *Film Fables*, 2.

94. Rancière, 25.

95. André Bazin, *What Is Cinema?*, trans. Timothy Barnard (Montreal: Caboose, 2009), 8.

96. Hugo Munsterberg, *The Film: A Psychological Study* (New York: Dover, 1970), 58.

97. Rancière, *Film Fables*, 8.

98. Rancière, 8.

99. Rancière, 9.

100. Mary Ann Doane, *The Emergence of Cinematic Time: Modernity, Contingency, the Archive* (Cambridge, Mass.: Harvard University Press, 2002), 178.

101. Rancière, *Film Fables*, 10.

102. Jacques Rancière, "The Life and Death of the Artist," in *Chronicles of Consensual Times*, trans. Steven Corcoran (London: Bloomsbury, 2010), 102.

103. Rancière, "Life and Death of the Artist," 31.

104. Rancière, 19.

105. See David Bordwell, *Narration in the Fiction Film* (Madison: University of Wisconsin Press, 1985).

106. See Benjamin, "Work of Art," and Rudolf Arnheim, "The Sad Future of Film" (1930), reprinted in Arnheim, *Film Essays and Criticism*, trans. Brenda Benthien (Madison: University of Wisconsin Press, 1997).

107. Rancière, *Film Fables*, 11.

108. Rancière, 19.

109. Rancière, 5.

110. Jacques Rancière, *Mute Speech*, trans. James Swenson (New York: Columbia University Press, 2011), 31.

111. Rancière, *Intervals of Cinema*, 7.

2. CINEMA'S THOUGHT

1. See, for example, Gilles Deleuze, "What Is a Creative Act?," in *Two Regimes of Madness: Texts and Interviews 1975–1995* (New York: Columbia University Press, 2006), 312–324.

2. Alain Badiou, *Cinema*, ed. Antoine de Baecque, trans. Susan Spitzer (Malden, Mass.: Polity, 2013), 123.

3. The most obvious example of this backlash came in the form of the popularity of the so-called *Nouveaux Philosophes* or New Philosophers. This group of media savvy anti-Marxists (at least some of whom were former Marxists), which included André Glucksmann and Bernard-Henri Lévy, shared a rejection of the so-called pensée soixante huitarde.

4. Though Badiou is a defender of philosophy, many of the figures he most admires fall under his category of anti-philosophers—Lacan, Wittgenstein, Nietzsche, and Pascal, for example. The anti-philosopher constitutes a more worthy opponent than the figures Badiou dubs "sophists." It should be noted that for different reasons than Badiou, Rancière also prefers the word "philosophy" to theory.

5. See Alain Badiou, "The Flux and the Party," *Polygraph* 15/16 (2005). For a more nuanced but perhaps even more controversial critique of Deleuze by Badiou written in a rather different context and idiom, see *Deleuze: The Clamor of Being*, trans. Louise Burchill (Minneapolis: University of Minnesota Press, 2000).

6. Gilles Deleuze, *Cinema 2: The Time-Image*, trans. Hugh Tomlinson and Robert Galeta (Minneapolis: University of Minnesota Press, 1989), 280.

7. Alain Badiou, "Cinema as Democratic Emblem," trans. Alan Ling and Aurelien Mondon, *Parrhesia* no. 6 (2009): 1.

8. Alain Badiou, "The False Movements of Cinema," in *Handbook of Inaesthetics*, trans. Alberto Toscano (Stanford: Stanford University Press, 2005), 83. Stupidity, for Lacan, it should be made clear, is not a bad thing, as is argued, for example, by Dany Nobus and Malcolm Quinn in *Knowing Nothing, Staying Stupid* (London: Routledge, 2005). Badiou himself is not scornful of "opinions"; he considers them necessary but not the province of philosophy.

9. Badiou, "False Movements of Cinema," 84.

10. Badiou, *Logic of Worlds: Being and Event II*, trans. Alberto Toscano (London: Continuum, 2009), 1.

11. Badiou takes the concept of a "non-relation" from Lacan as a relation defined by difference without any form of synthesis in the faux-Hegelian sense. This is how Badiou interprets Lacan's famous formula, "There is no sexual relation." In the Maoist language of Badiou's youth, it is a relation in which two does not make one. In Deleuze's terms, we could call it a "disjunctive synthesis."

12. See *Handbook of Inaesthetics*, 3–4. Badiou highlights two other possible schemata that link art to philosophy that also have their academic variants. One is the didactic schema, which follows Plato's lead in treating art as incapable of truth but of value to the extent that it can educate in truths external to art. Unlike "aesthetic regionalism," art is treated no longer as an object of knowledge but rather as an instrument for knowledge. Finally, the romantic schema assumes *only* art is capable of truth. Here we say that knowledge of art is limited in importance compared to our ability to appreciate it.

13. Badiou, *Handbook of Inaesthetics*, 85.

14. See Bordwell and Carroll, *Post-Theory*.

15. Gledhill and Williams, *Reinventing Film Studies*, 5.

16. These statistics are based on my own survey on Amazon.com.

17. Mulvey, "Visual Pleasure and Narrative Cinema," 198.

18. Brinkema, *Forms of the Affects*, 31.

19. Lacan, *Écrits*, 76.

20. Baudry, "Ideological Effects," 296.

21. See, for example, Peter Wollen's "The Two Avant-Gardes," *Studio International*, November/December 1975, or the various debates between *Positif*, *Cahiers du Cinéma*, and *Cinéthique*. For the English reader, a good introduction to these debates can be found in Sylvia Harvey, *May '68 and Film Culture* (London: BFI, 1978).

22. Gilles Deleuze, *Cinema 1: The Movement-Image*, trans. Hugh Tomlinson and Barbara Haberjam (Minneapolis: University of Minnesota Press, 1991), x. From this perspective, it is interesting to consider that Deleuze never mentions Guy Debord or Chris Marker.

23. Agamben, *Infancy and History*, 153.

24. Gilles Deleuze, *Negotiations 1972–1990*, trans. Martin Joughin (New York: Columbia University Press, 1995), 65.

25. Deleuze, *Cinema 1*, 56.

26. See Gilles Deleuze, *Essays Critical and Clinical*, trans. Daniel W. Smith and Michael A. Greco (Minneapolis: University of Minnesota Press, 1997), 168.

27. See Deleuze, *Cinema 2*, 27–30.

28. Bertolt Brecht, *Brecht on Theater*, trans. John Willett (New York: Hill & Wang, 1992), 192.

29. Antonin Artaud, *The Theater and Its Double*, trans. Mary Caroline Richards (New York: Grove, 1958), 90.

30. Artaud, *Theater and Its Double*, 98.

31. Artaud, 126.

32. Jean-Luc Nancy, "The Deleuzian Fold of Thought," in *Deleuze: A Critical Reader*, ed. Paul Patton (Oxford: Blackwell, 1996), 110.

33. Nancy, "Deleuzian Fold of Thought," 111.

34. Deleuze, *Cinema 1*, 59.

35. See, for example, Patricia Pisters, *The Matrix of Visual Culture: Working with Deleuze in Film Theory* (Stanford: Stanford University Press, 2003). "With respect to film theory, I hope to have shown concretely that with Deleuze a new wind is blowing. . . . Deleuze's conception of cinema as a pure semiotics of movement, sound, and images offers an alternative for the traditional conception of images as representations or as language systems. The increasing digitalization of the audiovisual seriously jeopardizes the ontologic argument of photographic analogy. . . . In traditional representational thinking, this confusion leads to panic. . . . Deleuze's Bersonian/Peircian semiotics demonstrates that there is no reason to panic" (216–217). Pisters adds that "Deleuze confined himself strictly to the masterpieces of cinema history" (8) but that she will take him to "unknown territories"—in other words, "more popular and commercial cinema" (8).

See also Barbara M. Kennedy, *Deleuze and Cinema: The Aesthetics of Sensation* (Edinburgh: Edinburgh University Press, 2000). At the beginning of the new millennium, she says, "We need to rethink a post-semiotic space, a post-linguistic space, which provides new ways of understanding the screenic experience as a complex web of inter-relationalities. The look is never purely visual, but also tactile, sensory, material and embodied" (3).

Or see Steven Shaviro, *The Cinematic Body* (Minneapolis: University of Minnesota Press, 1993), who looks to Deleuze and Guattari because "the psychoanalytic model for film theory is at this point utterly bankrupt; it needs . . . to be discarded" (ix). He also insists that we must think of "bodies and pleasures" without reference to "language, signification and representation" if we wish to grasp "postmodern cinematic practice."

Shaviro, it must be noted, later reevaluated the position he took in his first book. See his very illuminating retrospective self-criticism "The Cinematic Body Redux" posted on his website: http://www.shaviro.com/Othertexts/Cinematic.pdf.

36. Why certain artists are thought to be Deleuzian but bear little relation to the artists Deleuze himself favored is an interesting subject for further research. In some cases, the "unfaithful" use of Deleuze has produced very interesting work. Laura U. Marks's *The Skin of the Film* (Durham, N.C.: Duke University Press, 1999), which focuses on a range of third-world diasporic filmmakers and video artists such as Walid Ra'ad and Rea Tajiri, is one encouraging exception to some of the more unfortunate trends in Deleuzian film theory. Kara Keeling's excellent *The Witch's Flight: The Cinematic, the Black Femme, and the Image of Common Sense* (Durham, N.C.: Duke University Press, 2007) also provides an original and surprising use of Deleuze that puts him in contact with Fanon and Gramsci, with feminism and queer theory, and shows his relevance for both popular and more avant-garde black cinema.

37. András Bálint Kovács, "The Film History of Thought," trans. Sandor Hervey, in *The Brain Is the Screen*, ed. Gregory Flaxman (Minneapolis: University of Minnesota Press, 2000), 166.

38. Gilles Deleuze, "Letter to Serge Daney: Optimism, Pessimism, Travel," in *Negotiations*, 68.

39. Deleuze, "Letter to Serge Daney," 68–69.

40. Deleuze, *Cinema 1*, 13.

41. Deleuze, "Letter to Serge Daney," 72.

42. The coining of the term "data-image" has been credited to Kenneth C. Laudon in *Dossier Society: Value Choices in the Design of National Information Systems* (New York: Columbia University Press, 1986). I did not have Laudon in mind when I chose this term, but his use of it is consonant with my understanding of Deleuze and Daney's third regime of cinema images.

43. Deleuze, "Letter to Serge Daney," 75.

44. Deleuze, *Cinema 2*, 136.

45. Deleuze, "Letter to Serge Daney," 75.

46. Gilles Deleuze, "Postscript on Control Societies," in *Negotiations*, 179.

47. See Deleuze, "Letter to Serge Daney," 68–79.

48. Deleuze, 76.

49. Gilles Deleuze and Félix Guattari, *What Is Philosophy?*, trans. Hugh Tomlinson and Graham Burchell (New York: Columbia University Press, 1994), 12.

50. Deleuze, *Cinema 2*, 265.

51. Deleuze, 266.

52. Daniel Frampton, *Filmosophy: A Manifesto for a Radically New Way of Understanding Cinema* (London: Wallflower Press, 2006), 169.

53. Frampton, *Filmosophy*, 175.

54. Frampton, 174.

55. Jacques Rancière, "Contemporary Art and the Politics of Aesthetics," in *Communities of Sense: Rethinking Aesthetics and Politics*, ed. Beth Hinderliter, William Kaizen, Vered Maison, Jaleh Mansoor, and Seth McCormick (Durham, N.C.: Duke University Press, 2009), 48.

56. Deleuze, *Cinema 2*, 27.

57. Deleuze, 43. About the time-image, Deleuze says, "To use a formula of Nietzsche's, it is never at the beginning that something new, a new art, is able to reveal its essence; what it was from the outset it can only reveal after a detour in its evolution."

58. Deleuze, 260.

59. See Friedrich Kittler, "The World of the Symbolic," in *Literature, Media, Information Systems*, trans. Stefanie Harris (Amsterdam: G & B Arts, 1997), 130–146. See also Jacques Lacan, *The Ego in Freud's Theory and in the Technique of Psychoanalysis 1954–1955: The Seminar of Jacques Lacan Book II*, trans. Sylvana Tomaselli (New York: Norton, 1991), 294–308.

60. See Deleuze and Guattari, *What Is Philosophy?*, 164.

61. Gilles Deleuze and Claire Parnet, *Dialogues II*, trans. Hugh Tomlinson and Barbara Habberjam (New York: Columbia University Press, 2002), 120.

62. Flaxman, *Brain Is the Screen*, 369.

63. Deleuze opposes the "information table" to the window in various writings. See, for example, *The Fold: Leibniz and the Baroque*, trans. Tom Conley (Minneapolis: University of Minnesota Press, 1992), 27.

64. It should be acknowledged that Deleuze insists that the time-image is *not* privileged over the movement-image. "It cannot be said that one is more important than the other, whether more beautiful or more profound" (*Cinema 2*, 270). But my claim is that the logic of his thought suggests otherwise. When he addresses the specificity of cinema, he says, "But the essence of cinema . . . has thought as his higher purpose, nothing but thought and its functioning" (168), and he goes on to propose that, as Artaud realized early on and Jean-Louis Schefer has articulated, "thought in cinema is brought face to face with its own impossibility" (168) as a result of the change in the image that emerges after the crisis of the movement-image.

65. Deleuze and Guattari, *What Is Philosophy?*, 108.

66. Gilles Deleuze, "Control and Becoming," in *Negotiations*, 174.

67. Gilles Deleuze, *Foucault*, trans. Sean Hand (Minneapolis: University of Minnesota Press, 1988), 89.

68. Deleuze, "What Is a Creative Act?," 320.

69. Deleuze, 322.

70. Alain Badiou, "Fifteen Theses on Contemporary Art," *Lacanian Ink* 23 (2004): 110.

71. Badiou, "Fifteen Theses," 111.

72. Stéphane Mallarmé, *Selected Letters of Stéphane Mallarmé*, ed. and trans. Rosemary Lloyd (Chicago: University of Chicago Press, 1988), 187.

73. The poem is quoted in various places in Badiou's writings. See, for example, the essay "Philosophy and Politics," in Alain Badiou, *Infinite Thought: Truth and the Return to Philosophy*, ed. and trans. Oliver Feltham and Justin Clemens (London: Continuum, 2003), 58.

74. Badiou, *Logic of Worlds*, 1.

75. Alain Badiou, *Ethics: An Essay on the Understanding of Evil*, trans. Peter Hallward (London: Verso, 2001), 12.

76. Badiou, *Cinema*, 233.

77. Peter Hallward, *Badiou: A Subject to Truth* (Saint Paul: University of Minnesota Press, 2003), 193.

78. Alain Badiou, *Manifesto for Philosophy*, trans. Norman Madarasz (Albany: SUNY Press, 1999), 141.

79. Badiou, *Manifesto for Philosophy*, 142.

80. Badiou, 144.

81. Badiou has written a screenplay titled *The Life of Plato* and has expressed his desire to direct it himself with Brad Pitt in the title role.

82. Badiou, *Handbook of Inaesthetics*, xiv.

83. Badiou, xiv.

84. Badiou, *Infinite Thought*, 91.

85. Badiou, 95–96.

86. Badiou, 94.

87. Badiou, 102.

88. Badiou, *Manifesto for Philosophy*, 142.

89. Badiou, 62–63.

90. As Badiou points out, this was also the case of the other great German philosopher of the twentieth century, Wittgenstein.

91. Badiou, *Manifesto for Philosophy*, 74.

92. Badiou, 69.

93. Badiou, 71.

94. Badiou, *Infinite Thought*, 92.

95. Badiou, *Manifesto for Philosophy*, 74.

96. Badiou, *Infinite Thought*, 92.

97. Badiou, 93.

98. Badiou, 93.

99. Alain Badiou, *Being and Event*, trans. Oliver Feltham (New York: Continuum, 2005), 23.

100. Badiou, *Infinite Thought*, 101.

101. Badiou, 101.

102. Badiou claims that Deleuze often tried to "pin on" him the label "Kantian," but he does not go into detail about Deleuze's justification for the criticism. See Badiou, *Deleuze*, 99.

103. Badiou, *Infinite Thought*, 104–105.

104. Badiou, 100. Emphasis in original.

105. Badiou, 104.

106. Badiou, 102.

107. For Lacan, jouissance is not identical to "imaginary captation," but when Badiou speaks of the jouissance of art that must be subtracted from philosophy, he aligns it with the pleasures of narrative, image, and rhythm.

108. See Hallward, *Badiou*, 198.

109. James Knowlson and Elizabeth Knowlson, eds., *Beckett Remembering, Remembering Beckett: A Centenary Celebration* (New York: Arcade, 2006), 47.

110. Alain Badiou, *The Century*, trans. Alberto Toscano (Malden, Mass.: Polity, 2007), 160.

111. Alain Badiou, *Polemics*, trans. Steve Corcoran (London: Verso, 2006), 144.

112. Hallward, *Badiou*, 196.

113. Badiou, "Fifteen Theses," 109.

114. Badiou, 109.

115. Badiou, 103.

116. One example in cinema is what J. Hoberman has identified as the ordeal film. See J. Hoberman, "Quid Est Veritas: The Reality of Unspeakable Suffering," in *Film after Film: or, What Became of 21st Century Cinema?)* (London: Verso, 2012), 27–34. Some examples include Mel Gibson's *The Passion of the Christ*, Steve McQueen's *Hunger* and *12 Years a Slave*, Lars von Trier's *Dogville* and *Dancer in the Dark*, exploitation films like the *Saw* and *Hostage* series, certain Japanese or Korean horror films, and even more commercial films like *United 93* and *127 Hours*. The diegetic ordeal is a physical ordeal, and the spectacle is directed at the suffering or wounded or humiliated body. The ordeal is of course given another form for the spectator, who is in effect dared to watch to anticipate how far the film will go.

117. Badiou, "Fifteen Theses," 105.

118. Badiou, 107.

119. Gilles Deleuze, "Mediators," in *Negotiations*, 132.

120. Badiou, "Fifteen Theses," 107.

121. Badiou, 107.

122. Badiou, 107.

123. Stéphane Mallarmé, "L'Action restreinte," in *Œuvres completes* (Paris, Gallimard, Bibliothèque de la Pléiade, 1945), 372.

124. Badiou, "Fifteen Theses," 107.

125. Badiou, 111.

126. In a later reworking of his Theses on Art, Badiou replaces the word "Empire" with "the West" to distinguish his conceptual framework from Michael Hardt and Toni Negri's concept of "Empire," which had initially inspired his use of the term. See Hardt and Negri, *Empire* (Cambridge, Mass.: Harvard University Press, 2001). I use the word

"Empire" because "the West" seems to open additional confusions considering it seems clear that Badiou means to adopt a generic concept for what he will later, in *Logic of Worlds*, call "democratic materialism," the dominant logic of life in contemporary global capitalism, not confined strictly to the geographic West.

127. Badiou, *Being and Event*, 522. To avoid confusion, "state" does not refer to (or does not refer only to) the state component of a nation-state. Rather, "state" refers to any counted situation that excludes the void.

128. Ludwig Wittgenstein, *Tractatus Logico-Philosophicus*, trans. Paul Kegan (New York: Harcourt Brace, 1922), 189.

129. Badiou, *Being and Event*, 389–409.

130. Badiou, *Handbook of Inaesthetics*, 105.

131. Alain Badiou, *Conditions*, trans. Steve Corcoran (New York: Continuum, 2008), 174.

132. Badiou, *Infinite Thought*, 111.

133. Badiou, "Cinema as Democratic Emblem," 4.

134. Badiou, *Polemics*, 147.

135. Badiou, 148.

136. Badiou, "Cinema as Democratic Emblem," 2.

137. Badiou, *Infinite Thought*, 113.

138. Theodor Adorno and Max Horkheimer, *Dialectic of Enlightenment*, trans. Edmund Jephcott (Stanford: Stanford University Press, 2002), 111.

139. Badiou, *Infinite Thought*, 116–117.

140. Badiou, 114.

141. Badiou, *The Century*, 132.

142. Badiou, *Infinite Thought*, 115.

143. Alain Badiou, "Cinema as Philosophical Experimentation," in *Cinema*, 226.

144. Badiou, *Infinite Thought*, 113.

145. André Bazin, *What Is Cinema?*, trans. Timothy Barnard (Montreal: Caboose, 2009), 107–137.

146. Badiou, "Cinema as a Democratic Emblem," 1.

147. Badiou, 2.

148. Alain Badiou, "Surplus Seeing: *Histoire(s) Du Cinema*," in *Cinema*, 137.

149. Alain Badiou, "Dialectics of the Fable: *The Matrix*," in *Cinema*, 201.

150. Badiou, "Cinema as a Democratic Emblem," 3.

151. Alain Badiou, *Second Manifesto for Philosophy*, trans. Louise Burchill (Malden, MA: Polity, 2011), 121–122.

152. Badiou, "Cinema as Philosophical Experimentation," 216.

153. Badiou, *Cinema*, 236, translation modified.

154. Badiou, 213.

155. Badiou, 89.

156. Theodor Adorno, "Transparencies on Film," in *The Culture Industry: Selected Essays on Mass Culture*, ed. J. M. Bernstein, trans. Thomas Y. Levin (London: Routledge, 1991), 157. Adorno's assumption is that film is "primarily representational" and that this is "the retarding aspect of film in the historical process of art." But more interestingly,

he proposes that this limitation is also intrinsic to film's potential as an art: "The aesthetics of film is thus inherently concerned with society" (157).

157. Painting, like music, has never been considered the same kind of threat to film's autonomy as an art. Commercial cinema has of course relied heavily on narrative, as well as theatrical and literary conventions, which is one reason that, like music, painting has played an important role in much cinema that is identified as avant-garde.

158. Manovich, *Language of New Media*, 243.

159. Rancière, *Aisthesis*, 260.

160. Badiou, *Century*, 48–57.

161. Jacques Rancière, "Aesthetics, Inaesthetics, Anti-Aesthetics," trans. Ray Brassier in *Think Again: Alain Badiou and the Future of Philosophy*, ed. Peter Hallward (London and New York: Continuum, 2014), 218.

162. Alain Badiou, *Metapolitics*, trans. Jason Barker (London: Verso, 2005), 109.

163. Badiou, *Century*, 150.

164. Badiou, *Cinema*, 113.

3. CINEMA AS EMERGENCY BRAKE

1. Kenneth Anger, "Kenneth Anger's Big Secret," *Guardian*, June 4, 2007, http://www.guardian.co.uk/film/filmblog/2007/jun/04/doyouwanttoknowasecret.

2. Giorgio Agamben, "Difference and Repetition," in *Guy Debord and the Situationist International: Texts and Documents*, ed. Tom McDonough (Cambridge, Mass.: MIT Press, 2002), 315.

3. Walter Benjamin, *Selected Writings Volume 4: 1938–1940*, trans. Edmond Jephcott and Harry Zohn (Cambridge, Mass.: Harvard University Press, 2003), 402.

4. Deleuze, *Cinema 2*, 17.

5. Giorgio Agamben, *Means Without Ends*, trans. Cesare Casarino and Vincenzo Binetti (Minneapolis: University of Minnesota Press, 2000), 55.

6. Agamben, *Means Without Ends*, 56.

7. Giorgio Agamben, *Profanations*, trans. Jeff Fort (New York: Zone Books, 2007), 69.

8. Agamben, *Means Without Ends*, 59.

9. Agamben, "Difference and Repetition," 314.

10. Agamben, *Infancy and History*, 139.

11. Giorgio Agamben, "For an Ethics of Cinema," trans. John V. Garner and Colin Williamson, in *Cinema and Agamben: Ethics, Biopolitics and the Moving Image*, ed. Henrik Gustafsson and Asbjørn Grønstad (New York: Bloomsbury, 2014), 23.

12. The phrase "weak messianic power" comes from Walter Benjamin's "On the Concept of History," in *Selected Writings Volume 4*, 390.

13. This trio does not all get equal treatment. I will be focusing on Benjamin's relation to Agamben and to a lesser extent on Deleuze because these figures have had a stronger influence on film studies. But, as will become clear, Debord is a central figure in Agamben's thought on cinema and media.

14. This can also be said about so-called apparatus theory of Baudry, Metz, and Comolli, of which Agamben's project is in many ways a continuation by other means.

15. Agamben, *Means Without Ends*, 55.

16. See Quentin Meillassoux, *After Finitude: An Essay on the Necessity of Contingency*, trans. Ray Brassier (Oxford: Bloomsbury, 2008), 5.

17. Rudolf Arnheim, *Film as Art* (Berkeley: University of California Press, 1957), 111.

18. Béla Balázs, *Theory of the Film: Character and Growth of a New Art*, trans. Edith Bone (New York: Dover, 1970), 42.

19. Balázs, *Theory of the Film*, 44.

20. Balázs, 45.

21. Balázs, 45.

22. Béla Balázs, *Early Film Theory*, ed. Erica Carter, trans. Rodney Livingstone (New York: Berghahn, 2010), 14.

23. Balázs, *Early Film Theory*, 13.

24. Vilém Flusser, *Gestures*, trans. Nancy Ann Roth (Minneapolis: University of Minnesota Press, 2014), 2, 55.

25. Giorgio Agamben, "Kommerell, or On Gesture," in *Potentialities: Collected Essays in Philosophy*, trans. Daniel Heller-Roazen (Stanford, Calif.: Stanford University Press, 2000), 78.

26. Agamben, *Infancy and History*, 156.

27. Jean-Louis Schefer, *The Enigmatic Body: Essays on the Arts*, ed. and trans. Paul Smith (New York: Cambridge University Press, 1995), 191.

28. See Agamben's essay "Magic and Happiness" in *Profanations*, 19–22.

29. Agamben, "Judgment Day," in *Profanations*, 26.

30. Agamben, *Infancy and History*, 156.

31. Agamben, "The Author as Gesture," in *Profanations*, 66.

32. The term "enigmatic signifiers" comes from Jean Laplanche, who defines them as "signifiers which are pregnant with unconscious sexual significations." Laplanche, *New Foundations for Psychoanalysis*, trans. David Macey (Oxford: Basil Blackwell, 1989), 126. As should be clear, I am not using the term in the precise psychoanalytic sense of Laplanche. Nonetheless, I would argue that the gesture is enigmatic in the sense of being pregnant with meaning that remains unconscious.

33. *De lingua Latina* 6.77, qtd. in Agamben, *Infancy and History*, 154. This quotation is repeated in Agamben's *Opus Dei: An Archaeology of Duty*, trans. Adam Kotsko (Stanford, Calif.: Stanford University Press, 2013), where curiously Agamben provides a very different reading. In this later work, gerere "designates . . . the specifically Roman concept of the activity of the one who is invested with a public function of governance" (83). This new interpretation associates gerere "with the introduction of duty into ethics" and not, as in "Notes on Gesture," with the realm of pure means and play that would make duty and will inoperative. It is important to note that he does not use the word "gesture" in this context (only the Latin root) and he places the third sphere of action defined by Varro in a different genealogy directly antagonistic to how has used the term "gesture" elsewhere.

34. Bertolt Brecht, "A Short Organum for the Theater," in *Brecht on Theater*, 198.

35. Qtd. in "Brecht's Concept of Gestus and the American Performance" by Carl Weber, in *Brecht Sourcebook*, ed. Henry Bial and Carol Martin (London: Routledge, 2005), 44.

36. Walter Benjamin, "What Is the Epic Theater? (II)," in *Selected Writings Volume 4: 1938–1940*, 305.

37. Walter Benjamin, *Selected Writings Volume 2: 1927–1934*, trans. Rodney Livingstone et al. (Cambridge, Mass.: Harvard University Press, 1999), 802.

38. Benjamin, *Selected Writings Volume 2*, 814.

39. Agamben, "Judgment Day," 27.

40. Agamben, "Notes on Gesture," in *Infancy and History*, 151.

41. Agamben, *Potentialities*, 83.

42. Agamben, 83.

43. Agamben, "Notes on Gesture," 135.

44. Agamben, *Means Without Ends*, 53.

45. Agamben, 53.

46. Badiou, *Handbook of Inaesthetics*, 78.

47. Agamben, *Infancy and History*, 139.

48. Benjamin, *Selected Writings Volume 2*, 801.

49. For a good overview of the concept of "decreation" in both Weil and Agamben, see Libby Saxton, "*Passion*, Agamben and the Gestures of Work," in Gustafsson and Grønstad, *Cinema and Agamben*, 55–70.

50. Agamben, *Potentialities*, 270.

51. Giorgio Agamben, "Cinema and History: On Jean-Luc Godard," trans. John V. Garner and Colin Williamson, in Gustafsson and Grønstad, *Cinema and Agamben*, 26.

52. Agamben, *Profanations*, 25.

53. Bazin, *What Is Cinema?*, 9.

54. Benjamin, "What Is the Epic Theater? (II)," 305.

55. Étienne Souriau, "La structure de l'univers filmique et le vocabulaire de la filmologie," *Revue Internationale de Filmologie*, nos. 7–8 (1951): 234.

56. Benjamin, qtd. in Agamben, *Nymphs*, trans. Amanda Minervini (London: Seagull, 2013), 26.

57. Benjamin, "Author as Producer," in *Understanding Brecht*, 100.

58. Benjamin, 99.

59. Guy Debord, "A User's Guide to Détournement," in *Complete Cinematic Works: Scripts, Stills, Documents*, trans. and ed. Ken Knabb (Oakland, Calif.: AK Press, 2003), 209.

60. Naomi Klein's *No Logo* touches on the similarity at times between advertising and adbusting. Klein, *No Logo: Taking Aim at the Brand Bullies* (New York: St. Martin's, 2009).

61. Agamben, "Difference and Repetition," 314.

62. Giorgio Agamben, *The Coming Community*, trans. Michael Hardt (Minneapolis: University of Minnesota Press, 1993), 42.

63. See also André Leroi-Gourhan's *Gesture and Speech*, trans. Anne Bostock Berger (Cambridge, Mass.: MIT Press, 1993). For Leroi-Gourhan, tools are also intrinsic to gesture as "material action."

64. Agamben, "For an Ethics of Cinema," 19.

65. Benjamin qtd. in Agamben, *Nymphs*, 20.

66. Agamben, "For an Ethics of Cinema," 20.

67. Agamben, 20.

68. Agamben, 22.

69. Agamben, 22.

70. Agamben, 22–23.

71. Giorgio Agamben, *Nudities*, trans. David Kishik and Stefan Pedatella (Stanford: Stanford University Press, 2010), 44.

72. This analogy is intended only to be suggestive. Agamben provides hints about the ways that in a post-Fordist attention economy, the celebrity has a different relation to the value form than in the era or Marx or even Benjamin. And this shift has to do with how value is becoming untethered from work.

73. Walter Benjamin, "Critique of Violence," in *Selected Writings Volume 1: 1913–1926*, ed. Marcus Bullock and Michael W. Jennings (Cambridge, Mass.: Harvard University Press, 1996), 236.

74. Rancière, "Gaps of Cinema."

75. Theodor Adorno, Walter Benjamin, Ernst Bloch, Bertolt Brecht, and Georg Lukacs, *Aesthetics and Politics* (London: NLB, 1977), 129.

76. Agamben, *Infancy and History*, 118.

77. Althusser, *Reading Capital*, 186.

78. Agamben, *Infancy and History*, 119.

79. Agamben, 119–120.

80. Giorgio Agamben, "What Is a Destituent Power?," trans. Stephanie Wakefield, *Environment and Planning D: Society and Space* 32 (2014): 67.

81. See *Homo Sacer: Sovereign Power and Bare Life*, trans. Daniel Heller-Roazen, (Stanford, Calif.: Stanford University Press, 1998).

82. Deleuze, "Postscript on Control Societies," 180.

83. Deleuze, 182.

84. Agamben, "On Eternal Return," in *Means Without Ends*, 53.

85. Benjamin, *Selected Writings Volume 4*, 392.

86. Agamben, *What Is an Apparatus?*, 17.

87. Agamben, 15.

88. Agamben, 15.

89. Theodor Adorno, "The Culture Industry Reconsidered," in *The Culture Industry: Selected Essays on Mass Culture*, ed. J. M. Bernstein, trans. Thomas Y. Levin (London: Routledge, 1991), 102.

90. Giorgio Agamben, *The Open: Man and Animal*, trans. Kevin Attell (Stanford: Stanford University Press, 2004), 92.

91. Agamben, *Nymphs* 29.

92. See Francois Truffaut, Alfred Hitchcock, and Helen G. Scott, *Hitchcock* (New York: Simon & Schuster, 1984), 52.

93. This is the meaning of Hitchcock's well-known explanation of the MacGuffin.

94. This is Gershom Scholem's definition of the law in Kafka. Agamben discusses it in various places. See, for example, *Potentialities*, 98.

95. Chris Marker, "A Free Replay (notes sur *Vertigo*)," *Positif* 400 (June 1994): 79–84.

96. Agamben, "Cinema and History," 26.

97. These words are spoken during a sequence Godard calls "Introduction to the Method of Alfred Hitchcock" from chapter 4(a) of "Le Contrôle de l'univers" (1998) of *Histoire(s) du cinema*, directed by Jean-Luc Godard (1988–1998; Gaumont, 2007), DVD boxed set.

98. I use this example from Jean Epstein's 1921 *Bonjour Cinema* because it is part of the quotation that Rancière uses to open *Film Fables*. See *Film Fables*, 1.

99. See Rancière, "A Fable Without a Moral: Godard, Cinema, (Hi)stories," in *Film Fables*, 171–187.

100. There are some cases where Deleuze does mention a film in which there are images not made by the filmmaker—certain Godard films for example—but these instances are rare and he never discusses this aspect of them explicitly.

101. By referring to cinema as a form of "objectified memory" here, I am connecting Agamben's ideas about film and memory to Bernard Stiegler. See Stigeler, *Time and Technics, 3: Cinematic Time and the Question of Malaise*, trans. Stephen Barker (Stanford, Calif.: Stanford University Press, 2010).

102. Agamben, *Profanations*, 93–94.

103. According to Foucault, man has become an "entrepreneur of himself, being for himself his own capital, being for himself his own producer." See *The Birth of Biopolitics: Lectures at the Collège de France, 1978–1979*, ed. N. Senekkart, trans. Graham Burchell (New York: Palgrave Macmillan, 2008), 226.

104. Agamben, *Profanations*, 87.

105. Agamben, 82.

106. Agamben, 92.

107. Agamben, "For an Ethics of Cinema," 23.

108. For a good overview of debates about post-cinema, see Shane Denson and Julia Leyda, eds., *Post-Cinema: Theorizing 21st Century Film* (Falmer: Reframe, 2016). In my opinion, it is more useful to say that it is cinema and not film that persists in the twenty-first century. I am defining cinema broadly as moving images in general and film as the material substrate of the dominant form of moving image throughout much of the twentieth century. But "post-cinema," a term used by Agamben as far back as 1992, has been adopted to refer not to the end of cinema so much as the decline in the hegemony of the dominant forms of twentieth-century cinema. For a convincing argument about how the "experience" of cinema still persists in new mutations today, see Francesco Casetti, *The Lumiere Galaxy: Seven Keywords for a Cinema to Come* (New York: Columbia University Press, 2015).

109. Agamben, *Profanations*, 90.

110. https://vimeo.com/27488845. I wish to credit Erica Levin for making me aware of this video. See her brilliant analysis of it: "Toward a Social Cinema Revisited," *Millennium Film Journal* 58 (Fall 2013): 22–33.

111. Agamben, *Profanations*, 89.

4. RETHINKING THE POLITICS OF THE PHILOSOPHY OF CINEMA

1. It is worth noting that though the book was not published until 2001, it emerged out of a series of lectures given at London's National Film Theatre in 1998 at the invitation of Colin McCabe.

2. Žižek, *Fright of Real Tears*, 9.

3. Slavoj Žižek, *Enjoy Your Symptom: Jacques Lacan in Hollywood and Out* (New York: Psychology Press, 2001), xi.

4. See Slavoj Žižek, *For They Know Not What They Do: Enjoyment as a Political Factor* (London: Verso, 2002), xii.

5. Žižek evokes this scene frequently. See, for example, Slavoj Žižek, *The Sublime Object of Ideology* (London: Verso, 1989), 78–79.

6. Rancière, "The Pensive Image," in *Emancipated Spectator*, 107–132.

7. See Walter Benjamin, "The Work of Art in the Age of Its Technological Reproducibility, Second Version," trans. Edmund Jephcott and Harry Zohn, in Jennings, Doherty, and Levin, *Work of Art*, 28.

8. See Rancière, *Politics of Aesthetics*, 50.

9. See Roland Barthes, "Myth Today," in *Mythologies: The Complete Edition*, trans. Richard Howard and Annette Lavers (New York: Hill & Wang, 2012), and Althusser, "Ideology and Ideological State Apparatuses."

10. Paul Ricoeur, *Freud and Philosophy: An Essay on Interpretation*, trans. Denis Savage (New Haven, Conn.: Yale University Press, 1970), 32–36.

11. Laura Mulvey, "Visual Pleasure and Narrative Cinema," in *Narrative, Apparatus, Ideology*, ed. Philip Rosen (New York: Columbia University Press, 1986), 198.

12. Metz, *Imaginary Signifier*, 3.

13. Rancière has argued that so-called modernism is an especially restrictive interpretation of a new way of understanding art in what he calls "the aesthetic regime of art" that goes back to at least the late eighteenth century and includes the history of romanticism. See Rancière, *Politics of Aesthetics*, 10–11.

14. See Arnheim, *Film as Art*, and V. F. Perkins, *Film as Film: Understanding and Judging Movies* (London: Penguin, 1972).

15. David Bordwell and Kristin Thompson, *Film Art: An Introduction*, 8th ed. (New York: McGraw-Hill, 2008), xviii, 2–3.

16. For many examples of this logic in 1970s film theory, see Rodowick, *Crisis of Political Modernism*.

17. See Comolli and Narboni, "Cinema/Ideology/Criticism."

18. Rancière, *Emancipated Spectator*, 2.
19. See Stuart Hall, "Encoding/decoding," in *Culture, Media, Language: Working Papers in Cultural Studies*, ed. Stuart Hall, Dorothy Hobson, Andrew Lowe, and Paul Willis (London: Taylor & Francis, 1980), 126–127.
20. Andrew Sarris, "Preface," in *Directed by Allen Smithee*, ed. Jeremy Braddock and Stephen Hock (Minneapolis: University of Minnesota Press, 2001), x.
21. Susan Sontag, "A Century of Cinema," in *Where the Stress Falls: Essays* (New York: Picador, 2002), 118.
22. Stanley Cavell, *The World Viewed: Reflections on the Ontology of Film* (Cambridge, Mass.: Harvard University Press, 1979), 40–41.
23. I don't mean to suggest that the argument that film viewers are active emerges with digital culture. Benjamin was already arguing that film viewers were "experts" of a sort in the 1930s and the desire for an active spectator has a long history. But only recently has it become consensus that viewers are necessarily active.
24. Rancière, *Emancipated Spectator*, 13.
25. Rancière, 15.
26. See Glauber Rocha, "The Aesthetics of Hunger," in *Film Manifestos and Global Cinema Cultures: A Critical Anthology*, ed. Scott MacKenzie (Berkeley: University of California Press, 2014), 218–220.
27. Fernando Solanas and Octavio Getino, "Towards a Third Cinema: Notes and Experiences for the Development of a Cinema of Liberation in the Third World," in *Film Manifestos and Global Cinema Cultures: A Critical Anthology*, 248.

BIBLIOGRAPHY

Adorno, Theodor. *The Culture Industry: Selected Essays on Mass Culture*. Edited by J. M. Bernstein. Translated by Thomas Y. Levin. London: Routledge, 1991.

Adorno, Theodor and Walter Benjamin. *The Complete Correspondence*. Edited by Henri Lonitz. Translated by Nicholas Walker. Cambridge, Mass.: Harvard University Press, 2001.

Adorno, Theodor, Walter Benjamin, Ernst Bloch, Bertolt Brecht, and Georg Lukacs. Afterword by Fredric Jameson. *Aesthetics and Politics*. London: NLB, 1977.

Adorno, Theodor and Max Horkheimer. *Dialectic of Enlightenment*. Translated by Edmund Jephcott. Stanford, Calif.: Stanford University Press, 2002.

Agamben, Giorgio. "Cinema and History: On Jean-Luc Godard." Translated by John V. Garner and Colin Williamson. In *Cinema and Agamben: Ethics, Biopolitics and the Moving Image*, edited by Henrik Gustafsson and Asbjørn Grønstad, 25–26. New York: Bloomsbury, 2014.

——. *The Coming Community*. Translated by Michael Hardt. Minneapolis: University of Minnesota Press, 1993.

——. "Difference and Repetition." In *Guy Debord and the Situationist International: Texts and Documents*, edited by Tom McDonough, 313–319. Cambridge, Mass.: MIT Press, 2002.

——. "For an Ethics of Cinema." Translated by John V. Garner and Colin Williamson. In *Cinema and Agamben: Ethics, Biopolitics and the Moving Image*, edited by Henrik Gustafsson and Asbjørn Grønstad, 19–24. New York: Bloomsbury, 2014.

——. *Homo Sacer: Sovereign Power and Bare Life*. Translated by Daniel Heller-Roazen. Stanford, Calif.: Stanford University Press, 1998.

——. *Infancy and History: On the Destruction of Experience*. Translated by Liz Heron. London: Verso, 2007.

——. *Means Without Ends*. Translated by Cesare Casarino and Vincenzo Binetti. Minneapolis: University of Minnesota Press, 2000.

———. *Nudities.* Translated by David Kishik and Stefan Pedatella. Stanford, Calif.: Stanford University Press, 2010.

———. *Nymphs.* Translated by Amanda Minervini. London: Seagull, 2013.

———. *The Open: Man and Animal.* Translated by Kevin Attell. Stanford, Calif.: Stanford University Press, 2004.

———. *Opus Dei: An Archaeology of Duty.* Translated by Adam Kotsko. Stanford, Calif.: Stanford University Press, 2013.

———. *Potentialities: Collected Essays in Philosophy.* Translated by Daniel Heller-Roazen. Stanford, Calif.: Stanford University Press, 2000.

———. *Profanations.* Translated by Jeff Fort. New York: Zone Books, 2007.

———. *The Use of Bodies.* Translated by Adam Kotsko. Stanford, Calif.: Stanford University Press, 2016.

———. "What Is a Destituent Power?" Translated by Stephanie Wakefield. *Environment and Planning D: Society and Space* 32 (2014): 65–74.

———. *What Is an Apparatus? and Other Essays.* Translated by David Kishik and Stefan Pedatella. Stanford, Calif.: Stanford University Press, 2009.

Allen, Richard and Murray Smith, eds. *Film Theory and Philosophy.* Oxford: Oxford University Press, 1999.

Althusser, Louis. *For Marx.* Translated by Ben Brewster. London: Verso, 2005.

———. *The Humanist Controversy and Other Writings (1966–67).* Edited by François Matheron. Translated by G. M. Goshgarian. London: Verso, 2003.

———. *Lenin and Philosophy and Other Essays.* Translated by Ben Brewster. New York: Monthly Review Press, 1971.

———. "On Brecht and Marx." Translated by Max Statkiewicz. In *Louis Althusser (Transitions),* by Warren Montag, 136–149. New York: Palgrave, 2003.

———. *Philosophy of the Encounter: Later Writings, 1978–1987.* Translated by G. M. Goshgarian. New York: Verso, 2006.

Althusser, Louis and Étienne Balibar. *Reading Capital.* Translated by Ben Brewster. New York: Verso, 1997.

Andrew, Dudley with Herve Joubert-Laurencin, eds. *Opening Bazin: Postwar Film Theory and Its Afterlife.* Oxford: Oxford University Press, 2011.

Andrew, Dudley, Anton Kaes, Sarah Keller, Stuart Liebman, Annette Michelson, and Malcolm Turvey. "Roundtable on the Return to Classical Film Theory." *October* 148 (Spring 2014): 5–26.

Andrew, J. Dudley. *The Major Film Theories.* New York: Oxford University Press, 1976.

Anger, Kenneth. "Kenneth Anger's Big Secret," *Guardian,* June 4, 2007. http://www.guardian.co.uk/film/filmblog/2007/jun/04/doyouwanttoknowasecret.

Arnheim, Rudolf. *Film as Art.* Berkeley: University of California Press, 1957.

———. *Film Essays and Criticism.* Translated by Brenda Benthien. Madison: University of Wisconsin Press, 1997.

Arsenjuk, Luka. "On the Impossibility of Object-Oriented Film Theory." *Discourse* 38, no. 2 (2016): 197–214.

Artaud, Antonin. "Sorcery and the Cinema." In *The Avant-Garde Film: A Reader of Theory and Criticism*, edited and translated by P. Adams Sitney, 49–50. New York: New York University Press, 1978.

——. *The Theater and Its Double*. Translated by Mary Caroline Richards. New York: Grove, 1958.

Badiou, Alain. *The Age of the Poets, and Other Writings on Twentieth-Century Poetry and Prose*. Translated by Emily Apter and Bruno Bosteels. London: Verso, 2014.

——. *Being and Event*. Translated by Oliver Feltham. New York: Continuum, 2005.

——. *The Century*. Translated by Alberto Toscano. Malden, Mass.: Polity, 2007.

——. *Cinema*. Edited by Antoine de Baecque. Translated by Susan Spitzer. Malden, Mass.: Polity, 2013. Originally published as *Cinéma* (Paris: Nova, 2010).

——. "Cinema as a Democratic Emblem." Translated by Alan Ling and Aurelien Mondon. *Parrhesia*, no. 6 (2009): 1–6.

——. *Conditions*. Translated by Steve Corcoran. New York: Continuum, 2008.

——. *Deleuze: The Clamor of Being*. Translated by Louise Burchill. Minneapolis: University of Minnesota Press, 2000.

——. *Ethics: An Essay on the Understanding of Evil*. Translated by Peter Hallward. London: Verso, 2001.

——. "Fifteen Theses on Contemporary Art." *Lacanian Ink* 23 (2004): 103–119.

——. "The Flux and the Party." Translated by Laura Balladur and Simon Krysl. *Polygraph* 15/16 (2005): 75–92.

——. *Handbook of Inaesthetics*. Translated by Alberto Toscano. Stanford, Calif.: Stanford University Press, 2005.

——. *Infinite Thought: Truth and the Return to Philosophy*. Edited and translated by Oliver Feltham and Justin Clemens. London: Continuum, 2003.

——. *Logic of Worlds: Being and Event II*. Translated by Alberto Toscano. London: Continuum, 2009.

——. *Manifesto for Philosophy*. Translated by Norman Madarasz. Albany: SUNY Press, 1999.

——. *Metapolitics*. Translated by Jason Barker. London: Verso, 2005.

——. *Polemics*. Translated by Steve Corcoran. London: Verso, 2006.

——. *Second Manifesto for Philosophy*. Translated by Louise Burchill. Malden, Mass.: Polity, 2011.

——. "Three Negations." *Cardoza Law Review* 29, no. 5 (April 2008): 1877–1883.

Balázs, Béla. *Early Film Theory*. Edited by Erica Carter. Translated by Rodney Livingstone. New York: Berghahn, 2010.

——. *Theory of the Film: Character and Growth of a New Art*. Translated by Edith Bone. New York: Dover, 1970.

Barthes, Roland. *Camera Lucida*. Translated by Richard Howard. New York: Hill & Wang, 1982.

——. *Mythologies: The Complete Edition*. Translated by Richard Howard and Annette Lavers. New York: Hill & Wang, 2012.

Baudry, Jean-Louis. "Ideological Effects of the Basic Cinematographic Apparatus." Translated by Alan Williams. In *Narrative, Apparatus, Ideology,* edited by Philip Rosen, 286–298. New York: Columbia University Press, 1986.

Bazin, André. *Bazin at Work.* Translated by Bert Cardullo and Alain Piette. New York: Routledge, 1997.

———. *What Is Cinema?* Vol. 1. Translated by Hugo Gray. Berkeley: University of California Press, 2005.

———. *What Is Cinema?* Vol. 2. Translated by Hugo Gray. Berkeley: University of California Press, 1972.

———. *What Is Cinema?* Translated by Timothy Barnard. Montreal: Caboose, 2009.

Benjamin, Walter. *Selected Writings Volume 1: 1913–1926.* Edited by Marcus Bullock and Michael W. Jennings. Cambridge, Mass.: Harvard University Press, 1996.

———. *Selected Writings Volume 2: 1927–1934.* Translated by Rodney Livingstone et al. Cambridge, Mass.: Harvard University Press, 1999.

———. *Selected Writings Volume 3: 1935–1938.* Translated by Edmond Jephcott and Harry Zohn. Cambridge, Mass.: Harvard University Press, 2002.

———. *Selected Writings Volume 4: 1938–1940.* Translated by Edmond Jephcott and Harry Zohn. Cambridge, Mass.: Harvard University Press, 2003.

———. *Understanding Brecht.* Translated by Anna Bostock. London: Verso, 1998.

———. *The Work of Art in the Age of Its Technological Reproducibility.* Edited by Michael W. Jennings, Brigid Doherty, and Thomas Y. Levin. Cambridge, Mass.: Harvard University Press, 2008.

Bergson, Henri. *Matter and Memory.* Translated by N. M. Paul and W. S. Palmer. New York: Zone Books, 1990.

Best, Stephen and Sharon Marcus. "Surface Reading: An Introduction." *Representations* 108 (2009): 1–23.

Bordwell, David. *Figures Traced in Light.* Berkeley: University of California Press, 2005.

———. *Making Meaning: Inference and Rhetoric in the Interpretation of Cinema.* Cambridge, Mass: Harvard University Press, 1991.

———. *Narration in the Fiction Film.* Madison: University of Wisconsin Press, 1985.

———. "Never the Twain Shall Meet." *Film Comment,* May/June 2011. http://www.filmcomment.com/article/never-the-twain-shall-meet.

———. "Slavoj Zizek: Say Anything." April 2005. http://www.davidbordwell.net/essays/zizek.php.

———. *The Way Hollywood Tells It.* Berkeley: University of California Press, 2006.

Bordwell, David and Noël Carroll, eds. *Post-Theory: Reconstructing Film Studies.* Madison: University of Wisconsin Press, 1996.

Bordwell, David and Kristin Thompson. *Film Art: An Introduction.* 8th ed. New York: McGraw-Hill, 2008.

Bourriaud, Nicholas. *Relational Aesthetics.* Paris: Les Presses Du Reel, 1998.

Brecht, Bertolt. *Brecht on Theater.* Translated by John Willett. New York: Hill & Wang, 1992.

———. *On Art & Politics.* Edited by Tom Kuhn and Steve Giles. Translated by Laura Bradley, Steve Giles, and Tom Kuhn. London: Methuen, 2003.

——. *On Film & Radio*. Edited and Translated by Marc Silberman. London: Methuen, 2000.

Brinkema, Eugenie. *The Forms of the Affects*. Durham, N.C.: Duke University Press, 2014.

Burch, Noël. *Life to Those Shadows*. Berkeley: University of California Press, 1990.

——. "The Sadeian Aesthetic." In *The Philistine Controversy*, edited by Dave Beech and John Roberts, 175–200. London: Verso, 2002.

Carroll, Noël. *Mystifying Movies*. New York: Columbia University Press, 1988.

——. *Theorizing the Moving Image*. New York: Cambridge University Press, 1996.

Carroll, Noël and Jinhee Choi, eds. *Philosophy of Film Motion Pictures*. Malden, Mass.: Blackwell, 2005.

Casetti, Francesco. *The Lumiere Galaxy: Seven Keywords for a Cinema to Come*. New York: Columbia University Press, 2015.

——. "Theory, Post-theory, Neo-theories: Changes in Discourses, Changes in Objects." *Cinémas: Revue d'études cinématographiques/Cinémas: Journal of Film Studies* 17, nos. 2–3 (2007): 33–45.

Cavell, Stanley. *The World Viewed: Reflections on the Ontology of Film*. Cambridge, Mass.: Harvard University Press, 1979.

Comolli, Jean-Louis. *Cinema Against Spectacle: Technique and Ideology Revisited*. Edited and translated by Daniel Fairfax. Amsterdam: Amsterdam University Press, 2015.

Comolli, Jean-Louis and Jean Narboni. "Cinema/Ideology/Criticism." Translated by Susan Bennett. In *Cahiers du Cinéma Volume 3: The Politics of Representation*, edited by Nick Browne, 58–67. London: Routledge, 1996.

Daney, Serge. "Theorize/Terrorize (Godardian Pedagogy)." In *Cahiers du Cinéma Volume 4: 1973–1978: History, Ideology, Cultural Struggle*, edited by David Wilson, 116–123. New York: Routledge, 2000.

de Baecque, Antoine. *La Cinephilie: Invention d'un regard, histoire d'une culture (1944–1968)*. Paris: Fayard, 2003.

Debord, Guy. *La société du spectacle*. Paris: Buchet-Chastel, 1967.

Debord, Guy and Gil J. Wolman. "A User's Guide to Détournement." In Guy Debord, *Complete Cinematic Works: Scripts, Stills, Documents*, translated and edited by Ken Knabb, 207–209. Oakland, Calif: AK Press, 2003.

Deleuze, Gilles. *Cinema 1: The Movement-Image*. Translated by Hugh Tomlinson and Barbara Haberjam. Minneapolis: University of Minnesota Press, 1991.

——. *Cinema 2: The Time-Image*. Translated by Hugh Tomlinson and Robert Galeta. Minneapolis: University of Minnesota Press, 1989.

——. *Difference and Repetition*. Translated by Paul Patton. New York: Columbia University Press, 1994.

——. *Essays Critical and Clinical*. Translated by Daniel W. Smith and Michael A. Greco. Minneapolis: University of Minnesota Press, 1997.

——. *The Fold: Leibniz and the Baroque*. Translated by Tom Conley. Minneapolis: University of Minnesota Press, 1992.

——. *Foucault*. Translated by Sean Hand. Minneapolis: University of Minnesota Press, 1988.

———. *Negotiations 1972–1990*. Translated by Martin Joughin. New York: Columbia University Press, 1995.

———. *Two Regimes of Madness: Texts and Interviews 1975–1995*. New York: Columbia University Press, 2006.

Deleuze, Gilles and Félix Guattari. *Anti-Oedipus: Capitalism and Schizophrenia*. Translated by Mark Seem. Minneapolis: University of Minnesota Press, 1993.

———. *What Is Philosophy?* Translated by Hugh Tomlinson and Graham Burchell. New York: Columbia University Press, 1994.

Deleuze, Gilles and Claire Parnet. *Dialogues II*. Translated by Hugh Tomlinson and Barbara Habberjam. New York: Columbia University Press, 2002.

Denson, Shane and Julia Leyda, eds. *Post-Cinema: Theorizing 21st Century Film*. Falmer: Reframe, 2016.

Doane, Mary Ann. *The Emergence of Cinematic Time: Modernity, Contingency, the Archive*. Cambridge, Mass.: Harvard University Press, 2002.

———. "The Object of Theory." In *Rites of Realism: Essays on Corporeal Cinema*, edited by Ivone Margulies, 80–89. Durham, N.C.: Duke University Press, 2002.

Editors of *Cahiers du Cinéma*. "John Ford's *Young Mr. Lincoln*." Translated by Helen Lackner and Diana Matias. In *Narrative, Apparatus, Ideology*, edited by Philip Rosen, 444–482. New York: Columbia University Press, 1986.

Eisenstein, Sergei. *Film Form and Film Sense*. Edited and translated by Jay Leyda. Cleveland: Meridian, 1963.

Epstein, Jean. "On Certain Characteristics of Photogénie." Translated by Tom Milne. *Afterimage* 10 (Autumn 1981): 20–23.

———. "The Senses 1(b)." Translated by Tom Milne. *Afterimage* 10 (Autumn 1981): 9–19.

Flaxman, Gregory, ed. *The Brain Is the Screen: Deleuze and the Philosophy of Cinema*. Minneapolis: University of Minnesota Press, 2000.

Flusser, Vilém. *Gestures*. Translated by Nancy Ann Roth. Minneapolis: University of Minnesota Press, 2014.

Foster, Hal. "Post-Critical." *October* 139 (Winter 2012): 3–8.

Foucault, Michel. *The Birth of Biopolitics: Lectures at the Collège de France, 1978–1979*. Edited by Michel Senellart. Translated by Graham Burchell. New York: Palgrave Macmillan, 2008.

Frampton, Daniel. *Filmosophy: A Manifesto for a Radically New Way of Understanding Cinema*. London: Wallflower Press, 2006.

Gaines, Jane. "What Happened to the Philosophy of Film History?" *Film History* 25, nos. 1–2 (2013): 70–80.

Gledhill, Christine and Linda Williams, eds. *Reinventing Film Studies*. London: Arnold, 2000.

Habermas, Jürgen. *The Philosophical Discourse of Modernity: 12 Lectures*. Cambridge, Mass.: MIT Press, 1990.

Hall, Stuart. "Encoding/decoding." In *Culture, Media, Language: Working Papers in Cultural Studies*, edited by Stuart Hall, Dorothy Hobson, Andrew Lowe, and Paul Willis, 117–127. London: Taylor & Francis, 1980.

Hallward, Peter. *Badiou: A Subject to Truth*. Saint Paul: University of Minnesota Press, 2003.

———. "Staging Equality: On Rancière's Theatocracy." *New Left Review* 37 (January/February 2006): 109–129.

Hansen, Mark. *New Philosophy for New Media*. Cambridge, Mass.: MIT Press, 2006.

Hardt, Michael and Antonio Negri. *Empire*. Cambridge, Mass.: Harvard University Press, 2001.

Harvey, Sylvia. *May '68 and Film Culture*. London: BFI, 1978.

Hegel, Georg Wilhelm Friedrich. *Aesthetics: Lectures on Fine Art, Volume 1*. Translated by T. M. Knox. Oxford: Oxford University Press, 1975.

Higashi, Sumiko. "In-Focus: Film History, or a Baedeker Guide to the Historical Turn." *Cinema Journal* 44, no. 1 (2004): 94–100.

Hiller, Jim, ed. *Cahiers du Cinéma, the 1950s: Neo-realism, Hollywood, New Wave*. Cambridge, Mass.: Harvard University Press, 1985.

Hoberman, J. "Quid Est Veritas: The Reality of Unspeakable Suffering." In *Film after Film: or, What Became of 21st Century Cinema?*, 27–34. London: Verso, 2012.

Kael, Pauline. *I Lost It at the Movies*. New York: Bantam, 1965.

Kant, Immanuel. *Critique of Judgment*. Translated by Werner Pluhar. Indianapolis: Hackett, 1987.

Keeling, Kara. *The Witch's Flight: The Cinematic, the Black Femme, and the Image of Common Sense*. Durham, N.C.: Duke University Press, 2007.

Keller, Sarah and Jason N. Paul, eds. *Jean Epstein: Critical Essays and New Translations*. Amsterdam: Amsterdam University Press, 2012.

Kennedy, Barbara M. *Deleuze and Cinema: The Aesthetics of Sensation*. Edinburgh: Edinburgh University Press, 2000.

Kittler, Friedrich. *Literature, Media, Information Systems*. Translated by Stefanie Harris. Amsterdam: G & B Arts, 1997.

———. *Optical Media: Berlin Lectures 1999*. Translated by Anthony Enns. Cambridge: Polity, 2010.

Klein, Naomi. *No Logo: Taking Aim at the Brand Bullies*. New York: St. Martin's, 2009.

Knowlson, James and Elizabeth Knowlson, eds. *Beckett Remembering, Remembering Beckett: A Centenary Celebration*. New York: Arcade, 2006.

Koch, Gertrud. "Carnivore or Chameleon: The Fate of Cinema Studies." *Critical Inquiry* 35, no. 4 (Summer 2009): 918–928.

Kovács, András Bálint. "The Film History of Thought." Translated by Sandor Hervey. In *The Brain Is the Screen*, edited by Gregory Flaxman, 153–170. Minneapolis: University of Minnesota Press, 2000.

Kracauer, Siegfried. *Theory of Film: The Redemption of Physical Reality*. Princeton, N.J.: Princeton University Press, 1997.

Krauss, Rosalind. "Video: The Aesthetics of Narcissism." In *New Artists Video: A Critical Anthology*, edited by Gregory Battcock, 43–64. New York: Dutton, 1978.

Kuntzel, Thierry. "The Film-Work." *Enclitic* 2, no.1 (Spring 1978): 38–61.

Lacan, Jacques. *Écrits*. Translated by Bruce Fink. New York: Norton, 2006.

———. *The Ego in Freud's Theory and in the Technique of Psychoanalysis 1954–1955: The Seminar of Jacques Lacan Book II*. Translated by Sylvana Tomaselli. New York: Norton, 1991.

———. *The Four Fundamental Concepts of Psychoanalysis. The Seminar of Jacques Lacan Book XI*. Translated by Alan Sheridan. New York: Norton, 1978.

———. *The Other Side of Psychoanalysis: The Seminar of Jacques Lacan Book XVII*. Translated by Russell Grigg. New York: Norton, 2007.

Laplanche, Jean. *New Foundations for Psychoanalysis*. Translated by David Macey. Oxford: Basil Blackwell, 1989.

Latour, Bruno. "Why Has Critique Run Out of Steam? From Matters of Fact to Matters of Concern." *Critical Inquiry* 30, no. 2 (Winter 2004): 225–248.

Laudon, Kenneth C. *Dossier Society: Value Choices in the Design of National Information Systems*. New York: Columbia University Press, 1986.

Leroi-Gourhan, André. *Gesture and Speech*. Translated by Anne Bostock Berger. Cambridge, Mass.: MIT Press, 1993.

Levin, Erica. "Toward a Social Cinema Revisited." *Millennium Film Journal* 58 (Fall 2013): 22–33.

Lindsay, Vachel. *The Art of the Moving Picture*. New York: Modern Library, 2000.

Lyotard, Jean-François. *The Differend: Phrases in Dispute*. Translated by Georges Van Den Abbeele. Minneapolis: University of Minnesota Press, 1988.

———. *The Postmodern Condition: A Report on Knowledge*. Translated by Geoff Bennington and Brian Massumi. Minneapolis: University of Minnesota Press, 1984.

Mallarmé, Stéphane. "L'Action restreinte." In *Œuvres completes*, 370–373. Paris, Gallimard: Bibliothèque de la Pléiade, 1945).

———. *Selected Letters of Stéphane Mallarmé*. Edited and translated by Rosemary Lloyd. Chicago: University of Chicago Press, 1988.

Manovich, Lev. *The Language of New Media*. Cambridge, Mass.: MIT Press, 1998.

Marker, Chris. "A Free Replay (notes sur *Vertigo*)," *Positif* 400 (June 1994): 79–84.

Marks, Laura U. *The Skin of the Film: Intercultural Cinema, Embodiment and the Senses*. Durham, N.C.: Duke University Press, 1999.

Marx, Karl. *Capital Volume One: A Critique of Political Economy*. Translated by Ben Fowkes. New York: Vintage, 1977.

Meillassoux, Quentin. *After Finitude: An Essay on the Necessity of Contingency*. Translated by Ray Brassier. Oxford: Bloomsbury, 2008.

Metz, Christian. *Film Language: A Semiotics of the Cinema*. Translated by Michael Taylor. New York: Oxford University Press, 1974.

———. *The Imaginary Signifier: Psychoanalysis and the Cinema*. Translated by Celia Britton, Annwyl Williams, Ben Brewster, and Alfred Guzzetti. Bloomington: Indianan University Press, 1982.

———. *Language and Cinema*. Translated by Donna Jean Umiker-Sebeok. The Hague: Mouton de Gruyter, 1974.

Mills, C. Wright. *The Sociological Imagination*. Oxford: Oxford University Press, 1959.

Mitry, Jean. *The Aesthetics and Psychology of the Cinema*. Translated by Christopher King. Bloomington: University of Indiana Press, 1999.

Montag, Warren. *Althusser and His Contemporaries: Philosophy's Perpetual War*. Durham, N.C.: Duke University Press, 2013.

Morin, Edgar. *The Cinema, or The Imaginary Man*. Translated by Lorraine Mortimer. Minneapolis: University of Minnesota Press, 2005.

Mullarkey, John. *Refractions of Reality: Philosophy and the Moving Image*. New York: Palgrave, 2008.

Mulvey, Laura. "Visual Pleasure and Narrative Cinema." In *Narrative, Apparatus, Ideology*, edited by Philip Rosen, 198–209. New York: Columbia University Press, 1986.

Munsterberg, Hugo. *The Film: A Psychological Study*. New York: Dover, 1970.

Nancy, Jean-Luc. "The Deleuzian Fold of Thought." In *Deleuze: A Critical Reader*, edited by Paul Patton, 107–113. Oxford: Blackwell, 1996.

Nobus, Dany and Malcolm Quinn. *Knowing Nothing, Staying Stupid: Elements for a Psychoanalytic Epistemology*. London: Routledge, 2005.

Panofsky, Erwin. "Style and Medium in the Motion Pictures." In *Three Essays on Style*, edited by Irving Lavin with William S. Heckscher, 93–122. Cambridge, Mass.: MIT Press, 1995.

Pasolini, Pier Paolo. *Heretical Empiricism*. Translated by Ben Lawton and Louise K. Barnett. Bloomington: Indiana University Press, 1988.

Peirce, Charles S. "Logic as Semiotic: The Theory of Signs." In *Philosophical Writings*, edited by Justus Buchler, 98–119. New York: Dover, 1955.

Perkins, V. F. *Film as Film: Understanding and Judging Movies*. London: Penguin, 1972.

Peters, John Durham. *The Marvelous Clouds: Toward a Philosophy of Elemental Media*. Chicago: University of Chicago Press, 2015.

Pines, Jim and Paul Willemen, eds. *Questions of Third Cinema*. London: BFI, 1990.

Pisters, Patricia. *The Matrix of Visual Culture: Working with Deleuze in Film Theory*. Stanford, Calif.: Stanford University Press, 2003.

——. *The Neuro-Image: A Deleuzian Film-Philosophy of Digital Screen Culture*. Stanford, Calif.: Stanford University Press, 2012.

Rancière, Jacques. "The Aesthetic Dimension: Aesthetics, Politics, Knowledge." *Critical Inquiry* 36 (Autumn 2009): 1–19.

——. "The Aesthetic Revolution and Its Outcomes." *New Left Review* 14 (March/April 2002): 133–151.

——. "Aesthetics Against Incarnation: An Interview by Anne Marie Oliver." *Critical Inquiry* 35 (Autumn 2008): 172–190.

——. *Aesthetics and Its Discontents*. Translated by Steven Corcoran. Malden, Mass.: Polity, 2009.

——. "Aesthetics, Inaesthetics, Anti-Aesthetics." Translated by Ray Brassier. In *Think Again: Alain Badiou and the Future of Philosophy*, edited by Peter Hallward, 218–231. London: Continuum, 2014.

——. *Aisthesis: Scenes from the Aesthetic Regime of Art*. Translated by Zakir Paul. London: Verso, 2013.

——. *Althusser's Lesson*. Translated by Emiliano Battista. London: Bloomsbury, 2011.

——. *Bela Tarr: The Time After*. Translated by Eric Berensk. Minneapolis: Univocal, 2015.

———. *Chronicles of Consensual Times*. Translated by Steven Corcoran. London: Bloomsbury, 2010.

———. "Contemporary Art and the Politics of Aesthetics." In *Communities of Sense: Rethinking Aesthetics and Politics*, edited by Beth Hinderliter, William Kaizen, Vered Maison,
Jaleh Mansoor, and Seth McCormick, 31–50. Durham, N.C.: Duke University Press, 2009.

———. *Disagreement: Politics and Philosophy*. Translated by Julie Rose. Minneapolis: University of Minnesota Press, 1998.

———. *Dissensus: On Politics and Aesthetics*. Translated by Steven Corcoran. London: Continuum, 2010.

———. "Dissenting Words." *Diacritics* 30, no. 2 (Summer 2000): 113–126.

———. *Dissenting Words: Interviews with Jacques Rancière*. Edited and translated by Emiliano Battista. London: Bloomsbury, 2017.

———. "The Emancipated Spectator." *Art Forum*, March 2007, 271–280.

———. *The Emancipated Spectator*. Translated by Gregory Elliott. London: Verso, 2009.

———. *The Figures of History*. Translated by Julie Rose. Malden, Mass.: Polity, 2014.

———. *Film Fables*. Translated by Emiliano Battista. New York: Berg, 2006.

———. *The Flesh of Words: The Politics of Writing*. Translated by Charlotte Mandell. Stanford, Calif.: Stanford University Press, 2004.

———. *The Future of the Image*. Translated by Gregory Elliott. London: Verso, 2007.

———. "The Gaps of Cinema." Translated by Walter van der Star. Accessed June 6, 2018.
http://www.necsus-ejms.org/the-gaps-of-cinema-by-jacques-ranciere/.

———. *Hatred of Democracy*. Translated by Steven Corcoran. London: Verso, 2006.

———. *The Ignorant Schoolmaster: Five Lessons in Intellectual Emancipation*. Translated by
Kristin Ross. Stanford, Calif.: Stanford University Press, 1991.

———. *The Intervals of Cinema*. Translated by John Howe. London: Verso, 2014. Originally
published as *Les écarts du cinema* (Paris: La Fabrique, 2011).

———. "Jacques Rancière and Interdisciplinarity." Translated by Gregory Elliot. *Art & Research* 2, no. 1 (Summer 2008): 1–9.

———. *La Parole Ouvrière*. Paris: La Fabrique, 1976.

———. *Mute Speech*. Translated by James Swenson. New York: Columbia University Press,
2011.

———. *The Names of History: On the Poetics of Knowledge*. Translated by Hassan Melehy.
Minneapolis: University of Minnesota Press, 1994.

———. "On the Theory of Ideology—Althusser's Politics." In *Radical Philosophy Reader*,
edited by Roy Edgley and Richard Osborne, 101–136. London: Verso, 1985.

———. *The Philosopher and His Poor*. Translated by John Drury, Corinne Oster, and Andrew Parker. Durham, N.C.: Duke University Press, 2004.

———. "Politics, Identification, and Subjectivization." *October* 61 (1992): 58–64.

———. *The Politics of Aesthetics: The Distribution of the Sensible*. Translated by Gabriel
Rockhill. New York: Continuum, 2004.

———. "The Politics of Literature." *SubStance* 33, no. 1 (2004): 10–24.

———. *Proletarian Nights*. Translated by Donald Reid. London: Verso, 2014.

———. "Ten Theses on Politics." *Theory & Event* 5, no. 3 (2001). https://muse.jhu.edu/article /32639.

Ricoeur, Paul. *Freud and Philosophy: An Essay on Interpretation.* Translated by Denis Savage. New Haven, Conn.: Yale University Press, 1970.

Rocha, Glauber. "The Aesthetics of Hunger." In *Film Manifestos and Global Cinema Cultures: A Critical Anthology,* edited by Scott MacKenzie, 218–220. Berkeley: University of California Press, 2014.

Rodowick, D. N. *The Crisis of Political Modernism.* Berkeley: University of California Press, 1994.

———. *Elegy for Theory.* Cambridge, Mass.: Harvard University Press, 2014.

———. "An Elegy for Theory." *October* 122 (Fall 2007): 91–109.

———. *Gilles Deleuze's Time Machine.* Durham, N.C.: Duke University Press, 2011.

———. *Philosophy's Artful Conversation.* Cambridge, Mass.: Harvard University Press, 2015.

———. *The Virtual Life of Film.* Cambridge, Mass.: Harvard University Press, 2007.

Rosen, Philip. *Change Mummified.* Minneapolis: University of Minnesota Press, 2000.

———. "*Screen* and 70s Film Theory." In *Inventing Film Studies,* edited by Lee Grieveson and Haidee Wasson, 264–297. Durham, N.C.: Duke University Press, 2008.

Sarris, Andrew. "Forward: Allen Smithee Redux." In *Directed by Allen Smithee,* edited by Jeremy Braddock and Stephen Hock, vii–xv. Minneapolis: University of Minnesota Press, 2001.

Saxton, Libby. "*Passion,* Agamben, and the Gestures of Work." In *Cinema and Agamben: Ethics, Biopolitics and the Moving Image,* edited by Henrik Gustafsson and Asbjørn Grønstad, 55–70. New York: Bloomsbury, 2014.

Souriau, Étienne. "La structure de l'univers filmique et le vocabulaire de la filmologie." *Revue Internationale de Filmologie,* nos. 7–8 (1951): 231–240.

Schefer, Jean-Louis. *The Enigmatic Body: Essays on the Arts.* Edited and translated by Paul Smith. New York: Cambridge University Press, 1995.

Schiller, Friedrich. *On the Aesthetic Education of Man.* Translated by Reginald Snell. New York: Dover, 2004.

Shaviro, Steven. *The Cinematic Body.* Minneapolis: University of Minnesota Press, 1993.

———. "The Cinematic Body Redux." 2008. http://www.shaviro.com/Othertexts/Cinematic .pdf.

Sinnerbrink, Robert. *New Philosophies of Film: Thinking Images.* New York: Continuum, 2011.

Smith, Murray and Thomas E. Wartenberg, eds. *Thinking Through Cinema: Film as Philosophy.* Oxford: Blackwell, 2006.

Sobchack, Vivian. *Address of the Eye: A Phenomenology of Film Experience.* Princeton, N.J.: Princeton University Press, 1992.

Solanas, Fernando and Octavio Getino. "Towards a Third Cinema: Notes and Experiences for the Development of a Cinema of Liberation in the Third World." In *Film Manifestos and Global Cinema Cultures: A Critical Anthology,* edited by Scott MacKenzie, 230–250. Berkeley: University of California Press, 2014.

Sontag, Susan. "A Century of Cinema." In *Where the Stress Falls: Essays*, 117–122. New York: Picador, 2002.

Spivak, Gayatri Chakravorty. "Can the Subaltern Speak?" In *Marxism and the Interpretation of Culture*, edited by Cary Nelson and Lawrence Grossberg, 271–316. Chicago: University of Illinois Press, 1985.

——. *A Critique of Postcolonial Reason: Toward a History of the Vanishing Present* Cambridge, Mass.: Harvard University Press, 1999.

Stiegler, Bernard. *Time and Technics, 1: The Fault of Epimetheus*. Translated by Richard Beardsworth and George Collins. Stanford, Calif.: Stanford University Press, 1998.

——. *Time and Technics, 3: Cinematic Time and the Question of Malaise*. Translated by Stephen Barker. Stanford, Calif.: Stanford University Press, 2010.

Truffaut, Francois, Alfred Hitchcock, and Helen G. Scott. *Hitchcock*. New York: Simon & Schuster, 1984.

Turvey, Malcolm. "Theory, Philosophy, and Film Studies: A Response to D. N. Rodowick's 'An Elegy for Theory.'" *October* 122 (Fall 2007): 110–120.

Vertov, Dziga. *Kino-Eye: The Writings of Dziga Vertov*. Translated by Kevin O'Brien. Berkeley: University of California Press, 1984.

Weber, Carl. "Brecht's Concept of Gestus and the American Performance." In *Brecht Sourcebook*, edited by Henry Bial and Carol Martin, 41–46. London: Routledge, 2005.

Wittgenstein, Ludwig. *Tractatus Logico-Philosophicus*. Translated by Paul Kegan. New York: Harcourt Brace, 1922.

Wollen, Peter. "Godard and Counter-Cinema: Vent D'est." In *Narrative, Apparatus, Ideology*, edited by Philip Rosen, 120–129. New York: Columbia University Press, 1986.

——. "'Ontology' and 'Materialism' in Film." *Screen* 17, no. 1 (1976): 7–25.

——. "The Two Avant-Gardes." *Studio International*, November/December 1975, 171–175.

Žižek, Slavoj. *Enjoy Your Symptom: Jacques Lacan in Hollywood and Out*. New York: Psychology Press, 2001.

——. *For They Know Not What They Do: Enjoyment as a Political Factor*. London: Verso, 2002.

——. *The Fright of Real Tears: Krzysztof Kieślowski Between Theory and Post-Theory*. London: BFI, 2001.

——. *The Sublime Object of Ideology*. London: Verso, 1989.

——. "You May!" *London Review of Books* 21, no. 6 (March 18, 1999): 3–6.

INDEX

Adorno, Theodor, 113, 120, 150, 153–154, 157–158

advertising and pornography, Agamben on, 133, 150, 157, 166

aesthetics: Althusser conception of, 18–19, 22–25, 31–32; on narcissism, 166; politics of, 20–21, 39–42, 48, 49–50, 58–59, 67; Rancière break from Althusser over, 18–19, 58–59

affect, emphasis on, in film studies, 35–36

affect theory, 77

Agamben, Giorgio: on advertising and pornography, 133, 150, 157, 166; on art, 152–153, 177; "Bartleby, or On Contingency," 143; Benjamin and, 131–132, 163–164; on capitalism, 166; on Debord, 131–132, 142; on decreation, 142–143, 155, 164–165; Deleuze and, 80, 131–132, 143, 163; on end of cinema, 167; in film and media studies, 12–13; "For an Ethics of Cinema," 130, 149; on gesture, 131, 135–136, 137, 140–141, 172, 181; *Infancy and History*, 129, 155; on language, 136, 137; limitations of, 14; on magic, 136–137; on "moviegoing animal," 147–152; on museums, 169;

"Notes on Gesture," 129–130, 149, 153; on philosophy, 132, 143; on politics, 129, 155; on praxis and gesture, 153–158; on profanation, 130, 165; *Profanations*, 164; reading of Marx by, 153–155; on religion, 157; on repetition and stoppage, 129, 142–147, 168; strategy of suggestion of, 130–131; suspense and, 159–162; *The Use of Bodies*, 155

Akerman, Chantal, 88, 118

Alain-Miller, Jacques, 99

Alien (film), 171–172

Althusser, Louis: aesthetics and, 18–19, 22–25, 31–32; on ideology, 25, 26, 27, 52–53, 55–56; "Ideology and Ideological State Apparatuses," 43–44; influence of, 17; "knowledge effect" and, 3; "A Letter on Art," 24–25; Marxism and, 2; "On Brecht and Marx," 23–24, 31; Rancière and, 17–18, 53, 57–58; *Reading Capital* project of, 53; in seventies film theory, 17–18, 26–35; "structural causality" and, 154; symptomatic reading and, 22, 24, 56–59, 60

Alvarez, Santiago, 163

amateurism, 66–67

Melodrama and Modernity: Early Sensational Cinema and Its Contexts
Ben Singer

Wondrous Difference: Cinema, Anthropology, and Turn-of-the-Century Visual Culture
Alison Griffiths

Hearst Over Hollywood: Power, Passion, and Propaganda in the Movies
Louis Pizzitola

Masculine Interests: Homoerotics in Hollywood Film
Robert Lang

Special Effects: Still in Search of Wonder
Michele Pierson

Designing Women: Cinema, Art Deco, and the Female Form
Lucy Fischer

Cold War, Cool Medium: Television, McCarthyism, and American Culture
Thomas Doherty

Katharine Hepburn: Star as Feminist
Andrew Britton

Silent Film Sound
Rick Altman

Home in Hollywood: The Imaginary Geography of Cinema
Elisabeth Bronfen

Hollywood and the Culture Elite: How the Movies Became American
Peter Decherney

Taiwan Film Directors: A Treasure Island
Emilie Yueh-yu Yeh and Darrell William Davis

Shocking Representation: Historical Trauma, National Cinema, and the Modern Horror Film
Adam Lowenstein

China on Screen: Cinema and Nation
Chris Berry and Mary Farquhar

The New European Cinema: Redrawing the Map
Rosalind Galt

George Gallup in Hollywood
Susan Ohmer

Electric Sounds: Technological Change and the Rise of Corporate Mass Media
Steve J. Wurtzler

The Impossible David Lynch
Todd McGowan

Sentimental Fabulations, Contemporary Chinese Films: Attachment in the Age of Global Visibility
Rey Chow